Like,
Literally,
Dude

Like, Literally, Dude

Arguing for the Good in Bad English

VALERIE FRIDLAND

VIKING

VIKING
An imprint of Penguin Random House LLC
penguinrandomhouse.com

LIBRARY OF CONGRESS CATALOGING-IN-PUBLICATION DATA
Names: Fridland, Valerie, author.
Title: Like, literally, dude: arguing for the good in bad English /
Valerie Fridland.
Description: [New York]: Viking, [2023] | Includes biographical references
and index.
Identifiers: LCCN 2022030931 (print) | LCCN 2022030932 (ebook) |
ISBN 9780593298329 (hardcover) | ISBN 9780593298336 (ebook)
Subjects: LCSH: Discourse markers. | English language—Spoken English. |
English language—Social aspects. | English language—Rhetoric. |
English language—Usage. | Oral communication.
Classification: LCC PE1444.F75 2023 (print) | LCC PE1444 (ebook) |
DDC 420.1/41—dc23/eng/20220920
LC record available at https://lccn.loc.gov/2022030931
LC ebook record available at https://lccn.loc.gov/2022030932

Printed in the United States of America
1st Printing

Set in Sabon LT Std
Designed by Cassandra Garruzzo Mueller

To Cole and Taylor

In memory of Abram and Doba Frydland

Contents

Like,
Literally,
Dude

I hate when you say that!

Y ou know you have reached the end of your utility as a linguistic role model when your teenage son sighs as you explain the merits of using "will" instead of "going to" to express future tense, and then he nonchalantly dismisses your wizened wisdom with "Okay, boomer." He, for better or worse, has begun the timeless rite of passage known as adolescence. While perhaps the delivery of his message lacked diplomacy, he was on to something. It turns out that skin isn't the only thing that sags with age; our linguistic elasticity takes a serious hit as well. Perhaps even more surprising, the more educated and financially well off we are, the greater our linguistic rigidity. And it is the very fact that we think of ourselves as serving as some kind of role model that gives rise to our linguistic curmudgeon-ness.

Much of our problem with language—and especially the

parts of it that violate our sense of linguistic decorum—is that we have come to understand it from a singular point of view, the one provided by that ubiquitous red pen in English class. But if the pen is really mightier than the sword, how come every generation brings with it new forms and features that seem to cut down the ones that came before? The answer, as we will discover, is because language change is natural, built into the language system itself, and not just a way for teenagers to torture their parents. And trust me, as a parent I have had plenty of experience biting my tongue after being called "dude" and then being treated to "huh?" as the main conversational contribution. But whether one finds the innovations that come along in language useful (googling, tweeting, and facebooking) or useless (um . . . like . . . uh . . . you know), they are an inevitability. So we might as well try to understand where they come from, what they really mean, and why we use them.

MY OWN PATH TO LINGUISTIC REVELATION CAME IN THE FORM of early life experience. You see, when I was a child, I had no idea my parents had accents. Sure, they were born in Belgium and Montreal and cooked coq au vin instead of fried catfish and cornbread (haute cuisine in my hometown of Memphis, Tennessee), but to me, they sounded like everyone else—except when they argued, discussed critical issues like whether or not there was ice cream in the fridge, and debated child-related disciplinary action. That they did in French. Language became a game, a code for me to crack, especially when it involved dessert, or various forms of punishment. And so I learned French, to lift the parental veil of secrecy and to learn cusswords I wouldn't get in trouble for using at school.

My next great linguistic aha moment came when I was in college, at Georgetown University. I had signed up to be a Chinese major, and it wasn't going well. The Chinese tone system did not get along with my Southern twang. In fact, my drill-master (otherwise known as my professor) told me I sounded like I was singing Chinese opera, which he did not mean as a compliment. Nonetheless, I soldiered on. As part of my program, I had to take six linguistics courses, and on a whim I signed up for a course called Language and Gender. Truthfully, this said less about me than about the other classes on offer (Computational Linguistics and Theoretical Semantics, anyone?). I had no idea that this one class would change the way I looked at the world.

Starting from day one, we took a deep, hard look at the idea that speech defines and is defined by the gender we identify with and the ideologies we operate under. We considered why boys say *f@#k* while girls say *fudge*, how power and language are intimately connected, and why this matters long past arguments at playgrounds and into negotiations in boardrooms. Up to this point, I had never really considered how linguistic differences were so dependent on social conditioning. I had never stopped to think about how age, gender, ethnicity, economics, and even politics could play a part in how we talked and how we sounded. The class held history, current affairs, and my own conception of self up to a mirror I never knew existed.

And even more revealing to my eighteen-year-old insecure self, this first linguistics class gave me a better understanding of why I spoke the way I did and how it was not only tied to where I hailed from—the *y'all* usually gave that away pretty quickly—but was also a way to establish who I was and how I fit in. For instance, why my overly polite way of apologizing for imposition that some found annoying reflected a broader nineteenth-century shift in the form of our politeness, or how my use of "I've got to" instead of "must" reflected a larger deescalation of deontic modality this century.* All this before I even got into the nitty-gritty of phonological and morphosyntactic theory.†

For every seeming linguistic quirk or curiosity, I discovered a much more fascinating historical and scientific explanation. And so, instead of becoming a Chinese opera singer, I began my illustrious career as a linguist—a decision I have never regretted, and one that provided a perfect way to meld my scientific

---

* In simplest terms, deontic modality refers to how language expresses obligation, permissibility, or possibility.

† Morphology is the field of linguistics concerned with how words are formed. Syntax is the area of linguistics that focuses on how sentences are structured. Morphosyntax refers to the study of the interaction between morphology and syntax, such as when words are put into sentences. For instance, case is often marked on pronoun forms (e.g., *he* versus *him*) depending on whether it serves as a subject or object in the sentence.

curiosity and my desire to bring what I learned outside the hallowed halls of the academy to the people who live language every day.

Since these early college days, I have taught untold numbers of linguistics courses and written an embarrassing number of articles that would put most nonlinguists to sleep. But I have never forgotten how it felt to see behind the linguistic curtain for the first time, or the eye-opening thrill it was to suddenly understand that speech science could explain my inability to successfully master pronouncing the rounded front vowels of French in words like *deux* or *tu*. Admittedly, it took a bit longer to convince my mother of the scientific validity of my mispronunciation, but eventually, after pointing out her replacement of *th* sounds with *z*, i.e., *ze* for *the*, we came to an understanding. In both cases, our native language's phonological system lacks sounds (or phonemes) that exist in the other language. Since we acquire our native sound systems as babies, it makes it extremely hard to learn a different one once we are older. This is why, for a somewhat similar underlying linguistic reason, Japanese speakers sometimes have problems with *r*'s and *l*'s in English. Though Japanese does contain both sounds, they are variants of the same sound, not two separate sounds as in English, which makes it very hard to distinguish them.* These are not so much errors as

---

* English speakers also produce a number of variations of sounds that we hear as the same but that function as separate sounds in other languages. For instance, in English there is a very subtle difference between the *p* sound in the word *pit* and

they are beautiful examples of how our conceptual system and our social system work together to make us native language speakers.

MUCH TO THE CONSTERNATION OF THOSE WHO HAVE FOUND it quite the tongue twister when introducing me at talks, my fascination with the social side of language inspired me to become what is referred to as a sociolinguist. A sociolinguist is interested in empirically investigating speech features such as those we will talk about in this book, and even more subtle speech differences still—like whether we choose to say *wha . . .?* or *what?*—with a specific interest in how they function socially. But why should we even care about such seemingly tiny things?

Because, in viewing how these small linguistic choices help us craft social identities and affect how we are perceived when we use them, we come to find they have a surprisingly powerful impact. Take, for example, the variations in the way we pronounce the *t* sound in the word *what* mentioned above. There are three very common ways this sound is realized in English—a

---

that in the word *spit*, though most of us are blissfully unaware of it. This is referred to as aspiration—in word initial positions, *p* is pronounced with more expelled air. In languages like Thai or Hindi, this type of tiny difference makes a meaningful distinction between sounds that it doesn't in English. In other words, *p* and aspirated *p* are understood as completely different sounds—just like *p* and *b* would be heard in English.

fully released *t* version that sounds a bit like *what-hh?* with a puff of air at the end (the release); another less intense version where the tongue tip makes contact with the top of the mouth without subsequent air puffing (*what?*), and, finally, a variant known as a glottal stop, which has become a shibboleth of some less well-regarded varieties as in *wha . . .?* (or the more familiar *bu'ah* for "butter").

The version we choose is governed not by linguistic dictum but rather by our social background and our goals in conversation. *What-hh* can often be a signal of exasperation, annoyance, or impatience (e.g., in response to the cheeky child who keeps saying "Mom, mom, mom"), while *what* would tend to emerge when we are talking to someone less familiar or in a context like when we are at work. In contrast, *wha?* communicates either casual familiarity (e.g., a query when your friend gives you a funny look) or an orientation to a specific group or dialect in which this feature is recognizable (a Cockney speaker or a youthful Californian). In each case, the English sound system offers options for producing the *t* sound that don't change the conceptual meaning (e.g., it's still *what* no matter how we say it) but instead can be put to work to communicate social or stylistic meaning.*

In examining how real speakers put these options to work, sociolinguistic research confirms that this one tiny little difference

---

* These variants of a single sound (like those slightly different *p* sounds in English mentioned in the previous footnote) are called allophones by linguists.

in the way we say a *t* is very much tied to the needs and aims of speakers. For instance, one study found self-described "nerd" girls used the released *t* (*what* with a little release of air) at a higher rate than the frequently *t*-glottalizing cool girls as a way of sounding hyperarticulate and "nerdy." Another study found that Orthodox Jewish boys who were more focused on studying Talmud increased their rate of released *t* sounds to come across as more insistent and authoritative, especially when trying to mark a strong point. Girls in the same study did not, likely because the gendered expectations put on them in such communities were quite different, a division of vocal labor we will learn is far from unusual.

Your speech says a lot more about you than you probably realize, because you, like every other speaker on the planet, unconsciously vary the features you use. It is the job of a sociolinguist to figure out the meaning and pattern behind the forms, and why they have come to be used in that way over time.

FOR MANY YEARS AFTER BECOMING A LINGUISTICS PROFESsor, I happily puttered away as an academic, content to have my work read solely by the other fifty scholars who, like me, couldn't ever get enough research on the hot topic of American vowel movements. While it is fair to say that my publications on this topic might not have been big sellers outside of the academy, this probably wasn't helped by the fact that I was often mistaken for a gastroenterologist hawking books about bowels rather than vowels.* But still, for a language nerd like me, I was content in my corner of the world, unraveling the mystery behind some pretty fascinating sound changes affecting contemporary English.

But as I became older, wiser, and safely tenured, I was reminded of my own early linguistic curiosity when I was lecturing to students or giving talks about sociolinguistics to nonacademics. The concerns they expressed and the questions they asked were not the ones those of us researching sociolinguistics or phonetics tended to spend much time on. We had become focused on the internal mechanics of how language works, forgetting to serve as translators of this knowledge to the very people that language works *for*. Over the years, the idea for the topics covered in this book took form as I started to pay attention to what those who are in the language trenches—parents, employers, students, and, often, just friends—truly wanted to know.

---

* Alas, this easy perceptual confusion between *b* sounds and *v* sounds stems from the way the two sounds are both articulated with the lips. To make a *b* sound, we use both lips (bilateral), while a *v* involves the lip and the teeth (labiodental). But given the similarity in lip involvement, they can come out sounding rather similar in rapid articulation—a bane for those of us who happen to say "vowel movements" a lot in everyday speech.

Choices, choices, choices!

Although on the surface the topics I was asked about were wide-ranging, most questions lobbed my way centered around a common theme—that of the unceasing rise of what are viewed as annoying tics in the speech people heard around them—be it saying *like* all the time, vocal fry, or just the perceived decline of formality in contemporary English more generally. Often people would tell me about their own speech quirks, like the podcaster who felt self-conscious about what others had called out as his overly frequent use of "right?" Other times, I would hear about what drove people crazy in others' speech, e.g., the omnipresent "so" that one woman said she had banned her subordinates from using in front of her. In sociolinguistics, of course, we don't view these as tics at all, but rather as important linguistic features that developed the same way all the other forms we use on a regular basis have come to us—through the evolution of earlier forms shaped by changing social and linguistic pressures.

Though parents, teachers, and even speakers themselves see these contemporary features as arising from ignorance, laziness, or the sad decay of our grammatical principles, it is only because they lack the perspective that a full linguistic account can provide. After all, while the popular conception might be that we are moving in the wrong direction, few would suggest that the language of *Beowulf* represented the apex of English. Providing a perspective that is a world away from the grammar lessons drilled into us since elementary school, the fascinating stories that these features bring with them—shaped by historical conflicts, class struggles, gender norms, and generational gaps—offer an enjoyable and often humorous romp through our language past and straight into our present.

There have been a great many more speech forms brought up over the years than chapters possible here, but the choice of which ones to include was driven by those that have gotten a lot of attention in the media as well as fueled heated discussions over nightly dinner tables—and the ones that invariably get asked about in my classes and lectures. These features have come to be embedded in our everyday talk because, as annoying as some might find them, they appeal to us at a fundamental level. They are the ones that have steadily crept into the speech of those who live under our roofs and work in our offices, and despite firm convictions to the contrary, have made inroads into our own. In short, they are the tics that bug us precisely because they seem to be squarely central to what we will be saying well into our linguistic future.

Of course, beyond these examples, there are a lot of other speech features that have been called out as "bad" English. Many of these are associated with disfavored groups in American society and subject to a form of linguistic elitism that has very real consequences for speakers who use them. This devaluation is often tied to larger issues of race, class, and nation, and the reasons why they elicit the kinds of discriminatory responses they do involves more dedicated and complex theoretical unpacking than there is space for here, but a key point that I hope emerges is that there's no "right" way to speak English. As with many of the features covered in these pages, things like double negatives, which are strongly ethnically marked or classed and, as a result, often regarded as incorrect, have an equally interesting (and often surprising) derivational history and were once looked at very differently in earlier forms of English. What we will learn in this journey we are about to take together is that the difference between the features we embrace and those we can't tolerate is really just one of power and perspective.

Language rules!

There is no doubt that, by the time we reach adulthood, most of us know a lot about our language and how to speak it. After all, English rules have been drilled into us since our earliest school days, when we learn to use "may" instead of "can" and sing catchy little ditties about the myriad functions of our conjunctions. But if we want to really understand how language is used to express our social selves, we have to completely reimagine the way we think about language in the first place. In other words, we have to start thinking about language like a linguist.

When linguists study language, they look at how language is structured and how that structure guides the way it is used and how it changes. We examine what's possible and impossible cognitively and what we actually do as speakers, rather than relying on our socialized conceptions about language. For instance, can you tell me, quickly, how many vowels you use when you speak? Is a chorus of "*a, e, i, o, u*" running through your head? Then the lessons of first grade have clearly stuck.

But what if I told you that, from a linguist's point of view, you were absolutely wrong? Say *beat, bit, bait, bet, bat, bought, bout, boat, bot, but, boy, bite, book,* and *boot.** That's more than five, isn't it? Without all these vowel differences, most of these words would sound the same, leaving an arrest warrant the only difference between *betting* someone and *beating* them.†

---

* Depending on the dialect you speak, you may have slightly more (as in the British English *f-ah-ther* vowel) or slightly fewer (West Coast varieties) as a result of changes that have taken place over time. If some of these words sound the same to you (*bought* and *bot*) then you are what we refer to as a low-back vowel merger. Historically (and for many modern speakers still), these words contain different vowels.

† As mentioned in an earlier footnote, languages vary in which phonemes (sounds) mean something to speakers of that language, and English has an unusually large vowel inventory. For example, for an English speaker, the vowels *i* and *I* (*beat* versus *bit*) are meaningfully distinct and are the only reason words like *sheet* and *shit* are discernably different to us, but many languages, including Italian and Spanish, do not have this long and short (or more accurately, tense versus lax) vowel distinction. Given our relentless enjoyment of language-related humor, this difference provides fodder for many a joke involving the *shit/sheet* and

Clearly, we have been serious vowel deniers, all because we have been taught, since we were little, to think about language in a very particular way—one influenced strongly by how we write rather than how we talk. We write with five letters to represent English vowels, the ones you so perfectly recited just above, but we *say* many more vowel sounds than this. Looking at language like a linguist requires focusing not on what we've learned language "should" be, but on the units, rules, and principles that allow humans the capacity to speak, and on the psychological, social, and historical influences that shape how we do so.*

While learning how to follow grammar rules in school is certainly not without merit, we forget we were speaking to each other centuries before we were reading, writing, or sending texts, and we did pretty well at organizing and advancing long before prescriptive conventions came around. Indeed, most of what we tend to think of as language "rules" were actually just social preferences, decided on by those invested in codifying English usage so that it could be transmitted across time and space. A noble and necessary aim, to be sure, but over time we have confused such externally imposed standards—often molded on the model of Latin and based on the speech of the upper crust—with inherent goodness and correctness.

---

beach/bitch confusion of those who have learned to speak more languages than most Americans do.

* These units (e.g., sounds, word parts like *-ing* and *-ed*; and syntactic categories like nouns and verbs) and the rules and principles that guide how we combine them make up what we refer to as a speaker's (linguistic) grammar.

These ideas about what is "right" and what is "wrong" were very much influenced by who was steering English as it emerged from the shadow of classical languages. Written words and forms used at court became elevated, while plain old everyday speech, especially of those without the right pedigree or skin color, paled in comparison. But we forget that we love, work, forge friendships, and raise children not in formal standard English, but by using language that allows us to express ourselves and establish connections. While writing and public speaking might call for erasing our *like*s and *um*s, everyday speech follows our internal linguistic grammar—the rules and principles that dictate the possible form that languages and dialects will take as they evolve over time—rather than prescriptivist preferences. This doesn't mean that speech has no rules—in contrast there are many constraints built into our linguistic system—but only by exploring the range of human languages and what speech patterns are possible and impossible across them can we come to understand what the rules are and how they work.*

Thus, when teens adopt new intensifiers like *hella*, when Southerners drop a *g* or when adults use *literally*, well, nonliterally, it may feel like they are precipitously close to inciting grammar apocalypse. But they are actually adhering to solid linguistic principles—just not the ones we're typically schooled on (like not

---

* As we will discover in the next chapter, linguistic rules and constraints stem from how language is organized in our brains, how we process and encode our experience in the world, and how sounds are produced using our vocal anatomy.

ending a sentence with a preposition). These underlying linguistic rules, and the social forces that engage with them, paved the path of our language long before Grammarly or even Jonathan Swift came onto the scene.* So we can leave our modifiers to dangle, split our infinitives without remorse, and strand our prepositions out on the edges of our sentences without violating any linguistic rules, though perhaps recklessly abandoning some socially inscribed ones.

There can be little debate that the linguistic choices we make are not always everyone's cup of tea. Yet, despite legislation, shaming, and vociferous threats of professional ruin, best efforts at eradicating what's new and novel rarely do much more than spawn a flurry of headlines about the decline of English, only to be forgotten decades later once they have become de rigueur in even our own speech. The reality is that we are all the products of centuries of similar linguistic innovations, but we were just not witness to the process as we are with the current crop du jour of speech habits people are talking about. Before we join the chorus that cringes at the creak in Kim Kardashian's voice or we give up because our office mate refuses to accept our wise counsel that "irregardless" is not a word, let's take a look at what a long history of language change might be able to teach us.

---

* Eighteenth-century writer Jonathan Swift, more widely known today as the author of *Gulliver's Travels*, was a firm believer that language reform was necessary in order to protect it from the detrimental ravages of change.

Nowadays, do you say "It is I" instead of "It's me"? And if so, do your friends bow or curtsy out of deference for your royal ways? Do you regularly *whom*, or do you feel okay about *who* and just hope they remember the wine when invited to dinner? And do you have strong feelings about people who say *artic* for "arctic," or does the lack of a *k* sound not even cause you to break a sweat? Many of us have gotten so used to these so-called violations of prescriptivist no-nos that we don't even think they sound bad anymore.

And often, our notion of what's correct and what's not is not even accurate—a reflection of our prioritizing the written word over the spoken one. For example, according to the *Oxford English Dictionary*, the go-to authority on first known uses of words, the *c*-less *artic* is the original form, dating back to the fourteenth century from Old French *artique*. The pronunciation with a *k* sound viewed as correct today was a (mis)pronunciation arising from a spelling change adopted in the seventeenth century.* So naysayers beware. Living only in our modern language moments, we lose sight of the valuable lessons that we should take from our language past. As we uncover the history

---

* It was not until the seventeenth century that the word was revised in spelling to be more similar to its Greek root *Arctos*, originally meaning "bear," as part of a larger effort to mold English spelling in the image of classical languages. The pronunciation shifted because people then started mistakenly pronouncing the *c* that now appeared in writing. For the full story, check out Arnold Zwicky, "Ar(c)tic." *Language Log*, July 22, 2008, languagelog.ldc.upenn.edu/nll/?p=342.

and patterns behind contemporary tics such as seemingly incessant *like* use, pauses packed with *um*s and *uh*s, and the creaking
vocal fry that sounds like popping corn at the ends of phrases,
we will learn how the language of our future is really built on
the linguistic and social forces of our past. We might still hate
it when someone says these things, but at least we will better
understand why they do.

I speak therefore I am?

Remember the iconic "Wassup?" commercial from Budweiser,
featuring an endless tongue-wagging "Wasssssssssssssup" back
and forth among a bunch of friends? If an alien beamed down to
earth and tried to figure out what heck was going on, we would
be hard-pressed to explain it. The allure of that commercial, if
one can even use the word *allure* in this context, is how that
phrase captured the way we use language to "get" each other in
a hey-how-ya-doing-just-watching-football-bonding kind of way.
I get it and I don't even like football. Once a phrase like that
gains momentum, and we start to associate a certain feature
with a particular identity or personality, it offers us a shorthand
way to communicate who we are.

Such shared aspects of talk are an integral part of how we
build connection with others. For example, when I lived and

taught in Istanbul early in my career, I learned as much as I could about Turkish culture and, with the exception of one unfortunate run-in with lamb intestines that involved wild dogs, explored Turkish cuisine quite enthusiastically. And though most Turkish two-year-olds would have had me at *merhaba*, I tried, albeit badly, to learn the language. While I never managed even remote competence, my efforts at speaking Turkish, even if limited to tossing a few *Tamam* ("okay") into my lectures, made a huge difference in how I was received: not as an outsider but as someone genuine in my desire to fit in. Still, when I ran into another American English speaker, we were much faster friends than we would have been upon a similar chance meeting in the United States, quickly launching into a gleeful recounting of things we missed (Skippy peanut butter and drip coffee!) or funny stories from back home. Why? Because sharing a dialect intimates that we view things with a similar interpretive lens, that we have a shared perspective on the world and on the others in it that comes from growing up speaking the same code. An important lesson here too is that our identity is not static. So why should our language be?

Though we might have strong opinions about what makes for good language, and what makes for bad, this rarely influences how we speak when we are getting through our day-to-day lives. While speech features that become strongly associated with a certain type of speaker might take some heat in the hallowed halls of the English Department building, such as the teen phe-nomenon *like* or a class-based feature like *ain't*, on the runway of everyday life, we use them to project different attitudes and stances toward what we talk about and who we talk with. Think of the teacher who interprets a *Yo!* as an invitation to engage with her students, the *y'all* that we perceive as down to earth and friendly, the hyperarticulate *t* release at the end of our indignant *What?* or the emotional or excited expletives we use when talk-ing to our friends (though maybe not in front of our parents). All of these forms and features had histories before we used them, and without consciously realizing it, we draw on these associa-tions to bring home our points, relate to friends, and sometimes even impress prospective dates. It's this uptake by others that tends to really draw notice and gets the social meaning ball fully rolling.

For example, we didn't hear a lot of broader commentary about the term *bro*—or its vast utility as a prefix (*bromance, broflake, bromiserate*)—despite its long-standing use in African American English, until its fairly recent appropriation by young white speakers drawing on its sense of a brotherhood born through shared experience (but unfortunately erasing the racial-ized struggles that defined it). Many of the words or terms we use today, like *bruh* or *finna* or *zoom bombing*, enter English through initiating users in specific ethnic, regional, or special-ized groups. But then they get picked up by more and more speakers outside that community, often with piggybacking but shifted meaning, and get used for what they have come to communicate without recognition of where they started.*

We also lean on different features of language for the advantage it can give us as "insiders," whether it's to help us not get beaten up at lunch over our lack of cool, or to get noticed by the boss at the office. Margaret Thatcher famously changed her voice to fit the prevailing ideas about what a political leader should sound like—namely, powerful and male. Thatcher had to convince people that she was capable, strong, and intelligent, rather than accommodating, soft, and weak, qualities often associated with the way women speak (whether true or not). While she was often accused of sounding too much like a man, a criticism commonly faced by women in positions of power (e.g., Hillary Clinton), women's speech habits have long been held aside as less forceful and less convincing—two traits that most certainly don't instill a great deal of voter confidence. Despite the progress women have made in the years since the Iron Lady dropped her voice pitch, these ideas about gender and language still buttress our attitudes to the verbal habits we most love to hate. Women continue to get a lot of grief for using *like*, for over-apologizing, and for the frequent populating of our sentences

---

* For instance, *bro* and *bruh* originated in African American English, *finna* developed from southern *fixing to*, and *zoom bombing* was used predominately in online communities.

with intensifiers like *so*, *really*, or *totally*. Yet, as we will find out, the reality of why and how women and men use features like these is infinitely more complicated and arrives by way of a fascinating and unexpected history.

The idea of language as tying us to a community is key to understanding what drives our linguistic choices. It isn't usually sounding like you went to Yale or Cambridge that makes you tight with friends, voters, or colleagues. In fact, often it's the exact opposite. To be real, to reach people, to be approachable, now that requires people to feel like you are genuine. Such authenticity is communicated not by sounding smarter than everyone else in the room, but by sounding like you know a thing or two about life on the streets, on the farm, or in the valley. So instead of aiming for the voice of a news anchor, most of us prefer to take the opposite tack, especially since we don't generally hit the pub with the man in the boardroom or the woman on TV. Instead, we want to sound like somebody others can recognize and relate to. And there is no better way to do that than to use the speech equivalent of solidarity. A pleasant *y'all*, a laid-back *dude*, an unpretentious *whassup?*, now these are what tell people a bit about who we are and where we came from. Familiar speech habits are the grassroots of communication—they let us find common ground and establish relationships.

And, never short on finding an angle to help them be relatable, politicians have definitely jumped on this authentic speech bandwagon. In the United States, part of Donald Trump's persona was built on his brash speech style, his *we/they* pronominal dichotomizing, his frequent use of insults like *moron, stupid, loser,* and of course, his inventive word coinage. Much of his appeal came from sounding less like a president and more like just a regular Joe. In a similar effort to have more "everyman" appeal, former British Prime Minister Tony Blair blended features of Cockney with his otherwise posh accent, so much so that he has been accused of speaking "mockney." And of course, think of one-time vice-presidential hopeful Sarah Palin's appeal as a down-home Alaska gal.* Her noticeable accent, and her use of folksy terms like *Joe Six Pack* and *you betcha,* was a huge part of her appeal, and, as a bonus, provided great fodder for office water-cooler impressionists.

How we talk helps others see us the way we want them to, whether we do it consciously or not. It unites us, or sometimes divides us, it makes us cool, or at least fit in. It helps us build our identities by drawing on the linguistic forms and innovations that we collectively assign social meanings, like edgy, gendered, urban, smart, street, gangsta, conformist, hip, or geek. While

---

* Ms. Palin's accent has often been noted as having a Minnesotan twang, and, in fact, the area Ms. Palin hails from, namely, the Wasilla/Matanuska-Susitna Valley, does have a history of upper-midwestern settlement—but whether this truly accounts for her homey speech style is not entirely clear. Besides Palin's Mat-Su Valley English variety, there are a number of recognizable Alaskan English dialects, including Tlingit English, which, because of its Indigenous substrate origin, tends to be viewed negatively in contrast to the warm fuzzies that seem to be given off by Palin's accent.

these up-and-coming speech habits may not scream "correct," they reveal something even more important: our personality and our people.

Join the revolution, dude

Rather than point to any kind of absolutism, our linguistic likes and dislikes are spurred, instead, by our social needs and wants. Speech is deeply entwined with our sense of self, and with the way we feel about each other, which is why the nuances of language affect us all in deeply subconscious ways. Just like an older generation might judge a younger generation for wearing ripped jeans and sporting tattoos, so, too, it's likely to jump to conclusions based on different verbal trends.

Though many of the features discussed here might be most recognizable as belonging to American English, often their history begins much before colonists came to the New World, and their reach has traveled far beyond American shores. Whether one lives in New Dehli, Newcastle, or New York, the capacity for language to adapt and change is universal. In these pages, insights from historical linguistics, sociolinguistics, and other areas of linguistic science offer a window into where these features come from and where they are going. As these chapters will reveal, our linguistic choices are motivated by much more than simply transmitting information. Even the features that we love to hate construct an image so others can see who we are and where we fit in. Language, we will learn, is both function and fashion. And its most fashion-forward leaders—the stylistic icons that forge the linguistic path ahead—will surprise you.

1

Linguistic Fashionistas

Language change is an essential part of our language endowment, and like our opposable thumbs and lack of fur, it has evolved in the service of our needs, even if we don't all find the end results immediately attractive. Before we can talk about innovative linguistic forms like, well, *like*, *so*, *totally*, and singular *they*, we first have to tackle the larger idea of how and why language varies. Though it may seem counterintuitive given our notions of what constitutes "good" English, all the features we'll talk about in this book represent not a deterioration but a healthy progression of language. For some reason, we are often despondent about language change, despite the fact that, without it, English would all just sound like Icelandic to us.

Our language became the most powerful and far-flung language in the world not because it avoided changing, but because our eager tongues embraced it, at least in the earlier part of our history. As anyone who has attempted to read *Beowulf* already knows, Old English (OE) is as unintelligible to us modern English speakers as a foreign language. While some basics remain, between the Old and Middle English periods we shifted to a radically different system. How different? Well, for one thing, Old English would have made Yoda very happy, having a much looser word order than we have today. Liketh it, he would. And forget dropping the mic—the last thousand years have seen us drop pretty much every ending that previously existed in our language. So if you get upset with someone deleting *s* in plural forms, saying things like *three dollar*, you should really consider whether someone speaking a variety that shed hundreds of similar endings should be casting stones. In Old English, almost every word contained an ending that carried information about things like its gender, word class, case, and number, making its position in a sentence less constrained than is requisite today, as its endings helped us keep all that straight. But all of these slowly became obsolete as other languages like Old Norse, Latin, and Norman French introduced changes and, in particular, helped weaken the OE stress pattern, eventually leading to the loss of endings by destressing final syllables.

I mentioned Icelandic before not just because any language with names like Bjork and Eyjafjallajökull deserves mention, but as a reminder that language change is driven in great part by the social and linguistic behavior of speakers. Modern-day German, a sister language derivatively to modern English, has also changed substantively from the Proto-German that spawned both languages. In contrast, Icelandic, another relative on the Germanic family tree, is more conservative than either English or German, as it has been subject to overt linguistic governance in the form of regulating language bodies and written standardization.* As a result, it has retained more of the characteristic types of features that were prevalent in both Old English and Old Norse, such as the very complex inflectional system (it still has a mouthful of endings on words). However, we don't hear many Icelandic speakers lamenting what those vulgar English have done to their proto-language, or at least not in public. But even still, the Icelandic of today has had to keep up with the modern world and its new words, so even in the face of much more overt linguistic regulation, change cometh still, but just in different form. And though English has certainly altered its structure more than Icelandic, the changes we face today are miniscule compared to those that occurred many centuries ago. What has really shifted over the past three hundred years is not so much our language (in comparison to these earlier changes) but our ideas about linguistic correctness and authority.† So

---

* Though both English and Icelandic have Proto-Germanic roots, they are more like cousins than sisters. Icelandic is, along with Norwegian, Danish, and Faroese, of North Germanic descent. English and German are descended from West Germanic languages.

† Something that has also been discussed as the rise of a "complaint tradition" in English (e.g., Milroy and Milroy's classic *Authority in Language: Investigating Standard English*).

what, exactly, turned us from free-form speakers to prisoners beholden to grammar rules?

IN THE DAYS OF THE ANGLO-SAXONS, ENGLISH WAS THE word on the street (or horse path), it was the talk between friends, it was the curses hurled at one's enemies, but it was not so much the language associated with status, with God, or with learning. That honor belonged with the Romance languages—first Latin, and later French. Predating English, Latin had arrived with the Roman Legionnaires that occupied what they referred to as "Britannia" until the fifth century. And despite the crumbling of the Roman Empire, the legacy of Latin in the British Isles was far from over. A couple of centuries later, following the conversion to Christianity of the newly settled Germanic tribes whose tongues would end up as English's founding dialects, Latin rose again as the language of education and of religion. Important transactions were recorded not in English, but in Latin. As a result, grammar rules were not high on the list of what the Old English movers and shakers were worried about—at least not the rules of English. Latin, a classical language, had both a scholarly tradition and an elitist cachet that English at that time lacked, and it meant that English was free to develop unhindered by ideas about how it *should* be.

This view of English as not worthy of much literary or grammatical study was even more pronounced with the onset of the Middle English period and the invasion of the French-speaking Normans in 1066. For hundreds of years, Britain was ruled by people who did not speak the language of the common man or woman. English, a tongue considered vulgar and low class by the new social elite, might get you a position in the kitchen, but not in the court or government where documents were written in Anglo-Norman French or Latin. By not being the language of the elite, English was not constrained by top-down regulation, though it was still subject to substantial linguistic (and social) pressure from French.* As a result, English shed much of its Germanic word stock and changed up its sound system and morphology (combining Old-English roots with Old-French suffixes like -ance, as in "hindrance"). It took on loads of new words from French and Latin, gained several new sounds (welcome *v* and *z*), and said au revoir to many of its Old-English endings (good-bye -en†). It's a good thing the French also brought

---

* Sir Walter Scott's classic *Ivanhoe* nicely characterizes politics and language in post-Norman England and provides insight into how this inequitable relationship between the Anglo-Saxons and the French led to the dichotomous animal (Saxon) versus food (Norman) names still in play today, such as *swine* (*pig*)/*pork* and *cow*/*beef*.

† Ever wonder why we say *oxen* instead *oxes*? You can thank our German roots for that in the form of the Old English -an/-en plural suffix that coexisted with a -s plural ending. By the fourteenth century, -s had pretty much become the only way to pluralize, and -en was maintained in fewer and fewer word forms, like *oxen* and *children*. While this shift is not directly attributed to the influence of

us fashion, medicine, art, and music (as in literally brought us these words!), so we can forgive this intrusion into our language. In this melding of the speech of the common and the powerful, the foundation of the English we hold so dear today was laid. Notably, not from linguistic stasis or prescription but from nothing short of dynamic linguistic and social upheaval. But before English could fully ascend, it had to throw off the shackles of Norman French. And it is through its rise to prominence starting around the fifteenth century that English began to take on shackles of a different sort—that of standardization and prescription.

The transition to English as the language of power, education, and high society was greatly helped along by the increasing urbanization and cultural prominence of London in the early modern period. London's East Midland dialect became the fashionable dialect of those hobnobbing with the royals, those doing the work of government administration at the Chancery Court, as well as the "better brought up sort" for whom the city was home. Toss in William Caxton's introduction of the printing press in 1476, which led to the adoption of the London dialect as the literary standard, and you have a perfect prescriptivist storm in the making.

French, -s was adopted early by Anglo-Normans, likely helping usher this leveling along. (For more on this and other developments during this period, a good overview is provided in chapter 7 of the classic *A History of the English Language* by Albert C. Baugh and Thomas Cable.)

Still, it really took until the eighteenth century, with the increasing publication of dictionaries and usage guides and the focus on language "purification," for the guardians of culture to start caring about enshrining English *as it should be*. With new rules came more opportunities for linguistic rebellion, and evolving speech habits became the enemy. Perhaps not the same tics we complain about today (though you'll be surprised to learn that some have managed to annoy for centuries), but the same repugnance toward new forms, and, often, those who use them. These speech habits came about through the same old process of language change that existed for millennia, but for the first time, they butted up against some powerful social regulations. As a result, people really started to notice them and tried to eradicate them from the speech around them.

By the nineteenth century, upper-crust preferences for single *nots* instead of double negatives (*don't got none*), *asking* instead of *aksing*, and for dropping *r*'s but finding *t*'s (*bu'Tah* for "butter") were de rigueur, modeled by those most fashionable. Yet no matter how many times we try to get people to talk like we want them to, another tic we are not so fond of rises up to take its place. Like those irritating American *d* sounds where once there were *t*'s (*buD-er*), or our love affair with *so*, *well*, and *okay* as sentence starters, and the perpetual favorites *like* and *you know*. Instead of fighting it, at some point it makes sense to step back and consider why language just doesn't get the hint.

Behold the linguistic force

The bigger question is really why languages change, rather than what they look like at any one single point in time. Language change is born of a secret recipe that combines underlying and long-standing internal linguistic pressures with very au courant social ones—things like imperialism, urbanization, migration, ecological shift, social upheaval, and maybe even the sway of a social influencer or two. Key to why dialects evolve over time is understanding how our psychological and physical system of language engages with our social system.

There are always underlying cognitive and articulatory forces—i.e., the way our brains work and how our mouths operate—that guide the linguistic forms that languages tend to have and the shape that change will take when spurred on by a social "trigger" like those just mentioned. For example, preferences in syllable structure are thought to be universal, with syllables that take the form of one consonant + one vowel (like "me" or "do") found in all languages, but syllables with lots of consonants (like "widths" or "strengths") much less frequent. And as we see from such examples, English syllables can be very promiscuous when it comes to consonant clustering.

But when a bunch of consonants jump on the vowel bandwagon, a word is tricky to pronounce.* Just try saying "sixths" three times fast—it's right up there with Sally selling seashells. One inherent tendency, then, is to delete consonants in such clusters to get closer to more preferred (some even say more natural) and pronounceable syllables. But for some higher-status speakers of English, class ideology and the influence of institutionalized language norms artificially preserve consonant clustering, while speakers less tied to these social constraints reduce consonant complexity in line with intrinsic pressures, giving rise to pronunciations like *tes* for "test" or *tol* for "told."

Despite thinking that such pronunciation represents "bad" speech, all speakers actually delete consonants in this same pattern, for the same underlying reasons, but just not to the same degree.† For instance, rapidly say "I have a test Monday" and you'll find confirmation that everyone's speech follows a very similar route of consonant deletion in casual speech, here of the last *t* in *test*. This tendency is certainly nothing new in English. Haven't you ever wondered where the *d* in *handsome*, the *l* in *talk*, and the *t* in *often* went? All the result of a similar type of

---

* Often consonants end up in such clusters because words undergo various processes like suffixation or vowel deletion that result in consonants becoming newly adjacent (or they are borrowed from languages with somewhat different rules about which and how many consonants can cluster).

† Despite our tendency to ignore this pattern of deletion in our own speech, studies of consonant deletion have found such unanimity in this regard that linguist Gregory Guy wrote, "Every speaker ever studied does it at least occasionally," as cited in S. Tagliamonte and R. Temple, "New Perspectives on an Ol' Variable: (t,d) in British English," *Language Variation and Change* 17, no. 3 (2005): 281–302.

simplification process at work at an earlier point in our language's history. Luckily, since we've been deleting those consonants since about the fifteenth century, no one's around to judge us for it. But drop a little *l* from a word like *help* today, and you'd think #grammargeddon was upon you.

On the other end of the spectrum, sometimes we add instead of subtract to help make our consonants easier to say. For instance, do you say *ham-ster* or pop in a *p* as in *hamp-ster*? Or how about our Irish friends for whom *film* is broken into *fil-um* with an extra vowel to help manage the awkwardness between the *l* and the *m*?* And while we might naysay those who put the *uh* in *ath-uh-lete*, all of us can probably agree that *thuner* for *thunder* sounds weird. Yet it's much closer to the word's original pronunciation, at least until an extra *d* slipped in during the Middle-English period in pursuit of achieving a more harmonious syllable structure. So, while change might feel haphazard and incorrect, it's anything but unnatural or bad, motivated by underlying mental and articulatory constraints and principles. But when linguistic differences appear to go hand in hand with social differences, they tend to become a hot spot despite the fact that similar things have happened over and over in the course of our language.

A great example of how our reactions to recognizable fea-

---

* In *Romeo and Juliet,* Shakespeare spells the word *film* as *philome,* which hints of a similar pronunciation (though not used with the same meaning that *film* most often carries today).

tures are determined by how we feel about who is doing the talking rather than anything about the speech itself is the way some dialects of English don't pronounce the *r* sound when it follows a vowel in words like *heart, short,* or *better,* leaving them to sound more like *hot, shot,* and *betah.* This pattern can make for a merger in a number of word pairs like *god* and *guard, father* and *farther,* and most embarrassingly in polite company, *pawn* and *porn.* This difference is what linguists call rhoticity (which strangely always makes me hungry for chicken), and it sets apart posh British speech from most dialects in American English, where, with the exception of some New Yorkers, Southerners, and Bostonians, we pronounce our *r*'s in all the traditional places. But what's interesting is how the exact opposite pattern has emerged as to what's considered prestigious. In other words, what's good in Britain would be considered bad in America and vice versa, both simply falling out from the sociohistorical turn of events surrounding migration from Britain to the New World. You see, in the seventeenth and early eighteenth centuries, many British settlers arriving in the New World brought their *r*'s with them, as this was the norm at the time in Britain. But, during the eighteenth century, *r* deletion after vowel sounds (e.g., *here* as "he-ah") became increasingly popular among the London upper crust.* While this nonrhotic (*r*-less) southern

---

* Unlike southern British settlers, Irish and Scottish settlers contributed a strong rhotic influence throughout this period.

British style carried prestige in some areas of the United States for a time, by World War II the influence and allure of the British had greatly waned, and the American full *r* pattern solidified its position as the standard. As a result, *r*-lessness survives today mostly as a marked vernacular feature in some American dialects.

A crucial takeaway is that linguistic features have no inherent status qualities, meaning that there is no such thing as a particularly "good" feature or a particularly "bad" one. What gets picked up and spreads in a language is really more a measure of what gains traction in one group that serves as a model to other speakers. So, while dropping your *r* might be all the rage in London society, it might not get you far on your linguistic laurels elsewhere. The articulatory predisposition that caused the deletion of *r* in southern British dialects was by no means unique to speakers that relish tea and crumpets. Those of us who instead enjoy a venti latte with our cake pops simply developed different linguistic ideas, as well as strong feelings about where in Boston we should dump their tea.

No one ever said change was going to be easy

We are all comforted by our routines, so change is hard no matter how much good we know it might do us. I, for one, resist learning all the supposedly new and fantastical features my smartphone can perform as a matter of principle. Why would I ever need to have it track my location, admonish me for not moving often enough, or recognize my face and thumbprint? Did George Orwell design these things? But if I ever get lost in the woods, start having heart problems, or need to block my teenagers from accessing my phone, darn if I won't be happy to have them. In short, we often approach new things with dismay and disdain, but one day we might actually find ourselves using them with abandon.

Social forces like class, gender, and age are immense pressures on language; and though the same underlying linguistic pressures have existed through time, the changes they spark tend to occur only at some points and at some times but not others. Some of these social forces carry weapons. For example, the invasion of Britain by the Normans in 1066 instigated the end of an era—namely, the era of Old English. But the introduction of French alone was not the catalyst of change. A crucial component was the elevation of French in the royal court and among the elite, at the expense of English. The masses still spoke English, but now it was predominately the speech of the lower ranks. And when status gets involved, things start getting interesting, because some of the internal linguistic forces that have been quietly working behind the scenes (like the consonant deletion we just talked about) have more freedom to emerge in vernacular speech, when we aren't trying as hard to impress all those knightly types. As these variations start to take on some shared social meaning for speakers (i.e., let's unite to get rid of this interloping Anglo-Norman king!), they lay the foundation for the speech of our future. Class and conquest came together and inalterably changed how we spoke.

This question of why languages change in particular times and places, and for some speakers but not others, is often referred to as the actuation problem. The work of a sociolinguist is driven by an interest in why such changes take hold in one group and not another, despite the fact that our brains and tongues are wired the same way. In other words, we look for the magic combination of linguistic and social triggers that inspires the birth of a new word or feature in a particular time and place. Why did English shed its endings while Icelandic held fast? Why did *like* take over our linguistic nooks and crannies, while *love* is still so hard to find? What we find is often exactly the opposite of what you might expect, as it is the people on the edges of social space, not those in the center, who drive what language is to become.

Location, location, location

In 2013, *The New York Times* published a dialect quiz designed by graphics editor Josh Katz that went viral. It asked questions such as "How would you address a group of two or more people"? and provided multiple choice answers, such as *Youse*, *Ya'll*, *You Guys*, or *Yu'uns*. By interrogating a person on such plural pronoun choice and other terminological convictions, like how they described nightwear—as *pa-jaw-mas* or *pah-jam-as*—an algorithm determined where, in America, that person came from. The questions for the quiz were taken from professor Bert Vaux's Harvard Dialect Survey, inspired by his observation that, even without noticeable accents, his students still differed on what they called things.

This is, of course, not a big revelation. One of the most obvious forms of social distance is that arising from geography. In other words, if it is not that easy to hang out with one another, then our speech over time will naturally begin to vary as we experience the world differently. As a superficial example of this, consider the age-old question of what to call a carbonated beverage. Is it *soda*, *pop*, or *coke*? How you answer this is certainly very telling of where you grew up. As a self-respecting Southerner, the answer is undeniably *coke*. But those with a less fortunate geographic upbringing might say *soda* or even, if you were raised in the Midwest, *pop*.

This diversity in soft-drink names is not very surprising, as it is easy to see how differences in our names for things can come about just because we live apart but still need to call things something. For example, Coca-Cola was headquartered in Atlanta, so the first and most prominent soft drink for Southerners was called a *coke*. *Pop* is the sound the top makes when it gains

41

its freedom from the bottle, seemingly the inspiration behind the name in the Midwest. *Soda,* a derivative from the name "soda fountain," claimed classic fountain fans in the West. As a good Southerner, I defend my region's right to genericize *coke,* despite vociferous arguments to the contrary. After all, no one gets riled up when we call a generic cotton swab a Q-tip. Or a tissue a Kleenex. As it turns out, we often don't look past things that strike us as odd to see how many other instances of this same odd practice we already do without batting an eye.

Regional differences are deeply intertwined with the formative history of our country itself. The foundation of most early American dialects came in not with inventions of new products or regionally restricted naming practices, but instead, with diversity among the early colonists. In seventeenth-century Britain, significant differences existed in the British source dialects (namely, northern and southern British and Scots-Irish), which then helped established pockets of linguistically distinct dialects in the New World. Also, German, Dutch, French, and African influence were early contributors to the rich linguistic landscape of what would become the United States.

But beyond region, linguistic differences come about any time we have separation, be it geographic or social, among speakers. Regional dialects are really just proxies for ways that distance separates speakers, and how when we don't talk to one another, different internal pressures lead to the development of different ways of speaking. And even more important are the barriers that exist between speakers when they are separated instead by other types of social space.* We see how impactful these types of fractures are when we look at how conflicts around gender and race have played key roles in shaping our history and continue to do so. Likewise, though we look to the young to forge our future, at the same time, we often cast shade on them for butchering our language. So it should come as no shock that class, age, and gender, as well as ethnicity, are critical influences on how our language changes over time.

Talking up or talking down?

If you've never seen *My Cousin Vinny*, it should top your list of must-see classic movies. Not only because it features actor Joe Pesci in one of his funniest roles, but because it is a great example of how sometimes it's hard to look past the way people sound and dress, if black leather jackets and gold chains aren't your thing. There is a great scene where Pesci's "Vinny Gambini," a streetwise Italian American New York lawyer with no experience, appears before a rural Alabama judge and, impassionedly,

---

* Social distance as a harbinger of linguistic difference is most familiar to us in terms of geography, as who, for instance, hasn't attempted to "put on" a Southern drawl or a New "Yawk" accent. But most of the features we deem as "incorrect" are similarly socially derived differences—from divides created by ethnicity or class—that exist for the same reasons that Southern and Northern speech developed, namely, social separation that gave rise to the development of different linguistic forms.

keeps referring, in his thick New York City accent, to "the yutes" (meaning "youths"). The judge, of course, can't understand half of what he says and spends most of the movie offended or aghast at what comes out of Pesci's mouth. Much of the movie's success comes from how it comically contrasts his working-class speech and street sensibilities with the reserved and gentrified towns-people in the small-town South. And for a linguist, it beautifully exemplifies how the impact of what we are trying to say can often get lost because of the way we say it, especially if our ac-cent makes it sound like we don't "belong."

And this is not just the stuff of movies. A friend of mine is a very successful doctor and, not surprisingly, extremely articulate and well educated. She has never had any trouble growing a large specialty practice or building a big network of equally impressive friends. But much to her dismay, she has been less lucky in the romance department, often dating similarly career-oriented men but finding that nothing clicked. Then she met Tom, an incredibly kind and thoughtful man who works as a manager at a party store. The difficulty is, though, the way Tom sounds (and what he does) makes him stand out in her social circle, which is predominantly made up of upper-middle-class professionals. He uses past participles like "had went" instead of "gone" and lots of -in' endings, and leans heavily on contrac-tions like *gonna* or *wanna*. As they got more serious, he became a bit sensitive to feeling like he didn't fit in with her friends, and that he was just not as comfortable in her world as she was in his. While it may not be as stark as Tom's experience, we can all relate, whether at work or in a social setting, to feeling judged by the way we talk.

This clash of class culture is neither unique nor unusual in the social world of language. We have always used the way people speak as a gauge to their social standing. In fact, the upper-crust speech of eighteenth-century Britain formed the basis of much of what came to be considered proper written and spoken English, valorized in culturally defining dictionaries and writings of the time, such as those by Samuel Johnson and Jonathan Swift. In India, the traditional caste system that so sharply delineated class groups, prohibiting any mixing between them, was divided not only by social practices but also by language practices. Caste could be identified by simply hearing the dialect features someone used—for instance, in Bangalore in South India, a Brahmin speaker would say *ide* for "it is," while a non-Brahmin would say *ayti*. The existence of such caste dialects is the reason why speaking English has become so popular throughout India. Existing outside the linguistic shadow of caste, English has offered a way to move beyond the limitations imposed by this rigid status system.

Even without such sharp delineations, we still find language a window into the divide between the upper crust and the salt of the earth. In Boston, the highly recognizable Brahmin accent (actually a reference to the dialect of the highest Indian caste) typifies the speech of New England gentry (think *Haah-vahd* or the Kennedyesque Mayor Quimby from *The Simpsons*), while a "wicked" Southie accent marks you a person of the people (think *shawty* or *fawty*, which translate, for others, into "shorty" or "forty"). In London, we just as easily recognize the difference between a Cockney and a queen. After all, a Cockney accent can make *three pints* enticingly sound like "free" pints, which is surely the mark of a great accent. In other words, egalitarian as we may like to believe ourselves to be, our linguistic practices (and how they're perceived) still reveal a sharp class divide. Though we might pay homage to increasing equity across groups in society, our employment, social networks, and educational opportunities conspire to stratify us in ways that recognizably rank us by the work we do, the places we live, the styles we emulate, and the language we speak.

The big reveal here is that without this stratification and its resultant linguistic distinctions, our language would look very different today than the English we have come to know and love. Language evolution, it turns out, loves a mouth that isn't afraid to let it all hang out. And snooty talkers tend to be a bit too linguistically uptight. In the same way that increasing written standardization since the rise of the printing press has created less variation in how we write things, rising social-class affiliation seems to make us more guarded and regulatory about how we talk as well. If your bread and butter depends on making sure you sound like you belong at the top of the linguistic food chain, you will be more likely to suppress any tendencies toward change (especially the ones we talked about earlier that naturally arise in language) and be more inclined toward features that ooze social prestige rather than street smarts or camaraderie. Working-class or blue-collar speakers have more mixed pressures to respond to—sometimes a need to shift toward more high falutin' norms, or in other realms, the desire to use features that more intimately connect them within their social network, which tends to be more tight knit and locally drawn than upper-class speakers' social circles. Both of these forces, it turns out, are the secret sauce behind language change, as these tendencies propel speakers toward using features in less socially restrictive and more novel ways.

A striking and consistent finding in much language research is that lower-status speakers have with great regularity led the linguistic charge in many of the innovations that have become well-accepted parts of our language. To take a few examples, consider the dropping of the *y* sound (known as *yod*) before *oo* vowels (and especially after consonants like *n* or *d* made with the tip of the tongue), explaining why some speakers in the South or in Britain sound a bit snobbish when they say *nyooz* for "news," *djew* for "dew," or *tyoon* for "tune." This *yod*-dropping is something we Americans share with Cockney and other working-class dialects and, according to language historian Roger Lass, was decried as a corrupt and vulgar development in eighteenth-century speech.

Now even upper-class Brits are sometimes caught *yod*-less, following in the footsteps of us lowly, crass, and vulgar sorts. In America, we even find a decent number of speakers who have expanded this deletion pattern beyond the places where it most often occurs—for example, the sort (like me) who use *coo-pons* instead of *cue-pons*. While this pattern might be interpreted as American English clearly going to the dogs, I put to you the important question of whether you have ever found yourself held back in life by the absence of yod?

But this is just the tip of the proverbial iceberg of changes that have come full circle, led by those less bounded by the merely social rules we mistake for linguistic grammar. How about that dropping of *r* we just discussed? While this might be a mark of the Queen's English today, it began in the speech of the lower classes, gradually moving up the social hierarchy to become the prestige norm in England in the late nineteenth century. Though now simply just the way we speak, many of what we consider commonplace speech features like these were at one point associated with vernacularity and bemoaned as evidence of the decay of English. But, as with so many of the changes that have entered our language, they have ended up the linguistic legacies of our economically down-on-their-luck ancestors. Still, speakers in the lower classes didn't reshape English alone. To understand fully what drives our verbal habits, we have to sleuth out our most important linguistic partners in crime.

Let's just go ahead and blame the women and the children

As with so many things in life, it's good to have a scapegoat, and even better to have two. Especially when women and children (along with the lower classes) have long been held aside as linguistically questionable. But in what I view as a lovely twist, when it comes to language variation, these scapegoats may come to be seen as the greatest influencers of all time. *En garde*, YouTube!

Let's start with the most obvious place to lay the blame for language change—namely, with the young. Many social and linguistic novelties have taken shape under the influence of youth culture. What may surprise you, notwithstanding *twerking*, *VSCO girls*, and *TikTok*, is that many of the changes introduced by earlier whippersnappers have stood the test of time and become the norms by which we speak today. One might get hung up on the things that seem insulting (*cheugy*, *Karen*) or annoying (*like*, *duh*), but many other changes will happen right under our (sometimes wrinkled) noses without any notice, becoming what's normal in the speech of the next generation, and, to an often lesser degree, even in our own. How do these changes creep in without ever alerting our well-trained tongues? Primarily in our casual day-to-day interactions, where our focus is not so much on how we are speaking but rather on the social persona we are trying to project.

Informal spoken English, even for so-called standard speakers, is a far cry from the formal English norms that put more pressure on our speech in higher-stakes conversations like those we have at work or at school. But think for a minute about how you talk about regular aspects of daily life—things like going to the dentist or taking out the trash. Do you use "must" when describing your actions, i.e., "I must go to the dentist" or "I must take out the trash"? Probably not very often unless you are Scarlett O'Hara or have a very uptight relationship with your family. Instead, you say, "I hafta go to the dentist" or "I've got to take out the trash." In other words, you talk in a way that reflects the informal and more colloquial language we use when we are talking to friends, family, and neighbors.

So what happened to our long-hallowed and traditional verb of necessity *must*, a form that has been with us since the time of Old English? Has it disappeared into the linguistic sunset alongside *thou*, *whence*, and conditional *were*? In short, yes. And we might as well start pointing our fingers at someone for this sad state of deontic modality (what linguists call the linguistic embodiment of necessity). *Must* is no longer the preferred form to express obligation, being replaced in most of our speech, but particularly in the speech of younger speakers, with the verbs *have* or *got to*. This process of replacement has roots as far back as Middle English, but by the nineteenth century, *have to* and *have got to* came to be used more often, across more contexts, and by more and more speakers, until it became simply what we considered normal. Musty old *must* is now reserved for crafting legal statutes or in reference to little Maria's lack of homework during parent-teacher conferences.

Our verbs are not the only thing a-changing, and in fact, your speech probably already reflects massive shifts that are even further under way in the next generation. Namely, your vowels. Modern English varieties worldwide are all in the process of some pretty massive vowel shifts, but most of us probably have no idea how much different our vowel sounds are today compared to fifty years ago. Nor that younger speakers are at the forefront of these changes across the globe. Nowadays, young folks in California and Nevada put their groceries in *bogs* instead of *bags*, while in Ohio or Michigan, they *beg* their groceries. All because our *aa* (as in *bag*) vowel, the one we call ash, is being pronounced in different ways across regional American varieties. We find similar youthfully inspired vowel shifting not just in the United States, but across world Englishes. For example, in New Zealand, going to a *wedding* sounds more like you might be spending time in the garden "weeding."*

With all this shifty-ness, it's no wonder that when we listen to shows from earlier eras (think *Leave It to Beaver*), they sound

---

* Though the way that vowels are shifting in these varied Englishes is distinct, a common thread is that the changes are found to be more advanced in the speech of younger speakers.

quaint. It's not just the words they use that seem old-fashioned; other differences are more subtle, yet give a distinctly different flavor to their speech. As a result of generations of teenagers slightly changing the way they pronounced their vowels between then and now, even what we heard in the 1950s and '60s is different from the sounds of our vowels today—a shining example of the young leaving a powerful linguistic inheritance. And though a number of terms we've talked about here will soon fade into the linguistic sunset, especially those that are just single vocabulary items like *YOLO* or *yeet*, less one-off features, like those that come alongside deeper shifts in things such as deontic modality and vowel pronunciation (as well as most of those that drive the chapters of this book), will become part of the English of our future.

In fact, the list of changes that the young have ushered in and that are here to stay goes on and on. The move toward using *going to* instead of *will* for future tense? Yup. Led by the young. The shift from the American "tip-of-the-tongue" pronunciation of *r* sounds in Montreal toward the more back-of-the-throat, purr-like Parisian style *r*? Whippersnappers at it again. The adoption of less drawl-like speech in the South? You guessed it. The spread of *t*-glottalizing beyond Cockney and into London's posh Received Pronunciation dialect, otherwise known as the Queen's English? Tha's righ', youngsters to blame. And don't get me started on those who seem to be able to use *hella* or *hecka* naturally in a sentence. But these modernisms are just a small glimpse into linguistic innovations introduced by the young. Even the earliest records we have of linguistic change in communities show the young taking control of language and leaving the old folks in the linguistic dust.

You might wonder, why do the old and wizened not possess this awesome power of linguistic novelty? Well, like our ability to down tequila shots and do the macarena without breaking something, our dialect patterns seem to fossilize, or become more fixed, once we become adults. This is attributable in part to how language acquisition typically proceeds, as we seem to be most able to pick up on new linguistic patterns as children, especially in the period prior to brain lateralization.* One of the reasons we find languages learned by large numbers of speakers as adults (like English) tend to become less complex over time is because parent-to-child transmission allows for the learning of more involved linguistic forms that require children's ability to analyze and learn complex linguistic patterns.†

Once we hit adulthood, the very detailed analysis of the distributions of features in a language that young children seem to be able to do is lost, and we only pick up more transparent variants of the patterns (in grammatical terms). So, while kids are

---

* For those of us who still dream of retiring in Italy and ordering our primo and secondi piatti like a native, take heart: More recent research has suggested that the cutoff in language acquisition abilities may not be as sharp as first proposed, but that child learners are likely to achieve a higher level of fluency as well as more faithfully replicate complex grammatical rules.

† Here I refer to complexity in terms of how that language becomes differently structured over time (like losing case endings and relying instead on word order).

effortlessly able to acquire however many languages they hear regularly around them, those of us a little more mature don't quite get the hang of it as easily. In other words, kids are primed for what seems like automated linguistic acquisition, while adults are struggling to get by on the practice makes passable model. This is the reason why kids can move to another country and end up sounding native-like, while we old folks become reasonably fluent but carry our first language around like a scarlet letter, only this time the *A* is for accent.

Why this difference? Changes in cognitive plasticity, motivation, and our focus make us much better at evaluating risk, singing, driving, and board games, but pretty weak at linguistic prowess. This might explain why kids do better at picking up patterns they hear around them, but why do they also introduce new forms at such a high rate? Well, chalk that up to linguistic revolution, dude.

Don't lose all hope. We do have some impact on our kids' linguistic system. As babies and toddlers, children typically acquire a linguistic system like that of their parents. Unfortunately, our influence, like our coolness as parents more generally, wears off pretty quickly, and kids reorient to their much more interesting peers about the time they start primary school. Then, as with most everything else, kids turn away from the system imposed by their parents and start crafting their speech from what they hear around them. And this is where innovations incubate, spurred by the greater sensitivity of children to unpacking linguistic patterning and the attraction to anything that seems like it might be hip and offer the cool cred that they just can't find at home.

This is in large part because children's social world is nothing like the homogenizing social and class environments we surround ourselves with in adulthood. As grown-ups, we often live in communities and work in places where most of those we interact with look and talk a lot like we do. Schools, sports, and playgrounds expose kids to much more social and linguistic diversity than we have at home, giving them a pool of options to draw from when crafting their linguistic (and more general) identities. Since nonconformity with adult expectations is the hallmark of adolescence, language is a key way to forge a different path from one's parents. And the class barriers so carefully maintained by adults are more fluid and crossing them less problematic (and sometimes even stylistically advantageous) for kids.

While many of the variations that arise in the speech of the young are part and parcel of the natural inherent linguistic pressures that we talked about earlier, they can go the linguistic equivalent of viral when the "right" kids use them. Still, all of this (with the exception perhaps of using slang and trendy new terms) takes place with a surprising amount of subconscious processing. In other words, we don't think about what we are doing so much as we just *do* it. Sounds pretty much par for the course for most teens I've come to know and, on most days, love.

This process of fashioning a dialect using input from your

peer group is known in the fancy lingo of linguists as "vernacular reorganization." As kids age, getting into the teen years they integrate the social and the linguistic with greater success and are attracted to nonconformist or novel variants (think profanity or *like* or *brah* for "bro," for instance). As they overemphasize these changes in their speech, sounding like they use them a *lot*, we find what is called an adolescent peak of use (named after the peak we find in graphs when measuring the use of speech features across age groups). Though these teens tend to naturally adjust their use down a bit as they get older, this peak seems to highlight the use of the innovative sound, feature, or word form for younger kids, who begin to use it at an even higher rate (until they form a new adolescent peak).

If its use continues unhindered (and certainly not all changes do), by the end of a couple of decades, this peaking pattern will help put a new norm on our linguistic map, until eventually it is not a change anymore but even what the old fogeys say. We don't remember how this happened in our own speech because, well, what we say was always what was normal to us. A perfect example is the replacement of the aspirated *hw* pronunciation in words like *which* and *whine*, so that they now sound identical for most speakers to "witch" and "wine".* Didn't know there

---

* In looking at colonial dialects and how they have changed, a fun read that tracks the decline in older British forms in North America, including the long-sought answer to whether it's *to-mah-to* or *to-may-to* (duh—it's *to-may-to*), is linguist Jack Chambers' "Saying 'Tomato' in Postcolonial Canada," in *Variation and Change in Postcolonial Contexts*, ed. R. Calabrese, J. K. Chambers, and

was ever a difference? Blame the (now old) young'uns for that one too and stop *hwi*ning about it.

Hitting the catwalk

But it is not just being young that makes us linguistic hipsters. It is one particular group of youngsters who seem to be the trail-blazers, and if you take a minute to ponder our attraction to style icons, you might not be so surprised. When you think about who's strutting down the runways in Milan, New York, or Paris, who comes to mind? Tall, leggy women with strange makeup and outlandish hair wearing oddball outfits that cost thousands of dollars? Strange, that's what I think of too. But while we may have a hard time actually imagining wearing those clothes, by the time the looks inspired by those fashionistas hit the rack at Nordstrom, we buy them up like hot cakes. Why? Because fashion.

Along the same lines, it perhaps should not come as such a shock to us that women, long held as the standard bearers of that which is fashionable, should also be on the leading edge of

G. Leitner (Newcastle-upon-Tyne, UK: Cambridge Scholars Publishing, 2015). The source of the difference? According to Chambers, the importation of the fruit to Europe by Spanish explorers led to the adoption of the word with a simple vowel -*ah*-, as opposed to the separate development of the American long vowel pronunciation probably by analogy with *potato*. That difference we might not be able to blame on the young.

another type of sociostylistic marker—namely, that of language. When we talk about how kids are at the forefront of change, it is young women far more than young men who by and large are the movers and shakers in language. This takes a lot of people by surprise, because we often notice the speech of young boys on the playing fields and playgrounds more than we notice the speech of girls. That's only because boys tend to pick up on nonstandard forms more than girls do, which draws our attention to them.

In contrast to these bad boys, girls often get saddled with the pressure to use language considered proper or higher status. Using profanity or lower-class speech features will get girls called to the school office or kicked out of a boardroom faster than you can say fiddlesticks. This pressure on women to have more "refined" speech has a long history. In the eighteenth and nineteenth centuries, the height of the move toward prescriptivist notions of speech in England, a good and godly woman was one upholding the upper-class norms for speech. Usage guides were very popular during this period, and speech featured prominently as a place to aspire to higher-status norms. Women were policed both in dress and language, putting a substantial amount of weight on looking and speaking the part.* We still hear echoes of this deeply entrenched attitude when we tell our

---

* Just recall how well the phonetics professor Henry Higgins, from *My Fair Lady*, understood the power of linguistic retooling in upping a woman's social worth.

female children that they don't sound very "ladylike" or that they need to act more like a lady. While we might tell boys to be little gentlemen, the bar that sets, at least for language, is much lower than the one set for young women. As a result, when a community shows evidence of a shift toward a speech feature that appears to bring with it higher social prestige, women are most often the ones heading the charge.

This pressure on women to carry the linguistic torch has helped shape the direction of language over time, for example, ushering in the shift from Middle English *-th* to *-s* on verbs (*doth* to *does*) or the rise of periphrastic *do* (*I do not know* versus *I know not*), both forms that replaced more conservative and previously status-ful forms. What is fashionable is not always what's safe—sometimes you have to wear a little punk Vivienne Westwood alongside your classic Ralph Lauren. So women, both past and modern, do not only lead in changes that mark more high-status speech, but also lead in the use of novel forms that often become the new norms for their children's generation. In other words, they forge a new linguistic path, and these language trendsetters use what some may see initially as linguistic tics as tools for developing a linguistic style.

The list of more modern innovations inspired by young women's tongues is legend. For example, the switch from *must* to *have got* to express necessity is not just led by young speakers, but by young female speakers. The shift toward using *going to* for *will*, the rise of *t*-release in American English so that the end consonant of *what* sounds more like an indictment than a question, i.e., *what-tuhh!* Yup, all due to the linguistic ingenuity of women. The vowel changes sweeping across not just North American varieties of English, but also ones found in New Zealand, Australia, and Britain? The cot/caught merger that allows a world in which *collars* and *callers* converge? Yes! You've got it—women, women, women.

But why this strange paradoxical relationship between women and "proper" English on one hand, and women taking language by the figurative horns on the other? That is a good question, and one that linguists have been pondering for a while now. Women appear to be very sensitive to language forms and subtle variations that arise from the underlying articulatory and cognitive mechanisms that we talked about earlier. Often these percolating linguistic pressures and the subtle variations they create mean nothing socially, and we filter them out and ignore them as simply predictable by-products of our speech production. Sometimes, though, these variations become more prevalent or noticeable in the speech of some speakers rather than others, and it is in this space that they begin to take on associations with whatever qualities set those speakers apart.

And though these features may not be socially recognizable in and of themselves, the speakers or groups of speakers that use them imbue the features with an intangible appeal that attracts others to subconsciously imitate them. This can be something like urban-ness, ethnic-ness, popularity, or even something like a subtle "street" vibe, or perhaps, in the case of our sixteenth- and seventeenth-century women, showing yourself to be at the height of courtly linguistic style. Young women seem to be particularly cued into the value of subconsciously drawing on and adjusting these features in crafting and navigating their social identities. Good examples today would be the carefree and white SoCal association with the *euw* vowel in words like *dude* and *cool*, or, moving beyond just English, the gender neutrality offered to young Amish women increasingly using *es* (meaning "it") in Pennsylvania German instead of the more traditional *sie* ("she") to talk about each other. The social work of adolescence, the time when most of the linguistic groundwork for our adult speech is laid, involves making use of the resources around you. For boys, this might involve picking up features that build a tougher or more masculine identity—usually requiring slang or recognizably nonstandard language. For girls, it involves being sensitive to the possibilities that embryonic linguistic forms open up.

Since girls become women, and women tend to become moms, and moms often do more of the child-rearing duties in a household (we'll save discussion of the fairness of that whole system for another book), they become the role models for the next generation. With moms that sport the latest in linguistic fashion, kids get a head start in being linguistically modern. Language change, spurred by this new generation, jumps ahead, and boys catch up to girls by inheriting the system of their mother. Sometimes, of course, as girls and boys enter school, the social associations with some aspects of their speech get gendered, and boys retreat some from using high levels of "girly" language features (like using *totally* as an intensifying adverb). But overall, girls are a linguistic force to be reckoned with, and as innovations gain more steam as kids age, the adolescent peak cycle happens all over again. They become the next generation of parents and pass along the change, establishing the norms of the future, moving from being novel to being the norm in just a couple of generations. Sounding like a girl, it seems, is pretty much the pinnacle of linguistic achievement. But often, as we will see going forward, women are anything but rewarded for being the tour de force behind language change. And boys, we will learn, also bring a few things to the linguistic conversation.

Your language reinvented

So, how does all this relate to your verbal tics? Why does it matter whether women, children, and the financially less secure add the secret spice? Why should you care about the evolution of language when your kid's or employee's incessant *like* use drives you to distraction?

Because when we hear *so* and *totally* constantly ringing in our ears, when we get tripped up by how to use singular *they* or when uptalk and vocal fry plain confuse us—or if our own use

or misuse of these forms make us feel like we need to apologize—
it just means we are not yet at the point where we have forgotten
that there was once a different pattern. We might be getting a
glimpse of the future, but it is hard to stop clinging to the past.
Whether we are dropping our *r*'s or adding them back in, deleting our yods so that *do the dew* can become a soft drink's clever
catchphrase, saying *have got to* instead of dusty old *must*, or
blending our vowels so that, adding an unexpected twist to a
first date, *Don* gets confused with *Dawn*, language constantly
shows us that it was born to change. Despite our firm but mis-
guided belief in "right" or "wrong" ways of speaking, we have
all been subject to the exact same forces that have brought our
least favorite tics not only to see the light of day, but to thrive
and expand. And, my friend, prepare yourself, as these speech
habits are not going anywhere soon. In fact, they may in many
cases be some of the most rapidly expanding permanent changes
affecting English today.

We like to look only at the speech that is right in front of us,
but these features did not just appear out of thin air as wayward
linguistic orphans. In the rest of the book, we will come to know
the history that built these so-called tics, as the seeds for most of
these seemingly annoying habits were planted surprisingly far
back, and well before our kids (or we) started saying them. We
will also uncover why and how we use them, finding that what
seems random and chaotic is much more rule-governed and useful than it seems on the surface. Finally, we will shatter some

myths about who uses them and come to understand why we harbor such strong likes and dislikes when it comes to language, and more important, to the types of speakers who use them. As we begin our next chapter with a speech habit that is pretty much universal and move from there to cover others that have increasingly garnered attention, we will discover that these verbal tics we have been taught to erase from our speech are the very ones that might end up being our linguistic legacies.

2

Umloved

When your Amazon Alexa or Google Assistant asks you if you want the weather forecast or prompts you to order more Charmin bath tissue, what do you notice about the way they speak? Perhaps it's not really what they say, but what they *don't* say that's the tell that alerts us to their nonhuman nature, despite their unsettling familiarity with our toilet paper usage. The halting *um*s and hesitant *uh*s that pop into our pauses are absent from Alexa's text-to-speech-based delivery. But while our disfluency might be a dead giveaway to our side of conversations with machines, soon even our trademark *um*s and *uh*s might be imported into our digital assistant's repertoire. Google recently unveiled a voice AI that could fill pauses with the best of them. The result? A more natural-sounding conversational partner.

Still, despite the fact that to pause makes us more human, it doesn't seem to make us come across as more eloquent humans.

Business-oriented articles and speech improvement websites abound with dire warnings of how filled pauses and filler words are "killing your credibility," as one writer for *Inc.* puts it, or can "repel listeners," at least according to a site devoted to interviewing success. Toastmasters International, the organization that helps people develop public-speaking skills, even has an *uh* counter assigned to tally verbal pause transgressions of speakers—and then fines them a nickel per *uh*. I think it is safe to say that *um* and *uh* are not high on the list of ways to make a good impression. Nor, in the world of great speakers, do we find vocalized pauses listed among the qualities that make one memorable.

So it's no surprise that most of us regular folks cringe when forced to listen to a recording of ourselves talking. In the conversations of real life, we use a lot of overlapping speech, leave our sentences unfinished, make speech errors like inviting *Jarhead* instead of *Jarrod* over to dinner, and last but not least, slog our way through some serious *um*ing and *uh*ing. But we are far from alone—even the people we expect to be articulate, ranging from presidents to poets, still *um* and *uh* in nonscripted speech. Take a listen to Supreme Court arguments or White House press conferences, and you will find the most studied and erudite among us filling their pauses with packing peanuts. Which brings us to the bigger question—why do we all *um*? And, perhaps, even more importantly, should we?

What the *uh*?

In linguistic circles, *um* and *uh* are what are known, not so inventively, as filled pauses or FPs, also sometimes referred to as hesitation markers. They are typically taken as signs that a speaker is encountering some sort of trouble getting what they want to say out, i.e., pondering what to say next or frantically trying to remember the name of a new coworker who is politely waiting on an introduction. In short, we verbalize our pauses when we need a sec, linguistically speaking.

For a long time, research treated filled pauses as pretty much a vocalized form of a silent pause, rather than any kind of meaningful linguistic unit. What I mean by nonmeaningful here is that you could remove them without significantly altering the semantic or propositional information expressed by a sentence. "Dogs are really—uh—smart" and "Dogs are really smart" express an identical proposition about dogs. Yet filled pauses are also different from other types of nonsemantic additions we put in our sentences, such as "I mean" or "like," which, though they don't change the primary message we communicate, do provide information about a speaker's attitude to or knowledge about whatever they are saying. They are also what we traditionally consider to be actual words. *Um*, at least according to conventional wisdom, says nothing except "Yikes, I am struggling with what I was trying to say." And owing to their affinity with other speech hiccups like repeats, false starts, and self-corrections, researchers, on par with nonlinguists, have considered them as disfluencies rather than words.

Clearly, since we have established that they are not semantically contributory and they're not seen as a particularly attractive speech attribute either, we should absolutely have no compunction about judging anyone who uses them. After all, what is the point of public-speaking advice if not to help us sound clear, articulate, and employable? And "beware the *um*" ranks right up there with "don't use a monotone voice" in terms of top speaking tips. But what if this advice is dead wrong—at least for the type of talking most of us do? While for public speaking we may make a better impression if we limit our *um*s and *uh*s, research over the years has suggested that FPs might be more useful than they appear—both in terms of what they do for a speaker and, even more intriguingly, the benefits they offer for those willing to take a listen.

OUR *UMS* AND *UHS* HAVE RARELY BEEN GIVEN THEIR DUE, BUT a deeper look turns up some pretty remarkable stuff. First of all, filled pauses are universal. Not always in the same form exactly, but in that they exist in most languages studied. And for something so maligned, we use them quite a bit. It has been estimated that disfluencies constitute about 6 percent of what comes out of our mouths during spontaneous speech—that's about six out of every one hundred words we utter. In English, the form of our little verbalized pauses appears to have been inherited from our ancestor language. We surmise that this is the case since other modern Germanic-descended languages like Danish, German, and Faroese use similar forms of hesitation markers (e.g., *öh* and *öhm*), mainly differing in the quality of the vowel.

What's even more interesting is that not only do we find filled pauses the world over, but languages all seem to have more than just one form of filled pause—for example, *eh* and *ehm* in Dutch, *euh* and *euhm* in French, and *eh* and *ano* in Japanese. Plus, the form of these filled pauses is quite simple: a vowel sound (*uh*) or a vowel plus a nasalized sound (*um*), a commonality that would seem somewhat suspicious if there was not some underlying linguistic pattern we can blame. Sherlock Holmes might call me out here—being familiar with the British-derived *er* and *erm*—but, as Holmes would surely sleuth out, these are essentially just the same fillers Americans use, only appearing with an *r* in written form, a sound not pronounced in Standard British English.*
So, *erm* as written would essentially be *um* in spoken form. And

---

* Americans' erroneous view of *er* as a distinct hesitation form provides some humor for those better acquainted with the proper British *er* pronunciation, e.g., "How Americans imagine the pronunciation of *er* is not clear to me. I have never heard anyone go around saying *er* to rhyme with *her*," notes linguist Gunnel Tottie in a 2019 article that examined filled pauses in writing. Well, at least we know how to spell *color* and *flavor* right.

no matter how one writes it, such ubiquity strongly suggests filled pauses are serving a function, even if we don't think of them as particularly attractive.

The *um*s of antiquity?

Filled pauses are a bit hard to trace back, mainly because we only recently began using them for more than just filling our pauses. "Uh . . . that's awkward" or "Um . . . no" are now part of the scripted dialogue of our favorite comedies or snarky comments we tweet as we go about our day. For most of our history, though, *um* and *uh* were simply oral vocalizations, not literary treatises on our subjective take of a situation. Since most speeches written down for posterity were not verbatim records, we don't find documentation of such filled pauses in writings from antiquity. But neither do we find caution to avoid using them in early expositions on oration, suggesting that, if they were used back then (which in some form is likely), they were not the pariah they are now.

Even if we don't find any evidence that Cicero went up against Mark Antony replete with *um*s and *uh*s, we know that such markers of hesitation have been around for centuries at least. The *Oxford English Dictionary* notes *um* as a hesitating or inarticulate marker first appeared in the comedy *The Mistake* written in 1672. A differently spelled but similarly functioning *hum* was used even earlier by Shakespeare, for instance, "Hum: ha? Is this a vision?" from *The Merry Wives of Windsor*. Dickens gave us a *hum* here or there as well, with lines such as "I have a—hum—a spirit, sir, that will not endure it," which appeared in his novel *Little Dorrit*.* Presumably, as we tend to *um* more when we talk rather than when we write, filled pauses peppered our speech much longer than these written records suggest. What's more, these literary uses hint that they may not be as meaningless as long postulated, at least in how they help portray speechlike dialogue. Add to these literary chops the fact that we find *uh*s even on the earliest voice recordings from the likes of Thomas Edison and that early psychoanalysts pondered their ties to the subconscious, and the mystery of what these little linguistic features do for us grows deeper.

A Freudian *um*?

We have all heard of the Freudian slip—the telling speech errors we make that are somehow tied to our unconscious thoughts or desires. Like the slip when a host on the *Today* show accidentally introduced actress Amanda Seyfried as "titsy" rather than ditsy in her movie *Ted 2*. Of course, it was a film centered on a

---

* As this was an interjection used in writing and not the spontaneous oral form, its spelling was variable, but its intent seems to have been to indicate hesitation similar to what we use in speech.

teddy bear's right to procreate, so perhaps the bar was not set all that high. But in early psychoanalytic literature, particularly that of Sigmund Freud, such mistakes were not just embarrassing blunders, but were thought to reveal something of the inner workings of the mind. Freud's interest, as well as that of later analysts, was driven by the belief that such features revealed unmonitored flashes of the unconscious and expressed our repressed anxieties or worries.

Early psychological interest in the topic centered on whether speech "disturbances," as coined by Yale psychologist George Mahl in the 1950s, become more frequent during episodes of increased anxiety, a theory investigated in his research. Mahl thought that filled pauses, along with a complex of other disfluencies like false starts, repetitions, and slips of the tongue, might indicate that anxiety disrupted our processing of complex tasks, like speaking. While he found that most of the other disfluencies did increase with anxiety, filled pauses did just the opposite—decreasing in the high-anxiety groups. It appeared that filled pauses worked differently than these other disturbances.

Though research on filled pauses as part of a complex of nervous habits did not pan out, the idea that they were tied to some form of cognitive hang-up stuck around, with interest becoming more focused on the relationship between cognitive processing and language. As research has progressed on how and why we "um," two distinct lines of research emerged within the field known as psycholinguistics.*

One line of psycholinguistic research investigated whether filled pauses were symptoms not of anxiety but of the speech planning issues we encounter when searching for certain words or crafting impressively long sentences. In other words, our brain needs time to catch up to our mouth, particularly in the middle of processing tasks like trying to come up with the specific color that graced our latest bridesmaid's dress or discussing Machiavellian philosophy. Essentially, in this view, *um*s and *uh*s are the unintended verbal output that escapes, much like those words you shouldn't say in front of your children after smacking your head on the doorframe. Only here, it is your cognitive processing getting a bit of a bang trying to figure things out—and working it through in milliseconds rather than minutes.

If filled pauses are in fact symptoms of difficulties in speech processing or of increased cognitive load as surmised, then we should find that they most often occur right before points of greater complexity in sentence structure, or where a speaker is deliberating word choices. And in fact, this is exactly what we find. For instance, some of the earliest studies of how *um*s and

---

* Though it is tempting to take a Hitchcockian view of what a psycholinguist might do, linguists in this field of study are less concerned with showers and birds and more concerned with the mental processes that underlie speech production and comprehension.

*uh*s are inserted into our sentences suggest that pauses were more likely to occur before more complex syntactic structures (before starting long sentences, for instance). They are also more common right before infrequent or difficult vocabulary items, like, say, a *rhombus*, or a color term like *vermillion*, as opposed to frequent and familiar words like *square* or everyday basic *red*. As well, *um* and *uh* are found to occur more often before content words, or ones that carry a definable type of meaning, rather than conversational workhorses such as the words *a, and,* or *the*. It has been found, too, that if we use abstract terms, we are more likely to use *um*s or *uh*s compared to when we discuss concrete things.

Research has also discovered that we fill our pauses more when we are bringing up new topics or choosing among competing word options, rather than just the regular same old same old. We see this pattern borne out in a study that compared filled pause use per minute during lectures in the hard sciences versus those in the humanities. Want to take a guess which lectures came out on top in *um* and *uh* counts? Yup, the humanities. Why? Not because humanities lecturers just happen to be longer winded—in fact, when those giving the lectures were compared for filled pause use when not talking about their field, they didn't differ in use. Instead, it's because science has a more limited and constrained set of terminologies than we find in the humanities, something confirmed in a follow-up study comparing measures of vocabulary size in each of the fields.* As the researchers explain, when a science lecturer talks about E=mc², there's not a ton of wiggle room for wordplay, but discussing the Nine Circles of Hell in Dante's *Inferno* lends itself to a bit richer vocabulary.

Taken together, all these studies suggest that, from a speaker's perspective, filled pauses are uttered right before sudden increases in syntactic or semantic complexity or when encountering uncertainty or unfamiliarity during a speaking turn. In short, the harder we are having to think about formulating what we say, the more we show signs of this cognitive effort by using *um* and *uh*. The fact that we find a very high rate of filled pauses at the beginning of a sentence—as speakers work through both the words they will choose and the structure of the sentences they will create—further supports such a view. It is not such a surprise then that *um* and *uh* pop into our speech when it's our turn to talk in meetings or when called on by the teacher. It takes us some time to formulate what we are going to say, and the topics we are talking about are often complex and

---

* Psychologist Stanley Schachter and his colleagues compared professional publications, field-specific newspaper articles, and lectures from sciences and the humanities, finding: "Scientists consistently use fewer different words than do humanists," confirming my long-standing suspicion that hard scientists are at a loss for words. They also found that the number of different words correlated with the frequency of saying *uh* during lectures. In S. Schachter, F. Rauscher, N. Christenfeld, and K. Crone, "The Vocabularies of Academia," *Psychological Science 5*, no. 1 (1994): 37–41.

use highly specialized (and less frequent) vocabulary. Viewed in this light, maybe we should cut *uh*, and those who use it frequently, some slack.

But a good question is: Why don't we just take a silent pause? Why do we seem to have to alert everyone to our difficulties by *um*ing and *uh*ing our way out of them? And why do we have need of both *um* and *uh*? Shouldn't a single form of verbal time-out suffice? If it really were the case that filling our pauses is just a symptom of an increased cognitive load with no other benefit, then a silent pause or, at most, a single vocalized form would do the trick. And so the enigma behind the purpose of the filled pause endures, inspiring a new line of inquiry in the quest to understand our packed pauses.

Brain farts

These lingering questions suggest that maybe *um*s and *uh*s are not exclusively linguistic self-flagellation, displaying one's cognitive struggles for all the world to see. Instead, some researchers took it as impetus to consider hesitation phenomena from a more interactive vantage point—by looking at how filled pauses might also be a communicative strategy. In this line of thinking, we use filled pauses instead of silent ones precisely because we want to convey a message to our conversational partner. What's the message? A heads-up that there's going to be a delay.

Beyond being a symptom of our speech-planning difficulties, *um* and *uh* signal our listener to hang on a minute while we are working things out. We buy ourselves some processing time all while keeping the speaking ball in our court. If we paused silently, our talk buddy might get the wrong idea that we were done and make a move for the conversational floor. This may not paint a particularly positive view of how we perceive the motives of those we are conversing with, but it is resonant with the finding that filled pauses occur less often in constrained formats (such as lectures or speeches), where there is no risk of floor theft by coparticipants. When we are involved in back-and-forth chitchat, we have to pay more attention to what are called "turn transition cues," or places where a speaker is signaling it's our turn to jump in.* Pauses, at least silent ones, generally suggest the floor is up for grabs. By filling these pauses with *um* or *uh*, I am announcing both that I am doing some pretty hefty cognitive retrieval and that you should give me space to finish my thought.

And what of evidence that filled pauses are expressive signals directed at a listener? Well, for one, studies have shown that we use more filled pauses in conversational dialogue than in monologic contexts, like when we tell a story. When we are

---

* Things like falling intonation as we get to the end of our turn or making eye contact with a listener at the point where a transition is welcomed help us facilitate smooth conversational flow. When we stop talking, as when taking a silent pause, this too can be construed that we are finished with our turn.

directing tasks or giving instructions, we also use more filled pauses than when we are responding to them. Also, we use fewer *um*s and *uh*s when talking to computers than when talking to other humans, something that shows a bit more interpersonal intentionality than the automatic *um*ing and *uh*ing of a burdened mind. Further support for an account that includes a communicative angle is the finding that adults and children with autism spectrum disorder (ASD) use fewer filled pauses in general, which is consonant with the view that speakers have to take on a listener-oriented perspective when using them. Because those with ASD are oriented differently toward pragmatic language, or language that serves a communicative function, as well as subtle social cues, their use of filled pauses is reduced.

These findings on the communicative function of filled pauses led psycholinguists Herbert Clark and Jean Fox Tree to propose a pretty revolutionary idea in a paper they wrote in the early 2000s—that *um*s and *uh*s should be treated not as disfluencies but as words themselves, similar to interjections like *wow* or *oh*. This may not seem like a big deal, but it does have consequences for the type of linguistic behavior that we would expect from such pauses and for how they would be cognitively stored and processed. For instance, we would expect them to use sounds that already exist in a specific language (they do), to have specific points in syntactic structure where they tend to occur (often true), and to vary in form across languages (ditto).* But now for the rub: Why are there two of them? It's a bit odd that we need synonyms for our filled pauses.

Clark and Fox Tree wondered the same thing—perhaps there was a difference in how we use *um* and *uh* that hadn't been deeply explored before. They had a hypothesis that the fillers communicated information to a listener about how long a delay to expect. They based this on research done in the 1990s, in which college students were asked to give one-word answers to questions about various topics like, for example, in what sport the Stanley Cup was awarded. They discovered that students often used an *um* or an *uh* before answering and that the choice of filler seemed to indicate something about how long the student thought it would take them to answer, with *um* preceding longer delays than *uh* did. Following up this lead, Clark and Fox Tree examined a variety of different spontaneous speech collections (known as corpora) and lo and behold, they discovered that *um* generally occurred before longer speech delays than did *uh*. In other words, we use *uh* to indicate our listener might have to wait a second or two for an answer, but *um* indicates they

---

* This filler-as-word hypothesis is hotly debated, and while there is good support that filled pauses operate beyond simply being disfluencies, there is still a lot of space between being a cognitive by-product and having full status as a word where they could reside. As is often discussed in the literature, their role and function in syntax (e.g., as a part of speech) is not at all clear. In the end, which side of this fence one is on really depends on how "being a word" is defined.

might just have time to go get a sandwich. So, a filled pause appears to convey information at a meta level, over and above the specific content of a sentence.

It sure makes you wonder just what other helpful hints our verbalized pauses might be providing.

Comprendo?

Go to any public-speaking class and I can pretty much guarantee that they will not be advising you to "um" more. As a matter of fact, pretty much any public-speaking course worth its salt will give you tips and pointers on how not to be disfluent, rather than give you gold stars for how many *um*s you can produce during one PowerPoint presentation. But that is why they pay linguists the big bucks and public-speaking coaches get crickets. Um. Okay, maybe I have that backward. That's why they *should* be paying us the big bucks. Because we linguists have read the psycholinguistic research that suggests we have been wrong to ban hesitation from our talk. Just because we have been conditioned by our speech teacher to avoid using them or lost our lunch money to Toastmasters International, we find little scientific evidence that suggests they actually deserve such a negative reputation. In fact, the most fascinating area of hesitation research is not on why we "um" but on how our *um*s and *uh*s might actually be a speaking superpower.

How is this possible? Because our *um*s and *uh*s, along with other signs of disfluencies like false starts (sa—say what?), seem to signal to our listeners to be on alert that there is something requiring greater cognitive effort happening. Why would this be useful from a comprehension standpoint? Because it leads us to expect the unexpected; we don't get sidetracked by anticipating easy words or simple sentences, because we know disfluencies tend to accompany harder linguistic choices. Let's unpack this a bit by looking at what some of this research can tell us.

Our hesitations seem to act as pretty significant comprehension aids for our listeners. For instance, in one research study, participants were asked to move a mouse to select an object from two choices on a computer screen after hearing a prompt. The trick was that one of the objects had been previously mentioned during the study and the other had not. When the experimental instructions included an *um* before the name of the object to select, participants were not only more likely to be faster at identifying the unmentioned object, but they also started moving the cursor in that object's direction before the *um* was even finished. It seems the *um* clued the listener in to which word was more likely to be said (the unmentioned one) because they understood *um*'s role of marking something unfamiliar. This effect did not occur when the researchers used a same-length random background noise instead of the filled pause. The *um* made them do it.

And this tendency for filled pauses to help us anticipate what speakers will say next was not a one-off. It has been replicated in a variety of studies. A somewhat more complicated study using eye-tracking methodology asked participants to manipulate objects by giving them instructions like "Put the grapes over the candle. Now put the camel over the salt." They were shown images of both a candle and a camel, which, you might notice, both begin with a *ca* sound. Thus, when a listener hears the very beginning of the words, there is what is called cohort competition, which is a fancy way of saying we are not sure yet which one is meant because both of them sound the same at the onset of the word. Usually, assuming we don't tune out what someone says to us after the first couple of sounds, we figure out by the time they utter a few more sounds which word they meant. So we would have figured out that *cand* would be a *candle*, not a *camel*.

But if you stick eye-tracking equipment on somebody's face, as psycholinguistics tend to do, you will see that, as soon as they hear *ca*, listeners move their eyes first to the image they think is most likely meant based on whatever priming there was. This priming is usually contextual—for instance, something that was previously mentioned, or their knowledge that you tend to hang out a lot with camels, etc. So in this particular experiment, the researchers had already mentioned one of the objects but not the other in the experimental instructions; *candle* is referred to in the first line, "Put the grapes over the candle." As a result, when, in the second line, the *ca* sound starts, listeners indeed looked first toward the candle image, not the camel, as this is what they were expecting to hear. But, when the researchers gave instructions that included filler words like "Put the grapes over the candle, now put the *uh* ca . . . ," this led participants to look instead first at the unexpected object—the one that had not yet been mentioned—instead of the candle, which had been named. The disfluency here was taken by participants as a clue that the anticipated word involved more cognitive processing, such as required for integrating new information.

To look even more deeply at the effect of filled pauses on how we process and understand speech, several studies have also used event-related potential, or ERP, data to measure the effects of disfluency on comprehension.* For example, in one study, listeners heard recordings of sentences that ended with words that were predictable from the context. So, using a sentence like "Everyone's got bad habits and mine is biting my _____," one would more likely predict "nails" to fill in that blank than something like "tongue," the biting of which is usually an accident rather than a habit. Still, the sentence is plausible either way, even if habitual tongue-biting would make you slightly odd. Absent any kind of experimental manipulation, ERP results show what is called a N400 effect, a negative voltage change measured at the electrodes on the top of a subject's head, when an unpredictable word appears in the blank compared to a predictable one. But

---

* Using electrodes placed noninvasively on the scalp, the ERP technique measures voltage changes in the brain in response to stimuli, providing a glimpse into psychophysiological correlates of information processing.

when the experimenters put an *uh* prior to the unpredicted word, it reduced this N400 effect in listeners. Basically, subjects found it easier to integrate an unpredictable word in that sentence when a filled pause was present than when it wasn't.

Along the same lines, other studies have discovered that, when asked to choose between concrete or abstract items, or hard versus less-hard to describe objects like a square versus a squiggly shape, a filled pause in the instructions tended to encourage listeners to first look toward the abstract or harder option, with opposite effects when no fillers were present. Interestingly, when listeners were given information that provided an alternate explanation for why a speaker might be disfluent, such as they had a speech impairment, they were less likely to make any anticipatory shifts in which objects they looked at first. Likewise, another study found that listeners only made predictive inferences when hearing filled pauses in a native speaker's speech, but not when hearing them spoken by a nonnative speaker. All this suggests that we know that people typically use more filled pauses when talking about unfamiliar, difficult, unpredictable, or abstract things, and so we incorporate that knowledge into how we unpack what they say. But this is not automatic. If listeners don't think someone is using filled pauses in a communicative way—for instance, because of speaker-specific processing issues or as a second-language speaker—they don't rely on them in the same way they would in other contexts.

But assuming speakers and listeners are on the same page,

packed pauses can be unexpectedly useful. Not only does a bit of filled hesitation help us predict what people are going to say, but it also seems to help us more quickly recognize and remember what they already said. How does this work? Well, it seems that when hearing words preceded by *uh*s or *um*s in experimental tasks or recordings, participants perform better on later memory tests. For instance, in the ERP study just mentioned, subjects were also given a surprise recognition test about an hour after having listened to the speakers reading the experimental sentences. In that task, they were shown a word visually (e.g., *drink*), then asked whether it was old or new, meaning had they heard it or not during the previous listening task. When a word had been preceded by a filled pause in the recordings they had heard, listeners were better at recognizing it later, suggesting the vocalized pause actually helped make the word more memorable. Not only do listeners seem to get a mnemonic boost, but it also seems to speed up their processing time. For instance, when told to click a button as soon as they heard a particular target word in a speech stream, participants showed a faster response time when the word was proceeded by an *uh* or *um* compared to when that FP was filtered out.* The researchers suggest this is

---

* Psycholinguist Jean Fox Tree found that this faster response time effect was specific to *uh*, while *um* neither helped nor hindered word monitoring processes. This echoes some other studies that also suggest *uh* has a stronger comprehension benefit than *um*. This may be the result of the longer delay anticipated by listeners when hearing *um*, which draws their attention instead to try to help fill in missing words for speakers or simply does not allow them to focus sustained attention on the speech stream for the longer delay period. See Jean Fox Tree, "Listeners' Uses

because listeners integrate information more quickly when a filled pause is present. Had filled pauses instead hindered comprehension, as we might assume given their status as unwelcome speech interlopers, they should slow, not speed up, this speech-monitoring activity. But instead, adding filled pauses seems to be advantageous from a processing perspective for both speakers and listeners.

This advantage for memory and speed has been well studied—experiments testing disfluency effects on comprehension have pretty consistently illustrated recall and processing-time benefits when a filled pause is part of the stimuli. And the benefits are not just on word recall—we also seem to remember stories better when *uh* or *um* enter the picture. In an experiment testing how well people performed at recalling specific parts of the story *Alice in Wonderland*, participants showed better recall when they had heard recordings with filled pauses occurring before some plot points, such as "Meanwhile, . . . uh . . . , the cook keeps hurling plates and other items at the Duchess." Equivalently timed coughing inserted into the passages at the same points, though, didn't help them out in recalling those plot points later. In fact, the coughs seemed to impair recall. So it is specifically the *uh* that seems to do the trick.

That filled pauses help us in processing speech and in re-

of Um and Uh in Speech Comprehension," *Memory and Cognition* 29, no. 2 (2001): 320–26.

membering it seems pretty clearly established. The bigger question is why something we tend to think of as distracting and annoying might be so dang useful. There are a couple of possibilities. One is that inserting *um*s and *uh*s simply gives us more time to think about and focus on what is being said, so that it is not the *um* or *uh* per se, but simply the extra processing time it affords that is helping us. Certainly plausible, but research that has used other types of distracters like equivalently timed silent pauses or coughing doesn't produce the same effect. More likely, they work by alerting us to pay closer attention to what is being said. In other words, disfluencies suggest that what someone is saying is difficult to process in some way, so it jolts us into focusing more intently on the speech stream. This of course has some interesting real-world applications that we can put to work right away. For instance, next time I tell my teenager to remember to take his binder to school, I am going to give *uh* a shot in hopes it might actually help him remember. Of course, he would have to be listening in the first place, which unfortunately does not seem to be in *uh*'s bag of magic tricks.

Men-o-pausal patterns

There is evidence that *um* and *uh* are very much part of how we communicate out in the real world and not just when wired up with electrodes in a lab. Take a quick gander at Twitter and how many posts now start with "um," and you can see how it has moved past being just a ponderous pause to being transported into writing as a way to express confusion, surprise, and sarcasm.

Turns out, our packed pauses are quite the social butterflies, filling our conversational voids in unexpected ways. One might think that something that has long been treated as disfluency and verbal riffraff like filled pauses wouldn't show any social variation. After all, if *um* and *uh* are only subconscious indicators of cognitive load, it would seem a bit strange that they serve as any kind of social marker. But, given the listener-oriented message that research has suggested they carry, and the highlighting flags they seem to be, maybe it isn't such a leap to assume they might also tell us a thing or two about our social selves. And, as sociolinguistic luck (or historically long-evidenced patterns) would have it, our filled pauses are more similar in function to the more familiar fillers *like* and *so* than we might at first have surmised.

When looking at the use of filled pauses overall in a number of different large speech corpora across a variety of different studies, we find one pattern emerges pretty consistently: that men use more filled pauses than women. For example, in several posts from the popular *Language Log* blog that looked at filled pause use, University of Pennsylvania professor and well-respected linguist Mark Liberman found men had a higher overall rate of filled pauses in recordings of telephone conversations, using *uh* a whopping 250 percent more than women. This pattern of male pausing likewise prevails in other studies that examined speaking contexts ranging from sociolinguistic interviews to speed-dating events to assorted casual conversations.* Liberman also found older speakers using more *uh* forms, echoing other studies that found more mature speakers, especially those over sixty, using more filled pauses overall than younger ones.[†] And these patterns are not limited to American English. In fact, research comparing spoken-language corpora in Britain and the United States suggests that Brits use more filled pauses than Americans, with English men also populating their pauses with more *uh*s.

But here is where the old adage that looks can be deceiving is very apt, because looking at filled pause preferences over time reveals a surprising but perhaps not so unexpected twist: despite not using as much *uh*, women and younger speakers have greatly increased their use of *um* over the last century. Gradually at first, but at a much faster clip over the past fifty or so years. Not to be left in the *uh* dust, men have also been switching it up and using more *um*, but are, as one article estimates, still about twenty-two years behind women. So, while men's *uh*s might be more pervasive, women's and young folks' *um*s are changing up the

---

* These corpora of recorded speech are usually public (or academically available) collections. Interestingly, the type of speech (public speech versus private speech) has been found to affect the rate of filled pauses. Private speech shows fewer filled pauses than in task-oriented (e.g., work) speech, which makes sense if we assume *um* and *uh* increase under conditions when more speech planning is required.

† Though partly this might be related to a decrease in memory function as we age.

linguistic landscape. Most intriguing, in Germanic languages that share similar *uh*s and *um*s, like Dutch, Danish, German, Norwegian, and Faroese, a group of linguists found this pattern of a female- and youth-led shift toward *um* was prevalent across all the varied speech data sets.* As well, we find a similar trend when we look to studies of *um*ing and *uh*ing in British English. In short, women and younger speakers are driving the *um* train and leaving *uh* back at the station in a bit of an *um* revolution.

This leaves us, as all great research does, with some lingering questions. The big one, of course, is what's *um* got that *uh* doesn't? Why would we prefer one marker over the other, absent any evidence that we have taken up the cause of pausing longer? One idea bandied about has to do with how the two fillers are produced. *Uh*, as you can see if you make the sound, has a somewhat mouth hanging open, someone just punched you in the gut kind of articulation. *Um*, with a closed jaw and lips sealed articulation, is less likely to let the flies in and could come across as a more polite self-conscious form of a feature not well received to begin with. Alternatively, and the view put forth in a number of academic papers, is that *um* is rising because it has taken on some new functions in terms of how it is put to work in conversational structure. In other words, it's expanding beyond just being a signal of cognitive effort to also being a speech

---

* They also found confirmation of Clark and Fox Tree's hypothesis that *um* preceded longer pauses (e.g., longer delays) than *uh*.

feature that communicates the *meaning* of thinking or speech planning, much like *oh* at the beginning of a sentence communicates surprise when used more conventionally in speech ("Oh, really?") and not only when someone jumps out of the closet at you.

Staging an *um*-prising?

As mentioned in the last chapter, whenever we see young + female using more of something in language, it is usually a sign that change is a-coming. Still, haven't we had *um* and *uh* for quite a while to mark our pauses and alert our listeners? Sure seems a bit odd that speech disfluency would be subject to the same sorts of sociolinguistic forces that adorn more word-like words. But that is just it. The change that is coming might just be that the wordiness of *um* is breaking on through to the other side, functioning, as mentioned above, as a pointer to some meta-linguistic aspects of meaning being conveyed. Consider headlines like "Obama Is More, Um, Seasoned," in reference to the former president's graying hair, or an "Um, Senator . . ." signaling an oppositional stance to rebut something someone has said (as was used in a *New York Times* opinion piece), and we can see that our verbalized pauses have moved past being used as simply hesitations to being put to work for euphemistic intent or disagreement. The very fact that they are used in written language at all when not part of a disfluent quote tells us something is afoot. By tracking the rise of such features in what we write, we can get a sense of when they started to crystallize specific functions and meanings, identify jumps in frequency, and also get a sense of how they are perceived based on the types of writing they appear in or the attributes accorded to the characters who use them.*

Just take a look at the increase in filled pauses, and especially *um*, in our messages, tweets, movie dialogue, and journalistic reports over the past few decades. A quick search of the entire Corpus of Historical American English turns up a huge increase in the number of *um*s found in texts of various sorts from the early 1800s to the early 2000s—from less than one hundred mentions to over four thousand! And most of those early mentions are not today's *um*s at all, but rather along the lines of "give 'um hell!" A perfectly fun *um*, but no relation to the filled pauses of which we here speak, uh, I mean write. In fact, filled pauses don't seem to have even made a debut, at least in journalistic prose, until the 1950s, and even then, only rarely. Taking a look at the most recent *um*s that turned up, the majority are now filled pause uses, with splashy representation on the page and on the big screen, in magazines, and in newspapers. It would appear that *um* has found itself a very word-like employment not only when

---

* Even more useful in tracking how speech features have evolved and changed, as well as trends in who uses them, are forms of casual correspondence such as letters or diaries.

we chat, but when we are trying to get a bit of hesitation, attitude, or irony to come across in our writing. The question is why we suddenly have taken our pauses to the next level.

Remember how you sometimes *um* to start off a sentence when it might take a while to come up with the answer? Like when you randomly get asked, "What was that movie where Tom Cruise danced around in his underwear?" and your encyclopedic knowledge of Tom Cruise movies momentarily fails you. How much do you want to bet you started your answer off with "Um . . ."?* You might unintentionally *um* to announce a delay and hold the floor while you pondered, or, potentially, you might *um* right before you provide a snarky "Um, old much?" because you weren't even alive when that movie came out. You might also have responded with "Um . . ." before giving up just to make your friend feel like you at least gave it a go and thought about it for a sec. In other words, using filled pauses in writing brings in some of this same signaling work that pauses do for us in speech—like buy us thinking time, manage conversational turns, or highlight what we're about to say next. Though we use filled pauses in speech without much awareness as a thinking time-out or to search for a word, in our writing they have started to behave more like true discourse markers, or DMs as they are called by linguists, such as *well* or *like* that clue in listeners how

---

* Now that I have you trying to remember, did you come up with the movie *Risky Business* or did my *um* just buy you the time to google it?

to take what we are about to say. And it is this newer function that is also likely part of what is driving the shift to *um* in our speech, as its "working on it" and "planning" associations have acquired some meta awareness as more intentional pragmatic devices.

If we look at how changes in our speech have become part of our modern colloquial writing style—for instance, the use of *got* for passive *was*, as in "she got laid off," or *oh* to express surprise—it always follows the expanded use of those forms in speech. While in talking we use these forms fairly unconsciously, in writing we put them to work precisely because of the carry-over in meaning we can use to communicate a similar sense. We probably don't spend a lot of time thinking "How about I stick an um in here for effect," but that doesn't mean we don't notice that it's communicating that effect metalinguistically. So, when I answer your question about whether I like eggplant with an "Um . . . it's okay," it really translates into a considerate form of "Hell no." The *um* here showing via our knowledge of its hesitant-searching-for-the-right-word purpose that I am communicating something over and above what my words actually mean. And indeed, analysis of the use of *um* in instant message apps, a hybridized form of speech and writing, has actually found that messages often employ *um* to hedge their answers to express consideration or disalignment. This suggests that, in more speechlike written forums, our *um*s are taking on a discursive role beyond a flag for thinking or hesitation. And from a sound symbolism perspective, the closed-mouth, less yawn-like articulation for *um* may indeed make it come across as the somewhat politer option of the two filled pauses.

The use of filled pauses in speech and more speechlike messaging has also made inroads into more traditional nonhybrid contexts such as magazines, books, and newspapers. For instance, in her work examining how *um*, *uh*, and *er* were used over the past several decades in newspapers and magazines, linguist Gunnel Tottie finds that filled pauses at the very beginning of a sentence almost always function to express a "negative or contradictory attitude" to something previously said (e.g., "Uh, bullshit!" or the previous "Um, Senator" example). In contrast, filled pauses that occurred in the middle of sentences were used to convey, as she puts it, a "tongue-in-cheek" tone or to "put something delicately." We find such uses, for instance, in an attempt to humorously convey someone's less than stellar abilities, for example, "his dancing, um, skills," or to euphemistically call out an indelicate topic, as in "He was, um, taking care of business," in reference to what, in my kids' toddler days, we might have referred to as a nature pee.*

All of this suggests that filled pauses have started to become lexicalized, a big word for the concept of creating a new word

---

* Both of these examples were discussed in Gunnel Tottie's 2017 article, "From Pause to Word: *Uh*, *Um* and *Er* in Written American English." The first actually appeared in *USA Today* referencing boxing champ Evander Holyfield's lack of dancing grace, and the second appeared in a 1997 *Time* magazine article about a bear's entrance upending a camping jaunt.

with a recognizable meaning or sense, making it available for use in a somewhat more intentional way. The utility of filled pauses in speech to let our co-conversationalists know how to interpret or pay more attention to what we said has become a more prominent attribute, increasing their use as something more than just a pause. Once they start being pragmatically useful in our speech in this way, this, in turn, opens the door to bringing some of these signposting functions into our more colloquial forms of writing. In turn, they start to take on a more specialized function, where they communicate "faux" planning or hesitation. The course of change here is charted not by scholarly decree or grammatical edict, but, like so many of the shifts in our language that have occurred over the past thousand years, by the speakers in the trenches who use them to achieve a desired communicative effect.

Umdone

The biggest takeaway, though, is who forms the front line in the ever-evolving linguistic war of form and function. Much like what we will see for the other features covered in this book, our move toward *um* plows a well-worn and socially savvy path that has driven linguistic change for centuries. In other words, the young and female are leading the way, a pattern that, even back in the day of Middle English, has often been the harbinger of the language features that will soon be making the rounds. And a secondary pattern—where others lag behind but start to catch up as the shift percolates past the young and female—is usually the hallmark that something new and notable has fully taken root. Though not all features follow this same exact pattern, what doesn't change is the way that our social identities are always part of the magic mix of what rises to garner linguistic notice. But what we will come to realize is that language and social life have become entwined again and again over our history, and there is nothing random or flawed about the linguistic choices we make. As we venture deeper into the nitty-gritty of what lies underneath all the speech habits we notice and often deride, we will see that gender, age, and class have always fundamentally shaped the future of our talk in one way or another.

3

What's Not to Like?

Walk into any middle school in America and there's one word you'll hear echoing down the hallway that has taken on more than its fair share of shade. No, it doesn't rhyme with "luck" or "hit." This one rhymes with "hike" and should be wildly familiar to anyone who's seen the movies *Valley Girl* or *Clueless*. While "fer sure" and "totally gnarly" have faded into the SoCal sunset, the presence of *like* has only expanded, punctuating every sentence from Los Angeles to New York.

The frequent use of *like* may sound juvenile, but it has taken over our linguistic nooks and crannies in almost every variety of global English. It appears at the beginning of sentences, in the middle of clauses, and now it even introduces quotes. The funny thing is, despite its pervasiveness, hardly anyone claims to like this new type of *like*. Even those who admit to using it themselves rarely remark on it as a positive attribute. Case in point:

When I ask my college students to name the things that bug them the most about language, *like* is always at the top of the list, comically appearing in the very sentence that denigrates it: "I hate how people, like, use like all the time." Once the offending word is mentioned, the students can't stop noticing how often it pops up in everyone's speech for the rest of the class period—and then the rest of the day, week, month, and year. The fact is, like it or not, *like* use is here to stay. But before condemning it as a sign of impending linguistic ruin, let's take some time to consider why *like* might have entered our speech in the first place. As I tell my students, maybe, just maybe, there is more to *like* than we might at first believe.

Like, why?

This expanded use of *like* is so widespread that news outlets ranging from *The Atlantic* to *Time* to *Vanity Fair* to *The New York Times* have covered what seems to be its troubling and meteoric rise. One online college advice site has a post headlined "How to Stop Saying Like and Immediately Sound Smarter"; a speech-improvement service calls it "The Like Epidemic"; the *Chronicle of Higher Education* asks that we "Diss 'Like'"; and in *Vanity Fair* Christopher Hitchens called it "The *Other* L-word." Across global English varieties, concerned parents worry about this troublesome verbal habit. One mother, echoing the apprehensions of many, appeals for help from the advice expert at the UK's *The Guardian*, fretting that her teenager's *like* use sounds uneducated and will affect her success in the future. Teachers also report that its prevalent use in class is becoming problematic. In fact, a friend of mine who is a middle school teacher recently told me that it's her students' number one verbal tic.* This collective hand-wringing leaves little doubt that we have little love for *like*. So then why do we continue to use it?

Ask most parents and they'll probably say it has something to do with adolescent laziness or linguistic rebellion. Ask most employers and they'll probably say it has to do with a shift from a more formal workplace to a casual, less professional setting. Ask most linguists, though, and they'll probably tell you we're missing the mark. *Like* used in such contexts is not much different from other markers that we have used through the centuries to help us organize and structure our speech. In other words, there is nothing that unique or concerning about it.

Though we might not realize it, English has an arsenal of pragmatic-oriented features of speech, such as *so, you know, actually,* and *oh.* As with our now-beloved *um*s and *uh*s, these discourse markers don't directly contribute to the literal (semantic) content of a sentence. Instead, when added, they contribute

---

* In a proper-speech game she plays with her seventh graders, students populate their speech with *like* or *um* or other perceived infractions and the rest of the class guesses at what speaking violation is exemplified. The name of the game? "Permission to Speak Badly."

to how we understand each other by providing clues to a speaker's intentions. For instance, when I say, "Oh, I finally got a job!" my use of *oh* is a shorthand way to prompt a listener to mimic my surprise. Discourse markers provide the social greasing of the conversational wheel. Without them, our speech would sound less conversational and more computer-like. In fact, try having a conversation without using any discourse markers.* Not only will you find it quite difficult, but others will find you a less appealing speaker.

Discourse markers are by no means new or unusual. Shakespeare made liberal use of them, and the epic poem *Beowulf* even begins with one (*Hwæt!*). Suggestively, historical texts that date back to the Old English and Middle English periods (fifth to eleventh century and twelfth to fifteenth century, respectively) have shown evidence of words functioning similarly to modern discourse markers. For instance, the Old English word *þa*, meaning "then," served as a foregrounding discourse marker in narratives and was often associated with colloquial speech. As a matter of fact, some Old English scholars suggest *þa* occurred so often in some early texts that it can't have carried much semantic content, a complaint that echoes our modern assessment of excessive *like* use. Less controversial, Old English *hwæt*, meaning "what," seems to have served as an attention-getting device

---

* And in fact, the discourse marker *in fact* here very usefully makes the case for the utility of such markers in signposting as well as conversational flow and coherence.

roughly similar to the modern sentence's initial *so*.* As the opener to *Beowulf*, it's a signal to the audience that something worth paying attention to will follow. In more recent times—at least if you consider the early modern period (fifteenth through seventeenth century) recent—interjections such as *alas*, *ah*, and *fie*, among others, similarly functioned to give a sense of a speaker's intentions or emotions (alas, 'tis true). Though charming to our ears, these DMs may well have been painful to parents of the early modern era.

Looking back, we find that the origins of the word *like* are similarly rooted in the Middle English and early modern period. The *Oxford English Dictionary* (OED) first notes the use of *like* in its adjectival and verbal functions—as *līch* (adjective) and *lician* (verb), respectively—as early as 1200, with noun, conjunction, and prepositional uses noted around 1400–1500. The use of *like* as a conversational marker shows up later, though much earlier than we might have expected. The OED cites a passage from a text written in 1778 (F. Burney's *Evelina II*), where it is used to qualify the speaker's subsequent remark, "Father grew quite uneasy, like, for fear of his Lordship's taking offence." It also cites another example employing *like* in this way in 1840, in

---

* But even this is not without controversy—*hwæt* has been suggested to be the precursor of our modern discourse marker *you know*, carrying a similar "calling up our shared knowledge" sense. Of course, this "Hey, ya'll know what I'm talking about!" interpretation is a pretty radical departure from the conventional translation of this start to *Beowulf* as "Behold!" More edgy modern translations go so far as to translate this as "Bro!"

a magazine of the era: "Why like, it's gaily nigh like, to four mile like." And hinting at the source of *like*'s vibe of hip vernacularity, the OED gives a more recent example from a beat-influenced magazine, where we locate *like* occurring in its now familiar spot at the beginning of a sentence—"Like how much can you lay on (i.e., give) me?" (from *Neurotica* Autumn 45).

But even outside these literary uses, there are examples of many colloquial uses of the word throughout the centuries. In tracing the historical origins of our modern *like*, Canadian researcher, linguist, and *like* expert Alexandra D'Arcy finds evidence of a discourse-marking function back in the eighteenth century in the Old Bailey proceedings—documents and transcripts of British criminal court trials that go as far back as 1674.* She also finds octogenarian speakers in rural British villages using *like* in positions presaging modern discourse-marker usage: "Like it was a kind-of wee bit of tongue twister." Similarly, recordings made in the 1940s of elderly New Zealanders whose families hailed from the British Isles showed that *like* also dotted their linguistic landscape, often occurring at the leading edge of a sentence in much the same fashion as above. So while conventional wisdom might view *like* as a prime example of

---

* We find an example of such early discourse-marker use of *like* in this excerpt from a transcript in the Old Bailey collection of the trial of William Ward in 1789: "They were down both together, and the young man that is along with me now, he parted them, like one parted on one side the cart, and one on the other."

Americans going linguistically rogue, the idea that *like* is as American as apple pie is highly questionable. Given the British origin of the early examples just discussed, and the fact that New Zealanders used *like* long before it was a beat or SoCal thing, I think we can safely blame the British for planting the seeds of this one. After all, as D'Arcy notes, *like*'s presence across English varieties as far flung as Canada, New Zealand, North America, and Australia—all areas that share a lot of early British influx—is surely no coincidence.

Since we all use discourse markers and have, it seems, across the ocean and through the centuries, what's the big deal? Why are they so frowned upon in formal contexts, where we expect more prescribed speech? Just consider the negative press that swirled around Caroline Kennedy when, considering a run for Senate, she used the discourse marker *you know* frequently (which is a nice way of saying 138 times) in an interview with *New York Times* reporters. Likewise, Berkeley linguist Robin Lakoff noted in an article on Senator Hillary Clinton that she also used *you know* often during a press conference. In neither case were the ladies in question lauded for their eloquence and articulateness.

Why, despite the surprisingly long evolutionary history, are these speech features still perceived as an "emergent" and disastrous blight on modern speech? And why is *like* the worst offender of them all?

The trouble with *like*

To get to the bottom of our trouble with *like*, let's start by considering the word's traditional syntactic roles and semantic functions, meaning where it fits and what it usually means in sentences. *Like* is an incredibly amorphous word; even when it's "appropriately" used, it's a syntactical workhorse. Primarily, we hear *like* as a verb, to discuss a fondness for objects or people, as in, "I like Ameer because he is a nice guy," or, even better, "I like ice cream"; as a noun, to describe *likes* (ice cream) and *dislikes* (poison ivy); and as an adjective (*swanlike, buffoon-like*), to mean "similar to" or "in the manner of." We also see *like* used as a preposition, as found in a simile construction ("She has eyes like the sky") and as a conjunction to embed another clause, as in, "She rode the bike like she was on fire." Certainly, some of these *like* contexts might be more or less widely used or favored by speakers, but rarely do they earn the rebuke or commentary brought on by use of the word in contexts where it does not fulfill any of these roles, as in "I use like, like, all the time."

Still, that doesn't mean we have always been on board with *like* in all these syntactic forms either. Though most of us weren't around back in the 1950s when a Winston cigarette ad declared "Winston tastes good like a cigarette should," the grammar police certainly were. Prescriptivists denounced this "misuse" of *like* as a conjunction where, standardly, *as* should have reigned.

Ironically, they should have been more worried about the long-term effects on our health rather than our grammar. Nowadays, the conjunction *like* is so pervasive that its colloquial past is unknown to many of its users, despite the fact that traditional grammar books still label such use as incorrect in formal written English. Just consider the *like* that now pops in with zeal after *seems, appears, sounds, pretends,* or *feels,* as in, "He felt like he could go no further." Research examining the rise of this type of *like* in literature finds it pretty much unattested until the mid-nineteenth century, where it appeared mainly in the speech of vernacular sorts until about the 1930s, when it became more mainstream.

Hence, our continuing expansion of *like*—moving beyond even verb, conjunction, adjectival, and prepositional contexts—simply reflects its growing multifunctionality. The problem that looms large, of course, is convincing those who view its spread as a transmissible disease that, like our filled pauses, the discourse marker *like* serves the greater communicative good. To see how *like* indeed rises to the challenge, we'll take a closer look at its numerous forms and purposes.

Approximately something

Let's take a sentence like "I exercised for, like, ten hours." The *like* that appears in this example might not seem as if it is serving any strictly necessary role. In other words, it doesn't feel as useful as the *like* in "Let's take a sentence like," where it is doing hard labor as a respected part of speech. In fact, the *like* before "ten hours" could be deleted and the strict semantic sense of the sentence would remain ("I exercised for ten hours"). But you would lose some of what the speaker intends to convey, a certain linguistic je ne sais quoi. This use of *like* suggests the speaker is not completely certain of how long they exercised (or doesn't really care to be more specific) but is emphasizing the fact that the exercising period was impressively long. Researchers studying this type of *like* have referred to it as an approximating marker—a way for a speaker to communicate a certain impreciseness or looseness of meaning—and it is very commonly employed before some sort of numerical quantification or estimation.

Why might this function be important or useful in conversation? We will often state things strongly or weakly in order to persuade a listener about a position we present, or to resist making a strong claim, or even to share useful but potentially not exact information. In our example, "I exercised for, like, ten hours," the speaker's intent is to persuade the listener that the exercise was long and grueling, but probably not that it actually lasted ten hours. In fact, if taken literally, one might not have much interest in pursuing conversation with someone so obviously in need of alternate leisure-time pursuits. While often characterized as empty or meaningless in terms of the semantic contribution, such markers can be an important component of what we consider informative discourse.

Compare the sentence "John was, like, fourteen, when he left home" with the roughly equivalent utterance "John was fourteen when he left home." Should a listener know John, and also know that he actually left home at fifteen, the conversational import intended by the speaker (that he left home at an early age) may be missed because the listener is more concerned that the sentence violated what they know about John. In linguistics we call this the truth-conditional meaning of sentences. Native speakers have intuitions about how their statements will be received—if a listener will believe that they are true or false—and sarcasm and humor aside, speakers, and listeners, tend to aim for credibility. Thus, there is a subtle difference added by the use of *like* that may help a speaker make a point about John leaving home without getting sidelined by information regarding his age that could mess with our truth conditions.

Interestingly, what bothers people about "John was, like, fourteen, when he left home" seems not to be the intent, but the type of the discourse marker used. The speaker, of course, could use *about* instead of *like*, but this is just a matter of preference. For instance, one could easily have said "John left home when he was about fourteen," coming across as more reserved than carefree and hip. A recent study by Alexandra D'Arcy suggests that in such contexts where *about* might be more traditionally used as an approximating adverbial, younger speakers are moving toward using *like* in contrast to older speakers who use *about*. Here, it's important to note that the function of *like* is no different than the much less maligned *about*. Our unease with *like* use, then, is probably more about its association with casual, younger speech than with its functionality.

Just think about it this way: English speakers hedge and qualify all the time. The perfectly acceptable terms *think, may, possibly*, or *maybe* mitigate our commitment to certainty. Consider "It may rain tomorrow" versus "It will rain tomorrow"; your decision to bring an umbrella to work could hinge upon the choice of verb used by your co-conversationalist. In this form, *like* is just another way of expressing degrees of certainty. It may be disfavored, but it is certainly part of a much larger class that performs similarly useful linguistic tasks.

Laser pointers

My daughter (a model *like* user) and I were recently talking about a party she attended. When describing a fellow attendee, she said, "She's, like, one of the popular girls," and then proceeded to tell me about this tween Amazonian's death-defying acts of coolness. Now, I am doubtful that my daughter was trying to be vague about the girl's popularity. Instead, by introducing the noun phrase "one of the popular girls" with *like*, she was highlighting the point she was trying to make. In other words, she was using *like* not as an approximator, but as a linguistic focuser.

Rather than opening up a sentence by indicating looseness, *like*, instead, can tighten a sentence by indicating the focus. The interactional function alerts the listener to a speaker's emphasis on a particular aspect of the sentence. This is not by any means unique to English. The discourse marker *ba(ra)* in Swedish, *como* in Spanish, *genre* in French, or *liksom* in Norwegian can serve much the same function. All of these are conversational and youth-oriented equivalents to *like*, but somehow they sound a lot more sophisticated in another language.

The problem for some is that when *like* is used in its focuser role, it can seem to show up anywhere. But there is a method to the madness. Though there is flexibility in terms of exactly where *like* can go (known as syntactic detachability), its position in a sentence tends to follow a pattern, suggesting that its placement is linguistically governed. The majority of occurrences appear before syntactic units such as verb, noun, or adjectival phrases ("I was, like, so happy") or at the beginning of a sentence ("Like, I was happy").

Even more evidence that *like* has both a purpose and a pattern comes from a study that looked at how discourse marker functions of *like* were deployed by speakers when retelling stories. If *like*s appear at random, we should not expect them to occur in the same exact locations upon a repeat telling of a story. Testing this theory, it was discovered that when a personal story was retold by the original speaker, *like*s occurred in very close or even identical positions to where they had appeared the first time. For instance, "He's, like, legendary" was relayed in the second telling as "He's, like, a legend." Of course, one might surmise this overlap could just be the result of a speaker's intractable *like* habit and simple mathematical probability. But the same thing happened when a listener, and not just the original storyteller, was taken to a separate room and asked to retell the story. Both the original speaker and the listener tended to recycle *like*s at the same points in the story, suggesting that those specific *like*s really did matter in qualifying or supplementing the meaning at those points.* Like it or not (pun absolutely intended), *like* usage seems to be intentional and essential.

The plot thickens

While the above examples demonstrate the power of *like* as a discourse marker, the usage that seems to truly rally the grammar prescriptivists is *like* as a quotative verb. As in, "I was like, 'I can't stand it!' and she was like, 'I know! I don't like it either.'"

---

* In the same study, *like* use was also compared to *um*s and *uh*s, as *like* has been posited as a similar "filler" that indicates speech difficulties. In contrast to filled pauses, which did often co-occur with speech repetition and restarts (suggesting planning issues), *like*s did not. Nor was there any pattern of high FP users being high *like* users (or a high use–low use pattern where one replaces the other). This suggests that there is no connection, in function or placement pattern, between the two. *Like*, as study author Jean Fox Tree puts it, is not the modern *um*.

Though often all *like* use is seen as one and the same, quotative *like* is linguistically quite different. In contrast to the long history of discourse marker *like*, quotative *like* is a fairly recent development, with the OED first noting its use alongside a verb to introduce internalized speech in a *Time* magazine article from 1970, "And I thought like wow, this is for me." According to *like* experts, this reference is a throwback to the "Like, wow" phenomenon associated with beatniks in the 1950s and beat/jazz culture in New York City in the 1960s.

The popularity of quotative *like* use was mainstreamed by the popular song *Valley Girl* by Frank Zappa, with help from his daughter Moon Unit, in 1982. This song took popular culture by storm, drawing a caricature of the speech style used by girls from Southern California. Along with introducing the iconic phrase "Gag me with a spoon," it acquainted many of us with *like* in both its discourse marker and quotative functions, helping to accelerate its spread. Still, the song simply reflected, rather than started, an undercurrent already in play well before it came on the scene.

As a class, quotative verbs in English are used to introduce internal dialogue, for example, a speaker's reporting of their own thoughts, or as a preface to reporting something said by somebody else.* In standard formal practice, we use the verb *to*

---

* Linguist and well-known author Deborah Tannen was one of the first to examine different types of introducers to what she refers to as "constructed dialogue"

say in these contexts, as in, "And then I said, 'What's up?'" But, as one scholar puts it, *say* involves "quotation with no commitment." In other words, it is the unmarked way to report what has been said. So, to add some nuance and interest, we might use the verb *to go* ("Then she goes, 'What's up?'"), or even, in very colloquial speech, the verb *to be* + *all*, resulting in the somewhat awkward construction, "And I'm all, 'What's up?'" In the same vein as these quotatives, the verb *to be* + *like* also occurs when introducing reported or internalized speech, such as, "I'm like, 'No way am I taking another linguistics course!'"

This form of nonstandard *like* use seems to be the one people find most difficult to digest, which is unfortunate, since it's the most rapidly expanding one in English. Canadian researchers Sali Tagliamonte and Alexandra D'Arcy find the growth of this usage, at least in the Canadian English speech they examined, exponential—increasing from 13 percent to 58 percent of all quotatives used in less than a ten-year period. And further research on the appearance of *like* across English varieties globally suggests that it is this quotative *like*, and not discourse marker *like*, that might be the innovation that's "most vigorous and widespread in the history of the human language." In a study of its relentless advance in our speech across a number of world

---

in narratives. Her work suggested *be* + *like* allowed speakers to represent what someone said, while indicating that it was not literal, but just the general gist.

Englishes, Tagliamonte and her colleagues liken its diffusion to what is known as a Black Swan event—a unique, unprecedented event (like the internet, 9/11, or a pandemic) that fundamentally changes the way we behave.

When looking at how the *be-like* form is commonly used, Tagliamonte and D'Arcy find that it occurs most often with first-person narration of inner dialogue (e.g., "I was like" or "We were like") and mainly with the present tense or, especially for younger speakers, the historical present tense (using the present tense to describe past events, often used in fiction). Their findings echo research from the early 1990s that discovered speakers alternating between *say* and *like* to take on different narrating roles—using "they said" when directly reporting someone else's speech but "I was like" mainly when characterizing their own thoughts or feelings. This suggests that *be like* is used primarily to help us convey different perspectives while describing a story or an event, perhaps to heighten dramatic tension.

Intriguingly, this rapid uptake and selective replacement of the verb *to say* found across global Englishes appears to correspond with a fundamental shift in our narrative style during the latter half of the twentieth century. Prior to the rise of *be like*, our stories were primarily intended as retellings of events. Now, however, they have grown to include more "monologic performances" by speakers. In other words, we are also interested in dramatization and not just strict reportage, narrating our thoughts as if spoken out loud during the moments we are describing.* As a result, the focus has moved from the events themselves to our processing of these events. Such self-narration increased the need for us to "quote" ourselves, using the first person (I or we) instead of the third person (she, he, they). The problem? The verb *to say* didn't sufficiently capture the subjective sensibility this new approach required, which led to the rise of *be like*, serving to inject first-person reflections rather than simply the reported dialogue of the speaker. Gradually, these first-person uses of quotative *like* extended to use with all potential subjects, so that now she can be like, he can be like, and so can they.

In its quotative form, *like* is very limited in terms of where it can appear structurally in a sentence (unlike the promiscuous discourse marker). Namely, it can come only after the verb *to be* and before a quote.† Of course, since quotative *like* is often used by the same speakers who use discourse marker *like*, it can certainly seem as if *like* populates the speech of such users to an exceptionally high degree. All of which raises the question— who, exactly, are these linguistic renegades?

---

* Think of the difference between introducing speech with *to say*—e.g., "Then I said, 'Hello there!'" versus what's conveyed by using *like*, as in "Then I was like, 'Hello there!'" *To say* comes across as a verbatim quote while *be like* communicates a "something along the lines of" sentiment, and in fact might be taken here to describe what I was thinking rather than anything I actually said.

† Of course, in dialects with copula *be* deletion, one could simply use "he like" or "they like" to preface a quote, but the *be* is understood.

Old dogs, new tricks

Not surprisingly, most studies of the expansion of *like* in English varieties worldwide—ranging from British, Irish, and Scottish English, Australian and New Zealand English, to, of course, Canadian and American English—have definitively found a greater use of both discourse marker and quotative *like* by younger speakers, a pattern that is often the hallmark of a new speech norm. The big question now is whether it will remain the purview of the young or if it will continue to expand across the age divide.

Certainly, young speakers tend to be the most innovative when it comes to introducing new forms into language, and those forms are often oriented toward solidarity functions and appealing to their peer group. More commonly, older speakers use the verb *to say* for quotatives and *you know* as a discourse marker in the places where younger speakers use *be like* and *like*. Still, it is definitely not the case that we never find *like* in speakers over forty. Research suggests that *like* use is increasing, with speakers born in the late 1980s onward using *like* the most but locating an incremental increase in use by decade starting in speakers born as early as the 1960s. In other words, modern *like* use started slowly, hit the mainstream by the 1990s, and is becoming the new norm. As the millennials turn into parents and, eventually, grandparents, *like* may age along with them—leaving an opening for new generations to develop their own linguistic tells.

What women like

The young and the restless may use *like* more frequently than their parents, but the association with the word is particular to young women. After all, there aren't many references to Valley boys. Despite *like*'s cool cred coming in with the 1950s and '60s male-dominated counterculture (e.g., the beats and Shaggy from *Scooby-Doo*), many still tend to think of *like* use as a feminized linguistic style. This begs several questions. First, don't young men use *like*? And, second, if women do use it more, why is this the case?

The first thing to consider is that English does not have any extensive gender forms or gender marking, unlike some languages where men and women are expected to use socially appropriate forms for their sex. For example, in Japanese, there are specific vocabulary items that men use, such as *ore* or *boku* for "I," while women might use more feminine forms, such as *atashi*. In other languages, the gender of a speaker is marked by the addition of a specific ending to a word—e.g., in the (extinct) Native American language Yana, *ba* is the male speaker's version of "deer" and *ba-na* is the female speaker's form for "deer." In English, it is rare to have linguistic features that only men use or only women use. Unless there is something really unusual happening, chances are that whatever one sex is doing, the other is doing too, to some degree. What is likely to differ is the frequency, or the preferences, of word use by gender, driven in large part by various social pressures.* Which leads us to our first point: despite conventional wisdom, *like* use, both as a discourse marker and a quotative, appears in both men's and women's speech.

Why, then, do we so strongly associate *like* use with women's talk? This is much more than a personal bias; research on perception, such as that by linguists Jennifer Dailey-O'Cain and Isabelle Buchstaller, confirms that this is a widespread belief. Perhaps this is related to the ways society polices women's talk more than men's, and negatively characterizes features that women use more often. For instance, not only is it believed that women use *like* more often than men, but it is further believed that this indicates female users are vapid, airheaded, and clueless. Contrast this to the fact that men use the nonstandard *-in'* versus *-ing* forms at a higher rate than women, but there aren't a bunch of articles linking *-in'* with the decline of men's cognitive abilities. What, then, does this interrelation indicate?

Women's speech has historically been disparaged as chatty, gossipy, and less topically important than men's, something many contemporary researchers in the field of language and gender studies have interrogated. For instance, think of terms like *shrill* and *shrew*, or even the term *gossip*, all of which have been used for centuries to describe and devalue the talk of women.

---

* This is referred to in linguistic circles as frequency-based variation, in contrast to features that categorically only occur in one group or another (known, not surprisingly, as categorical variation).

Now throw in a speech feature that is associated with both young people and female speakers, and stereotypic associations make for appealingly convincing headlines.

Of course, the crucial question is: Is it even accurate to say that young women use more *like* than other speakers? This is where the facts get a little muddy. The findings on sex-based use of *like* are a bit more complicated than the findings on age. It is true that, on the whole, when a sex difference has been found, it has typically been women who use *like* more often. In particular, use of quotative *like* seems to be consistently favored by women. However, there are also a number of studies that have found that men use *like* more in some discourse marker contexts (such as when it is used in a sentence initially), or that there is no significant difference at all (when used as an approximating adverbial in lieu of *about*). Though the study was not rigorous in methodological design, Mark Liberman used data from almost twelve thousand recorded telephone conversations from 2003 to examine the distribution of nontraditional *like* use by age and sex, in what he referred to as a "Breakfast Experiment" on the *Language Log* blog. Counterintuitively, he found that men used *like* somewhat more in these conversations, but that the trend of *like* use in the sample was definitely more common among younger speakers. What this and other studies overwhelmingly suggest is that young men and women use *like* much more than older men and women, and despite Liberman's experiment, most researchers agree that it is somewhat more likely to be found in women's speech.

This gendered pattern is not a big surprise to most linguists, but neither is it an indication that women are the more feeble-minded sex. The conclusion is quite the contrary. It is a primary example of how most changes that have entered English and become new norms over the last century have been led by women. For example, linguist Louis Gauchat's 1905 work in the Swiss village of Charmey showed that young and female speakers were the most advanced in the sound changes affecting that community. His work was the earliest study to specifically investigate the sociolinguistic distribution of speech forms, rather than just chalk up any differences to women's lesser intellect and flightiness.* In the more recent (and voluminous) *Phonological Atlas of North American English*, sociolinguists Bill Labov, Sharon Ash, and Charles Boberg also found that almost all the sound changes that have affected the English vowel system over the last fifty years have been female led. Likewise, much work in between these two seminal studies has reinforced the role that women and young speakers play in linguistic change. For

---

* Unfortunately, he didn't start a trend. Danish linguist Otto Jespersen, who would in 1922 write what was considered a seminal text on the nature and structure of language, devoted an entire chapter to "The Woman," as if she were a separate (and inferior) species, at least linguistically speaking. While pointing to many differences in the way men and women spoke in the early twentieth century, Jespersen toed the androcentric party line that women's forms were less well developed and vacuous compared to those of men.

instance, this is the same pattern we saw at work in our previous chapter on changes in filled pause use over time. As was the trend with our increased tendency to *um*, only after changes pick up steam do males adopt the patterns, and at that point, the gender differences are almost nonexistent.

It is the men, then, and not the women, who are in a linguistic supporting role. We see this in an early study in Texas that looked at speakers across the 1990s, in which linguists Kathleen Ferrara and Barbara Bell found a trend of men's use "catching up" to women's as the study progressed. The caveat is that when a new linguistic form becomes too strongly associated with female use, it can instead reverse the behavior of men in what academics refer to as a linguistic retreat. This is the linguistic version of heteronormativity, or, in other words, acting macho. The desire to signal masculinity through language practices can also sometimes play a role in driving the adoption of other new forms, which we'll get into in the next chapter. But when it comes to *like*, it is a bit too early to tell if we will see a masculine retreat or if men are still playing catch-up. Personally, my money's on *like* staying the course.

To like or not to like?

As is the case with many other items we use regularly, *like* has a story, a linguistic pattern, and a large and growing population that finds its use agreeable. There is little evidence that its spread will be halted in either American English or other English varieties, and we would be wrong to dismiss *like* use as simply bad grammar. Its function, both as a discourse marker and a quotative verb, is well attested and deeply embedded in etymological history.

While understanding that the linguistic patterning and function behind such *like* use may not create a more harmonious relationship with its users, it should make us appreciate, at least a little, the marvel that is linguistic innovation. And for anyone who remains unconvinced, perhaps take solace in the fact that *like* may sound as quaint a hundred years from now as *fie* sounds to us today.

4

Dude, WTF!

When considering the trademark features of young men's talk, it usually involves words we don't say in polite company. But if most of what's new and noticed in modern speech is led by the young and female, what exactly is the role of men in forging the future of language?

The inexplicable success of Bill and Ted's endless saga across the universe and the enduring enigma of *Wayne's World* suggests the answer is indeed found in a four-letter word, though probably not the one that springs immediately to mind. Want a hint? It's a word that started off as an insult worthy of instigating a duel, but now epitomizes a state of enviable nonchalance. And similar to *like*, it has grown exponentially over the past fifty years in its communicative utility—employed as a greeting, a sign-off, a signal of disapproval, or just a marker of commiseration.

The term in question? Um, *dude*, of course. But while *um* and *like* might represent the linguistic cutting edge, the attraction of *dude* as a multifunctional sentential marker lies in its ethos of counterculture laid-back cool. The real surprise though is how *dude* transformed from a term of derision to one that populates our daily conversations, beer ads, and foreign movie dialogue, and how Gilded Age gender norms, subcultures, and vernacularity fueled its rise.

All the young dudes

Upon learning that there are college professors out there studying the meaning and function of *dude*, your first reaction might be the same as when you found out there were classes on the structure of Klingon or philosophy in *The Simpsons*, i.e., tuition dollars down the drain. But whoa, dude. It's not what you think. The point of studying *dude* is not just to pave a path to tenure, but to understand how the modern pervasiveness of *dude* among young men is tied to the larger cultural forces at work that drive the way we believe boys are supposed to talk and act. While young women are drawn to language features that make them come across as fashionable, urban, cool, or aloof, they tend to innovate in line with social norms that tell us that young ladies are still proper. In other words, using *like* or *totally* doesn't scream nonstandard nonconformist, but instead trendy hipness. For boys, though, the pressure to use speech that makes one appear rebellious, tough, and, crucially, heterosexual requires a very different pool of language resources. Think "Dude, what the f@#k?" and you've pretty much accomplished all of these things with one phrase.

For me, the story of *dude* lands close to home. Beginning when my son was in fifth grade, I noticed he started participating in a strange phenomenon that can only be referred to as dude-splaining. It went a little like: "Dude, UFOs are real!" or "Want some, dude?" or the simple but eloquent "Duuude!" when attention was critically needed. Sometimes I was even considered dudeworthy, as my son would call me *dude* in a momentary lapse caused by excitement. *Dude* had become a ubiquitous communication aide. While over the years my son's dude-splaining has decreased in frequency, once having dotted his sentences with almost *like*-like frequency, *dude* is still a mainstay of how he talks to his friends. But why *dude*? And what does it do for him and the millions of young men before him that "Hey" or "You know" just doesn't seem to? Though we might think of *dude* as just youthful slang, there is a lot more behind it, and how it came to represent cool masculinity, than one might imagine.

Dudes throughout history

When most of us think *dude* we envision familiar faces like Ashton Kutcher in the aptly named *Dude, Where's My Car?* or maybe most excellent dudes Bill and Ted. Or perhaps just the laid-back, naturally chill dude we all aspire to be. The sense that all these dudes encapsulate is the one drawn from a type of easygoing casual coolness—an esprit de corps that makes friends and influences people. But it turns out that the term's original meaning came from a certain style of dress and behavior that set the dude apart, and not in a good way. While the dude of today may separate the man from the boys, the dude of yesterday was more of the effeminate variety.

The *Oxford English Dictionary* describes the original meaning of *dude* as "a man who shows an ostentatious regard for fashion and style in regard to dress or appearance; a dandy, a fop," and suggests this early colloquial usage is now rare. And though we certainly do not use *dude* in this sense today, what current dudes and past dudes have in common is the way that both represent societal preoccupation with what it means to be masculine. In the nineteenth century, the term referred to men who concerned themselves with aesthetics, fashion, and beauty, and by pushing the envelope of what constituted manly preoccupations, they challenged existing social boundaries. Likewise, being a dude today also revolves around defying traditional expectations for behavior, though in a very different way.

Our first glimpse of the early dude came in a poem dating from 1883, "The True Origin and History of 'The Dude,'" that appeared in the influential newspaper *New York World*, mocking the effete and fashionable fop viewed as increasingly prevalent in New York at the time. Unlike the macho or burned-out image that we associate with dudes today, the dude of yesteryear was decidedly feminized, as the poem describes:

They do not care for cruel sports,
Like foot-ball, cricket, gunning,
But lemonade they drink by quarts,
Their girling's "real stunning!"

And if the image of a dude sipping lemonade and sitting out a good game seems the antithesis of the term today, imagine too that this dude was also replete with self-absorption, British affectation, and foolish self-indulgence. Think Oscar Wilde, referred to in the poem as an "imported dude," but with an American accent. In literature, Western itinerant Mark Twain introduced dudes in his *A Connecticut Yankee in King Arthur's Court*, employing this ostentatiously dressed sense when he famously describes King Arthur's knights as "iron dudes." Given how we use the term today, a modern reader would be easily forgiven for thinking this a recognition of their fierce constitution, à la our more familiar *ironman*. But in the *dude* lingo of the day, this is actually a reference to their overly showy attire and attitude, not their comportment.

Soon, fascination with the dude spread across the nation, and his style and demeanor became the Gilded Age equivalent of water cooler gossip and ridicule. According to an 1883 article, there was rarely a time where "what constitutes a dude is not daily discussed and where one or more young men do not lie under suspicion of dudity." In this era, being called a dude was no compliment. In one instance, a young gentleman aghast at being referred to as a dude sued his accuser in court for defamation, but only after first challenging him to a duel. Writing of the case, *The New York Times* found the very matter of the duel the deciding point, as a real dude "meek in spirit" would never "have invited a personal conflict."

This enduring public interest in the dude's foppish dandyism was a reaction to what appeared to many of the era as the effeminate and weak demeanor of the new breed of young American male. This uneasiness emerged out of a late nineteenth-century society upended by women's suffrage and increased gay male visibility, both perceived as threats to the sanctity of the family. By transgressing conventional masculine behavior, dudes presented social disruption that set conservative-leaning Americans on edge. In politics, cartoons used labeling of dude-ism as a tool to lampoon candidates pushing social reform, a particularly effective strategy in the 1884 election cycle. Thus, the tarnish of being a dude became quite an effective way to undermine those whose nontraditional approach posed a threat to the status quo in politics and society.

A dude and his duds

As they say, the clothes make the man, and they are also key to what sets a dude apart. Writing on the meaning of the term for *American Speech* in 1952, English professor Robert Knoll suggests our attention has always centered on a dude's duds, though mostly in mockery. Citing the 1897 *Oxford English Dictionary*'s definition of a dude, "a name given in ridicule to a man affecting an exaggerated fastidiousness in dress, speech and deportment," Knoll suggests that, by the 1950s, the showy sense of *dude* remained but had lost a bit of its foppish affectation to describe more of a well-dressed outsider. This is still a far cry from the sense it holds today of grungy slacker. While one could call the dude's rise from disparaging to decorated a rags-to-riches tale, in this case, it's really more like a riches-to-rags tale. So, how did a dainty dandy become a laid-back man's man in a matter of a century?

By the 1930s and '40s, *dude* was beginning to break from its British dandy pretension to be used more generally to describe men who stood out because of their duds—for instance, slang for a uniformed train conductor or an army recruit with a spanking new uniform. In the old West, calling someone a dude was a way to dis a tourist or city dweller as a nonlocal. As Knoll put it, "An over-dressed Californian is surely as much a dude in Wyoming as a Bostonian." And a suspicious lot these dudes were—linguist

Richard Hill notes that dishonest dudes were a staple of old Westerns, giving us movie dialogue like, "That dude slickered me outta muh ranch, Hoppy!"

In reality, perfectly well-mannered but inappropriately clad dude tourists inspired a flourishing cottage industry in the West. Our modern-day term *dude ranch* was coined from this mid-twentieth-century meaning of *dude*, an homage to the appeal of the West's rural, cow-wrangling lifestyle to fish-out-of-water over-dressed city folk. The awkward effort to assimilate the clothes and customs of the old West is aptly expressed in the 1991 bromance-inspired *City Slickers*, when Billy Crystal's character compares his friend's get-up to the cowboy in the Village People.

So when did being a dude finally start to become cool? Not until hipper people than trussed-up white folks started to use the term, and with much better music as a backdrop. Enter the jazz and jitterbug era of the 1930s and '40s. Though the Western tourist sense of *dude* was still around, *dude* was transported into counterculture slang as African American zoot-suiters and Mexican American pachucos began describing themselves as "dudes," drawing on the fashionably attired connotations of the term, but leaving behind the pejoration. The dandy was deconstructed, replaced by edgy fashion, and buoyed by rebellion all while maintaining the strong focus on appearance. And in the process of its reinvention, the dude went from dandy to dangerous, at least in the highly volatile racial climate at the time.

Like several language features we'll talk about in these pages, these early users adopted the term to address each other as a way to mark in-group membership. It's in this space where *dude* begins its life as a nonwhite solidarity symbol rather than a term of derision, a way to call out other dudes who shared one's outlook on life while facing down strong cultural prejudice. Soon, young white men from lower-income neighborhoods and with a sense of shared experience picked up the term. From there it quickly spread beyond the ethnic subcultures, given life by middle-class men attracted to the jazz and beatnik scene and resistant to dominant mainstream expectations. Groovy white dudes had become a thing.

By the 1970s, all men could be dudes, and most dudes were no longer defined by their duds, or at least not by caring about their duds. The showy, fastidious dresser connotation of the term had fallen away, and the nonconformism and cool camaraderie it represented was all that remained. *Dude* had become just another way of saying "man," only in a more counterculture (i.e., druggie/surfer/hippie) kind of way. And it was out of this redefinition that *dude*'s expansion into popular culture came to pass. By the 1980s and '90s, Hill suggests that *dude* had become the most ubiquitous slang term of the day, instigating "a virtual syntactic revolution in the English language." He claims *dude*'s usage patterns rival the impressive range of f@#k, which can be used as a filler, an exclamation, or as "virtually every part of speech." Only *dude* had the added bonus of being less hindered by indecency concerns. In other words, *dude* is no longer just a term of address, but a multifunctional means of wider expression that you can even say in front of your grandparents.

Cowabunga, dude!

Beyond this shift in meaning and use over time, a key question for etymologists has been where the word itself came from. Divining the origin of the word *dude* has not turned out to be all that easy. Early attempts at locating potential progenitors posited that it derived from the Middle English word *dudde*, meaning a rough cloak or rags. The same root form gave us the modern colloquial word for clothes, *duds*. This makes sense, given that clothes seemed to have always loomed large in the world of a dude. But recent etymological sleuthing has uncovered a more unexpected inception.

After spending ten years sifting through archival newspapers and periodicals, etymologists Barry Popik and Gerald Cohen uncovered a key piece of evidence on the origin of *dude* in an 1883 issue of *Clothier and Furnisher*. The article therein outlined the meaning of the recently coined term *dude*, suggesting it derived not from *duds*, but from a shortening of *doody*:

The word pronounced in two syllables as if spelled "dood-y" has been in occasional use in some New England towns for more than a score of years. It was probably born as a diminutive of dandy, and applied to the feeble personators of the real fop. . . . The name, now generally sounded to rhyme with rude, has been applied to one who . . . makes a feeble attempt to imitate the manners of some effeminate young nobleman about whom he has read in a foreign novel, but turns out to be only an emasculated penny edition of the despicable character he is trying to copy. The name is doubtless applied in familiar speech and in the press to some who have not all the essential features we have drawn; whatever may be the variations, there is one attribute common to all—they exist without any effort to recompense the world for their living.

So, the mystery of *dude* might seem to be solved, but how did *doody* come into nineteenth-century parlance to begin with? Here is the unexpected twist: it appears to be from the song "Yankee Doodle Dandy," the ditty originally sung by British soldiers during the War of Independence as a put-down to the ragtag, disheveled American soldiers. As the war tide turned, American soldiers allegedly sang it back to the British upon their defeat, earning the song both longevity and a patriotic flair.

But how did "Yankee Doodle Dandy" go from a song of soldiers to an ode to a dude? In a word, because macaroni.

Since you already have the song running through your head now that I've brought it up, take a minute to think through the lyrics. Recall that Yankee Doodle "stuck a feather in his cap and called it macaroni." After countless preschool recitations, have you never wondered what in tarnation a feather has to do with a piece of pasta? Today, perhaps not much. But back in the day, at least the eighteenth-century day, *macaroni* referred to a particular group of young British men with continental European airs who liked to eat the signature Italian dish. Nicknamed *macaronis* for this epicurean taste, these young men had a very keen and influential fashion sense—tight vests, tall wigs, and highly varnished shoes. Against this backdrop, our friend Yankee Doodle is cast as the bumpkin from across the pond trying unsuccessfully to aspire to this level of dandyism by attaching to his hat a feather. Eventually, the song's "doodle" and "dandy" came to be fused together in "doody" as another way of calling out the newly minted American dandy.

And this was just the first "doody" to be parlayed into the limelight. The Western-inspired 1950s children's show *Howdy Doody* is surmised to also have played a role in mainstreaming the term, particularly in surfing subculture, alongside the popular term *cowabunga*.* For those of us who were not yet born when *Howdy Doody* was prime time, *cowabunga* may be more familiar to us from the likes of Leonardo and Donatello—but *cowabunga* was a thing long before talking renegade reptile

---

* *Cowabunga* first made the rounds as "Kowabonga!" on *The Howdy Doody Show,* but then morphed to become popular not only out of the mouths of surfers but also allegedly from the mouths of American soldiers on the battlefields of Vietnam.

dudes hit the scene. And from Yankee Doodle to *Howdy Doody*, the modern meaning of *dude* had finally arrived.

Behold the dude

As used today, the power of *dude* is that it helps form bonds with other dudes while maintaining a macho straight-guy image. To dig into this, let's start with who is a dude. If I asked you for a top ten dude list, who would be on it? Perhaps it would be "the Dude" from Jeff Bridges' incarnation of a pot-smoking easy-living slacker in the cult hit *The Big Lebowski*. Or the chillaxed surfer dude Spicoli from *Fast Times at Ridgemont High* who really brought *dude*'s full expressiveness into pop culture? Maybe. But for those under forty, it will just as likely be the people you hang with that most exemplify the trait of "cool solidarity," as coined by linguist and dude scholar Scott Kiesling. According to Kiesling's research, *dude* has become the go-to term for young men when they want to show camaraderie but at a nonthreatening heterosexual distance. And as a bonus, drawing on its more recent association with carefree slacker subcultures like surfing, skating, and pot smoking, it also brings nonconformist connotations along for the ride. All things that seem to help young men navigate the masculine minefields of adolescence and early adulthood.

Of course, being liked and having a tight social network is

key to both men and women, especially during this period. But how they accomplish this linguistically seems to be quite distinct, resulting in a significant impact on the course of language over time. It's not being a boy or a girl that biologically predispositions you toward one form or another, but the social currency that forms provide—the types of self-expression that boys and girls favor—that seems to drive this difference. And much of this is driven by the expectations that larger society puts on them. Boys will be boys, but girls are expected to be ladies. As a result, girls are sanctioned more for aberrant behavior and also tend to end up pushed toward roles that require more outward-facing language skills—i.e., less slang, more cachet. While the new features that women introduce into language often go on to become the standard norms over time, the features that men use tend to draw upon vernacular dialects, especially ethnic or working-class varieties that carry street cred. The forms trumpeted by men will often not move up the ranks to achieve institutionally sanctioned status, but that is exactly what makes them attractive. Telling someone to "F@#k off" might not impress your parents, but it sure as hell might impress your friends. In other words, some words and language features have power precisely because they draw on an association with nonstandard talk and advertise certain kinds of in-group membership.

In Britain, we see this at work in the popularity of Cockney features, peppering the speech of princes and politicians alike. Often, they have adopted nonstandard features from what's called Estuary English to help them be relatable as an "every-man." And they are far from alone. Dropping a few *g*'s and swallowing one's *t*'s give off a "don' mess with me bu' how 'bout we grab a pint or somefin'" sort of mystique, as does calling someone a *mate* or a *bloke*. More recently, Multicultural London English (MLE), with its unique slang such as *whagwan* for "what's up" and unusual use of "man" as a pronoun ("man does it"), has infused youth speech through its association with Caribbean-inspired hip-hop music and its urban working-class multicultural vibe.* While it is certainly not only men who find such speech appealing or useful, it's typically men who gain the most social power from using it.

In the United States, as with *dude*'s repurposing, we find that young men often draw from inner-city varieties because such features effuse an air of rebellious nonconformity. This, of course, has more to do with cultural stereotypes about the speakers people think use such features than anything inherent in these linguistic forms. In truth, urban varieties are multifac-eted and diverse—not just comprised of the "gangsta" talk as-sociated with rough characters in movies and music. Innovative features arise in ethnic varieties in large part because language is a key way to establish in-group community and solidarity,

---

* MLE is a dialect now widely spoken in inner-city London, having developed in the 1980s under the substantial influence of Cockney as well as multiple immi-grant varieties. Some of the notable features of this variety are the use of *man* for the first-person singular pronoun *I* and for the use of a new quotative form, "This is me [saying X]."

something crucially important when faced with threats from another group in power. But out-group beliefs about what being a young black male constitutes—e.g., physical strength and dangerousness—are extrapolated to the features that get associated with their talk, giving rise to an attached sense of "toughness." As a result, we find that recognizably vernacular speech like *ain't* and *aks* and *thang* from rap and hip-hop culture have strong appeal to white boys in the burbs wanting to exude tough coolness. Obviously, no one told them that *aks* was even more hip in Chaucer's day and that literary greats like Dickens made fair use of an *ain't* or two, or that African American English varieties are as complex and rule governed as any others. But would that ruin the allure? Probably not.

The power of using slang features comes from the streetwise currency they provide, which is what attracted boys to their use in the first place. So, while girls' talk also draws from existing linguistic features, they are usually ones that start with little stigma or social awareness, like *um* or vocal fry. By using them in novel ways to take a certain stance or to contrast or fit in with others, they develop social meaning. But boys adopt new features often *because* they already have stigma or social meaning attached, the very thing that makes them enticing. This is why *dude* is not the only four-letter word that makes frequent appearances in teen boy's talk, and often in the same sentence. This appeal of vernacularity is exactly that it is the counterculture language—seen as a slightly rebellious response to the kind of speaker your parents want you to be. Though it limits the potential of these features to become larger standard norms, the uptake of such forms spurs on new adherents as it takes on new aspects of meaning (like signaling slackerdom or aloofness) that others find appealing.* It moves from fringe to functional for people far beyond its originating group.

And this seems to be exactly the force that has driven the popularity of dude-ing. *Dude* gives off an air of laid-back masculine solidarity, while also invoking the image of someone only marginally or not at all concerned with fitting in. Too cool to care. Kiesling suggests that *dude*'s association with druggie subculture "connects the term to counter-culture, nonserious masculinity." And even before its association with slacker culture, *dude*, like *bro*, was primed to be popularized precisely because of its use outside the mainstream. *Dude* has traveled the same path from an in-group to more generalized marker as happened with *like* and *um* as discourse markers—and as we will find happens a lot over the course of language change.

It might be odd to think of those who *dude* as the masculinized equivalent of our linguistic fashionistas from previous pages, but young men appropriated *dude* to accomplish the same

---

* Though this is often the pattern we find for the features in which men lead, this is largely dependent on social and ecological roles assumed by men and women in a particular culture. In communities where, for instance, women do not have access to education or employment opportunities, men will more often lead in linguistic change toward prestige norms and women will instead seek forms that express solidarity.

social persona building that we have seen women do. They just don't get called out as being trivial or airheaded because of it. How much newspaper ink have you seen devoted to warning young men that *dude* use will be the end of their professional careers or that pathologize its use as an "epidemic"? Not a whole lot. Instead, we find websites devoted to "dudeism" as a philosophical journey and spreads in magazines like *Rolling Stone* devoted to "The Decade of the Dude." Do we see comparable iconicity for Reese Witherspoon's *like*-spouting Elle Woods? Not unless you count widespread adoration of her pet chihuahua, Bruiser, in the win column.

A friendly dude

It might have all started with "Yankee Doodle Dandy," but how about Aerosmith's more modern take on *dude* in their song "Dude Looks Like a Lady"? Pretty apropos given that the original dude was in fact an effeminate dandy. Unlikely to be fans of *Clothier and Furnisher*, it is doubtful the band's use was intended to take us back to its earlier meaning. More likely the song uses it in a guy commenting to another guy "We're cool so can talk about other men" sort of way. And that is the essence of today's dude.

In the years since Aerosmith sang this little tune and the mutant ninja turtles hit the big screen, *dude* has only increased in popularity. To analyze this modern use of dude, Scott Kiesling had his students compile what he referred to as the "Dude Corpus," a collection of *dude* used in context. For three days, each of his students detailed the specifics about the uses of *dude* they heard—things like who said it, who received it, and what the surrounding conversation was. To get a full picture, he also looked at how *dude* was used in recordings from his year of ethnographic fieldwork in a college fraternity. Now this is a researcher seriously willing to go into the trenches in the name of linguistic discovery.

In addition to getting quite an education on what college students do when not in class, he discovered that *dude* had expanded into being the sort of duct tape of conversation, a fix-it for everything. Beyond the well-known greeting function, he found it used in a commiserating sense—when lamenting a hard class, "Dude, that test was killer," and as an exclamation of excitement, "Dude!" (higher pitch), or disgust, "Dude!" (lower pitch). Dude was also used to offset what could be taken as something confrontational or bossy, as in, "Dude, don't do that" or "Your turn to do the laundry, dude." And a simple, well-placed *dude* could sometimes say it all, as when being empathetic to someone's really shitty day. "Dude," woefully spoken.

Fundamental to all these *dude* uses was that they signaled solidarity and a sense of equality while also shielding the speaker from any suggestion of inappropriate sexual intimacy.

This pressure toward finding verbal means to express one's heteronormativity seems to be a particularly salient one for adolescent males. It's a key part of what drives the attraction to ethnic or working-class features that come to be associated with a figurative brotherhood as well as physicality or toughness, fundamental traits in the American cultural model for what it is to be a man.

And who do we dude? Not surprisingly, Kiesling found men rarely used *dude* when talking to their girlfriends and used it most when talking to other men. Somehow calling your date *dude* does not bode well for future encounters or a good-night kiss. But calling your female pal *dude* doesn't seem to be a problem. The fact that men also reported calling female friends *dude* tells us that it can signal nonromantic connections apart from its sense of masculinity. Since students often used *dude* as an exclamatory word or an empathizer, as in "Duuuudde," accompanied by a sympathetic side-to-side head shake, it was only a matter of time before *dude* became unisex.

And, indeed, the days of the dude's *dude* appear to be waning. Dudes now don't just look like ladies, they are ladies. In the most recent incarnation of the seemingly endless Bill and Ted sequels, the title characters' daughters are the next-generation dudes—invoking *dude*'s expressive power as often as their fathers before them. As *dude*'s meaning takes on more social nuance, no longer so strongly connoting masculinity, its appeal is more global. The masculine attachment it carries has been surpassed by its ability to just intimate laid-back camaraderie or call attention to a friend's transgression, as in "Dude, WTF? That was my pizza!" In other words, being a dude is not always part of what it means to *dude* someone. As we will discover with many of the tics we will talk about, once a feature becomes emblematic of a social identity that others recognize and relate to, it becomes both more frequent and more diffused across speaker groups seeking to invoke that quality. And as it is adopted by more and more speakers over time, new norms—and new meanings—get established.

It might seem odd that women would be attracted to a feature that seemed so gendered initially. But we don't have to look far to see examples of terms once referring exclusively to males being extended to refer to women. Lacking a plural form of second-person pronoun *you*, English speakers have come up with a veritable cornucopia of pluralizing additions to make up for this gap. *Youse, yinz, you folks, ya'll,* and of course, the increasingly popular *you guys*. Now, last time I checked, guys were typically male, but this doesn't seem to have stopped us from liberally using it to address mixed gender groups everywhere.

But if you think about it, we don't tend to see many female terms that expand to encompass men, unless we consider the use of *girl* as a campy term of endearment. But this is really no surprise. The shift from gendered to generic has tended to travel only in one direction over the course of history, with men's terms fine for women, but women's terms not a big hit with men or, even worse, considered an insult. Almost makes you wonder if there is some underlying hierarchy at work that puts dudes on top.* Like a place where men run the country, control the boardrooms, and get paid more than women for the same work.

Even with this spread beyond gender lines, we might make the mistake of imagining *dude* is a relatively limited speech resource that, in the tradition of short-lived *manbuns* and *broflakes*, will soon fade from popular use. But we would be tremendously underestimating the power and the proliferation of modern-day *dude*. To see the full range for which *dude* is useful, one merely has to watch Super Bowl commercials, read the comics, or hang out in a high school—all places where the multifunctionality of *dude* is prolifically displayed.

To get a sense of *dude*'s limitless potential, just google the series of Bud Light commercials featuring a "day in the life" of a guy who uses only *dude* to communicate. When his roommate sits too close to him? Admonitory "Dude!" When the milk carton smells bad? Ugh, "Duuude." At a baseball game signaling his availability to catch the ball? Attention-getting "Dude. Dude!" When he wants his roommate to get lost when getting cozy on the couch with a girl? Psst, "Dude." And finally, when his office mate won't stop tapping his pencil repetitively? Annoyed "Dude." In fact, through the entire commercial nothing but *dude*, in

---

* And though its rise began in ethnic vernacular trenches, the modern dude lifestyle is also one that has become classed and racialized. While middle-class white frat boys—or the grown men they become, as epitomized by Jeff Bridges in *The Big Lebowski*—might live it, many others don't have the social power, safety, or financial resources to live as a dude.

varying pitch and tone, is uttered, though so much is said. Part an attempt to poke fun at men's stereotypical lack of expressiveness and part an ode to the omnipresence of *dude* in modern speech, the genius of the ad is that we all completely get it.

A dude of destiny

Whether you use it yourself or just watch from the sidelines in dismay, you have to appreciate just how far this dude has come. What seems like just another four-letter word has forged a path through history from a term of derision to a term with an impressive ability to convey a complex array of meanings. From effeminate dandy to flashy zoot-suiter to laid-back surfer to just a pal that is a gal, the dude, it would seem, abides.

5

Wha' You Talkin' Bout?

anguage changes over time—we've established that. But not all of the variations in the speech around us can be explained by looking at these permanent, tectonic shifts in our language. Sometimes we switch up how we pronounce things or the words we choose simply because we want to express different things in different circumstances—much like wearing a dress instead of jeans and a T-shirt when heading out to a fancy dinner. After all, although the need to wear clothes is at its core to uphold public decency, the type of clothes we choose is really more about intended social performance rather than just keeping the fig leaf in place.

So why are we so quick to judge when we find people doing the very same thing with language? That is, why do we insist on labeling speakers' linguistic flexibility as nonstandard sloppiness?

Take, for example, the widely used *-in'* pronunciation of English words that end in ING, often equated with "swallowing consonants." While those who lean more toward the *-in'* are chastised for being lazy and inarticulate, the reality is that *-ing* is like your formal attire while *-in'* is like your pair of comfortable sweatpants.* Both do the trick from a purely linguistic perspective, but the fact that these two forms have coexisted for centuries tells us something else must be afoot that keeps both these looks in fashion.

The real OG

We often associate omitting sounds with sloppy or uneducated speech, especially when it makes what we say deviate from the written form, believing of course that we ourselves never violate such rules. To those I say, please explain to me how you pronounce *often, knight,* or *gnaw* and then we'll talk. Those unpronounced sounds we blissfully ignore when we are the ones doing it are the consonantal ghosts of our English past. The only reason *g* sticks in our craw is because the option of an *-in'* or an *-ing*

---

* A quick overview on the notation used in this chapter: I will be using the capitalized ING when discussing the notion of the *-ing* ending regardless of how it is pronounced—in other words, just the suffix in abstract. The lowercase *-ing* is used when I want to represent the standard or preferred twenty-first-century "full" pronunciation, while *-in'* represents the colloquialized so-called "dropped *g*" pronunciation.

pronunciation still exists in modern English and we allow ourselves to be fooled by the spelling.

The even bigger reveal is that we are all *g* droppers because the alternation between the *-ing* and the *-in'* form does not actually involve what we think of as a regular *g* sound in either case (written as /g/ in phonetic notion). Though spelling might suggest otherwise, both endings are actually pronounced with just a vowel + a single nasal consonant, and it's the consonant that varies. The *-ing* version involves a nasal sound made with the middle of the tongue lifted toward the fleshy part of the top of your mouth (the velum). In ling lingo, we refer to this sound as a velar nasal, which is written phonetically as /ŋ/. Say "king" or "sing" and you can get a sense of where this articulatory magic happens. In contrast, the *-in'* variant involves the nasal consonant we know and love as the *n* sound, or /n/ using phonetic notation. In linguistics, we refer to it as an alveolar nasal because it's made when your tongue tip makes contact with the alveolar ridge right behind your teeth, also known as that spot you burn when you eat pizza. Try saying "kin" then "king" and "sin" then "sing" and feel the difference in your tongue position. Notice how it is a single sound in both instances, not an *n* + *g*. You don't say *kin* then *g*, do you?

If you are still not convinced that there is no actual /g/ there, compare how you say *finger*, which we often say with a *g* sound in the middle (fing-ger), to *singer* (sing-er), which is also just a velar nasal rather than /n + g/. Even better, just go listen to

American Idol judge Luke Bryan's pronunciation of "sing-Ger," which audibly adds a *g* that isn't supposed to be there in the middle. This dedication to a belief that a /g/ is dropped is based on the way the ending is spelled, a residual trace of the Old English root suffix from whence it cameth.*

We alternate between the velar and alveolar form not because we're lazy or because our tongue piercings inhibit proper contact with the roof of our mouths, but because these two forms help communicate different social meaning. In fact, we all have a set of linguistic features we use that can be said in more than one way, with the main drive for using them in one form or the other being social. Think *wanna* for *want to,* *donchu* for *don't you,* and, of course, *-in'* for *-ing.* These alternations are not changes— meaning one form is not gradually taking over for another over time.† Rather they coexist to help us be more socially expressive.

Socially adapt-ING?

In sociolinguistics, we talk about features being socially marked. As in, they give hints as to one's identity, and they become so-

---

* Sticklers might find using "from" with "whence" redundant, but, in keeping with our recurring theme that language changes to keep up with modern times, adding the preposition just keeps us on our linguistic toes. Plus, Shakespeare and Jane Austen seemed to find using "from whence" quite agreeable.

† In sociolinguistics, this situation is referred to as stable variation, as opposed to change in progress, as we find no evidence that a "new" variant is taking over. Instead, each form develops a more nuanced or contextually based use.

cially salient precisely because they deviate from the "norm" we expect. Often, we start to notice a pattern of a certain group of speakers using that same feature more than others, and whatever we associate with those speakers becomes associated with that feature. So, if we hear -*in'* mostly from our friends but not from our bosses, we get the hint that -*in'* helps set the mood for casual banter but not for office negotiations. When we pick up our car from the body shop and -*in'* is being bandied about, it can become associated with a close-knit blue-collar sensibility in contrast to the more anxious-sounding -*ing*.

When we speak to each other, we have many variable linguistic features at our command to signal our communicative and social intent, allowing our speech to move far beyond simply conveying core informational content. For instance, if I say "Whatcha doin'?" I am representing our relationship as informal, relaxed, and probably close. But instead, saying "What are you doing?" is much colder and distant. You could just as easily be yelling at me as simply inquiring as to my current occupational status. By deviating from this standard formal structure, we clue each other in to who we are and how we relate to each other.

Our everyday speech is peppered with these small social hints we give each other—cues we provide about how serious we should be taken, how intimate our relationship, where we come from, how old we are, and our social standing, among other things. And in this vein, the alternation between -*in'* and -*ing* is one of the most common ways to do all these things and more.

What the ING?

Right after Christmas a couple of years ago, I walked into a UPS store to return a package. Looking up at their overhead service banner, I felt a moment of total sympatico with my friends in the brown uniforms. Now a shipping store and a linguist might not normally have all that much in common. And, in fact, I'm usually more of a FedEx girl, being raised in Memphis, home of its headquarters. But ING had brought us together. You see, UPS has unveiled a new motto, "Every ing, all in one place," and by golly if that doesn't suggest we are a match made in heaven, I don't know what does. After all, this chapter makes much the same argument: That ING plays an important role in our linguistic and social lives. Not sure that packing, shipping, and printing are the most important INGs in my life, but the creative verbiage behind them certainly is.

Linguistically speaking, ING is a suffix, or word ending, that is used whenever we are trying to describe an ongoing activity. *Thinking, dancing, eating, screaming, dreaming,* and *breathing* are all things accomplished with great ING. And, of course, *posting, mailing,* and *shredding.* To get a bit more grammatically technical, the ING suffix attaches to verbs when we are expressing the progressive aspect, i.e., a continuing action or something in progress, such as *he is singing loudly* or *I am always eating Oreos.* When we have a particular suffix that denotes a specific grammatical function like this, we say this meaning has become "grammaticized," that is, it's instantly recognizable by the use of that form. So, for instance, we all understand that when we see -ed on a verb it means past tense, and likewise, that to be + ING on a verb signals progressive.

We can also find the ING suffix on nouns, but generally ones that at some point in their derivational history came from verbs. We usually call such nominal forms gerunds in modern English, as in "His singing that song made my ears hurt." But keep in mind that Old English was quite different in the way it was structured, and though we do find OE nouns with the ING ending, such as *gaderung* ("gathering"), it is not clear whether any functioned like gerunds.* You see, even in modern English, there is a cline of "verb-iness" that nouns with the -*ing* ending can show. On one side, we find some functioning as ho-hum everyday nouns, like *the evening* and *the ceiling*, that have no verbal characteristics at all. On the other side of the spectrum, we have nouns that show some verbal qualities in that they can have things like objects, though they are used as nouns in a sentence, and these are referred to as gerunds. For instance, in the sentence "Learning life lessons makes us stronger," *learning* allows for an object (like a verb) but it serves as subject of the sentence (a noun-like employment). Change the noun phrase to "The

---

* The -*ung* form of the -*ing* ending is the feminine form and was widely used in OE, but it was supplanted by the masculine -*ing* by the twelfth or thirteenth century.

learning of life lessons," and *learning* behaves a little less verbally (as it takes a prepositional phrase as its object), so it is referred to instead as a nominal gerund. There is debate as to whether any kinds of gerunds were used in Old English, but the strongly verbal gerund is undoubtably more recent and developed sometime in the Middle English period.

As we will see, this grammatical difference between using ING for progressive verb forms and using ING for nouns and gerunds plays a big role in both how *-ing* developed to be what it is today and how we pronounce the ending, i.e., as *walkin'* or *walking.* Turns out, that colloquial flair we thought was reserved for chatting with friends is actually the legacy of a great battle between Old English word endings. And here's the spoiler, ING won. But how it won is the stuff of linguistic legend.

(K)ing Slayer

If you have ever read George R. R. Martin's A Song of Ice and Fire series (or watched *Game of Thrones*), you'll recognize this allusion to Sir Jaime Lannister, known as the "king slayer" for his, shall we say, specific skill set. Back in the medieval day, the ING suffix did some slaying of its own—of other endings that vied for space in early English. In fact, such early English morpho-syntactic bloodletting led to the almost wholesale loss of our elaborate inflectional system on the way to the morphologically simpler language that we have today.* And the rise of modern ING is a particularly revealing example of how life and language in the British Isles changed from the ninth to fifteenth centuries.

As in Westeros, the mythical setting for *Game of Thrones* based loosely on medieval Britain, English found itself spread into a number of different kingdoms in its early days, the legacy of the different Germanic tribes that settled the isles starting in the fifth century. They spoke related yet distinct languages, and from which descended not only English but modern German and Dutch. Though united by the Anglo-Saxon king Æthelstan in the early tenth century, these early kingdoms established long-lasting linguistic variation.

Northern Britain was settled by the West Germanic tribe, the Angles, and subsequently in the eighth century, by our Viking friends who brought with them substantial influence from Old Norse. In the south of England, at the helm of political and economic influence, was Wessex, primarily settled by the Saxons. This early settlement pattern is where the term *Anglo-Saxon* originates, a reflection of the two most influential Germanic tribes who made the island home. Southerners tended to turn a wary eye to the north (and vice versa), and travel was quite

---

* Old English was replete with endings on nouns and verbs allowing one to understand how each word related to the rest of the sentence (i.e., as in "he" for subjects and "him" for objects). In modern English, we generally now do this by putting subjects first and objects after the verb, rendering such morphologically inflected forms unnecessary as long as consistent word order patterns are used so everyone understands who was doing what to whom.

treacherous, slowing the spread of linguistic influence for changes begun in one area of Britain to another. This division still echoes in the northern-southern British distinctions, like whether one says *bath* or *bahth*, and as we will see, affected our ING.

As today, the south of England wielded more power and prestige, giving their language forms a bit more cachet by the Middle Ages, and led them to badmouth northerners. For instance, in the riveting twelfth-century read *The Chronicle of English Bishops*, Benedictine monk William of Malmesbury attributes the incomprehensibleness of northerners to their close proximity to barbarous folk. Seems that William could stand to learn a thing or two about appreciating the wellspring of linguistic innovation.

On being progressive

So, what does all this have to do with our progressive participle? A lot, it turns out. But to understand how requires a short trip down memory lane to sixth-grade grammar class.

Unlike our English today, Old English had an extensive inflectional system, which boiled down to having a lot of suffixes to tack on the end of root forms. We have no spoken recordings obviously, so our knowledge of these features comes from their use in written documents, mainly religious texts, manuscripts, chronicles, and literary sources. The variations in spelling are the only indicators we have that reflect spoken variation, since spelling did not start to become standardized until well after the printing press made a splash in the late 1400s. Instead, most of these texts were written in regional dialects, and differences in the way words were written were a window into how things were said in those areas. Until we get into the Middle English period, all those endings on words that we no longer say today, like those *e*'s on words like *stone* and *tale*, were fully pronounced,* and in fact provided critical linguistic information, like what the role of the word was in the sentence (case), how many there were (number), and which (grammatical) gender it was.

Looking back at Old English homilies and texts, we find -*ing* (or -*ung*) was a suffix that formed nouns from verbs, as in OE *masse sinnynge*, "mass singing," or *hergiung*, "the act of plundering," both, one supposes, illustrative of the range of ninth-century proclivities.† Verbal forms like modern *walking* and *talking*, referred to as participles, were instead created with the OE suffix -*ende*, as in *weren specende* or *singende,* meaning "were speaking" or "singing." According to language historian Roger Lass, this ending was sometimes written as -*ande*, especially in northern areas influenced by Old Norse. An -*inde* spelling, on the other hand, was common in the south. These

---

* In Old English, the *e* on these words would have denoted information about number and case, i.e., *tale* would be singular accusative, while *tala* would be plural accusative, meaning someone was telling a lot of tales, as opposed to just one.
† Only certain classes of verbs in OE took the ING ending, though it applied to more and more verbs as time progressed. Also, especially in later writings, the letter *y* was often found instead of the letter *i* (as in *sinnynge*) to represent the same sound.

differences in how the suffix was written hint of variation in how the vowel was likely pronounced across early English dialects. Regardless of spelling, in Old English, participles with the -*e/inde* suffix commonly appeared in adjectival or adverbial contexts (e.g., "Swooning, he fell"), rather than as a progressive participle with *beon*, the precursor to our modern "to be." While nouns formed with -*ing* were fairly common, evolving into modern words like *evening*, *gathering*, and *blessing*, verbs formed with -*e/inde* to indicate a continuing action don't tend to appear very often, reflecting the lack of a grammaticized progressive marker in this period. In fact, the only examples of the participle form co-occurring with "to be" (referred to as a copula) during this period were generally OE translations of Latin texts.

What this means is that, in older forms of English, there were a variety of ways to get across the idea of a continuous action, but no one grammatically obligatory way as we have today (via "to be" + *verb*-ING). For instance, OE didn't directly express things like "He is hunting," which is a main use of progressive participles in modern English. Instead, in Old English to say something was in process like this, you would have said "He wæs on huntinge," meaning roughly he was on a hunt, where hunting was a noun, not a verb, thus taking the more common -*inge* nominal ending.* This may allow it to read with a progressive sense, but

---

* This is also the origin of relic expressions like "he was a-hunting," where the *a*- prefix is a reduced form of "on" or "of."

it is not the same as the modern progressive aspect, and instead grammatically considered a locative construction (something that indicates a location). In addition, in early literary works, we find writers often just used the simple present even when describing a continuous process. We see this in Chaucer's *Canterbury Tales* in clear ongoing action lines like "Ye goon to Canterbury (l. 769)," translating in modern parlance to "You are going to Canterbury."

If all this sounds pretty confusing, it was, and our Middle English ancestors apparently thought so too. By the time we arrive in Chaucer's London in the fourteenth century, *-inge* (often written at the time as *-ynge*) had become the more commonly used suffix in his Midland dialect regardless of whether one meant a gerund or a progressive. So, while *-ende* was actually the real OG for progressive participles in Old English, by Middle English, the OE noun forming *-ing* suffix was showing signs of mission creep into progressive-like territory.

The end of *-ende*?

You've heard of the expression "Shit happens," right? Well, that pretty much sums up what happened to *-ende* from the ninth through the twelfth centuries in Britain. A lot happened in that period to affect the course of English, most of it coming in the form of interlopers who spoke Old Norse or Norman French.

The end result of all this linguistic mixing was that it was the final straw in a long line of percolating linguistic pressures that had decreased the emphasis speakers put on unstressed syllables, something referred to as weakening. Consequently, the morphological endings that tended to inhabit those syllables, like those on the ends of words clueing us into case, gender, or number, were no longer fully pronounced. This change eventually led, in the late Middle English period, to the complete loss of word final vowel sounds, such as the final *e* that had remained as the last vestige of such inflectional endings. We are able to observe this change happening over time by noting the increasing absence of written *e* in texts after the thirteenth century (e.g., *-inge* became variably written as *-ing or -yng*).*

After the loss of final vowels, the consonants figured they just couldn't go on, so they might as well drop off too. As early as the fourteenth century, both suffixes are sometimes written simply as *-in* (*drynkyn* for "drinking"). The absence of these final consonants orthographically tells us that, while they were likely pronounced in Old English, by the Middle English period it's not clear they always stuck around or, if they did, in what form.†

---

* This shift, of course, was the impetus for a much more consistent word ordering in English, where subjects go first, objects go last, and prepositions help tell us to what direction all these subjects and objects are going.
† For instance, we find examples of variably absent consonants ("att the makyn of this letter") in a fifteenth-century collection of correspondence among members of the Paston family (*The Paston Letters*).

But regardless of when these final consonants were deleted, with all this stress shifting and phonetic weakening, the once distinct noun and verb suffixes were becoming more similar in the way they would have sounded, making it hard to tell them apart. One potential but very subtle difference being the way the nasal sound might have been pronounced, that is, as an alveolar nasal /n/ on the verb participle versus as a velar nasal /ŋ/ on the noun-forming ending. Thus, the seeds of the -in'/-ing alternation seems to have been planted centuries before we were even a glimmer in our great-grandparents' eyes.

When function becomes the fashion

Not only did these endings sound confusingly similar in the Middle English period, but they also began to overlap in terms of how they functioned in the grammar. While only -ende/-inde had been employed as a verbal participle in Old English, by Middle English, the formerly very noun-like -ing began to show verb-like ways—for instance, tacking on to more types of verbs and behaving like a gerund or providing a progressive reading. And while true be + participle- (e.g., beon + -ende-) type progressive forms had been quite rare in Old English, they were becoming more common in Middle English. The increasing role of progressives in the syntax of Middle English was driven by linguistic innovations such as the development of the infinitival progressive ("to be going") and the perfect progressive ("have been going"), both of which had not existed in Old English. These new progressive expressions gave more opportunity in the Middle English period for a more verbal-acting -*ing* to expand its domain. Especially in the south of England, where the very close sounding -*ind* and -*ing* coexisted, this spelled trouble for -e/*inde*.

Between the twelfth and fifteenth centuries, we find the -*ing* suffix written more and more where a progressive sense was intended, and these once separate endings were not coalescing randomly, but rather in the direction of -*ing*. This, of course, didn't happen overnight or in all areas of Britain at the same time. In the north of England, we often find -*ande* in regional spelling, suggesting their version of the suffix had an *a* vowel instead. Because this regional form was more distinct, northerners took another century or so to warm up to writing all -*ing* all the time, but by the fifteenth century, the original OE participial form was pretty much toast across Britain, at least in writing. By the time the sixteenth century rolls around, people had pretty much forgotten which had been the true original. For -*inde*, winter had indeed come and, much like the undead White Walkers in *Game of Thrones*, the suffix was not completely lost, but had become a shell of what it once was.

Despite the shift toward the -*ing* ending as the norm in writing, even in the eighteenth century we find evidence that an *-in* pronunciation was still a prevalent form. So prevalent, in fact, that in the very succinctly titled *Critical Spelling Book: An Introduction to Reading and Writing Readily and Correctly in a Manner More Commodious Than Any*, grammarian Solomon Lowe makes mention of the homophony (fancy for "same pronunciation") between words like "herring" and "heron" and "coughing" and "coffin." An overlap that, one imagines, could have led to some rather unfortunate misunderstandings.

The ghosts of endings past?

And out of this complicated suffixal development history arose the variation we find in our talk today—though widely misjudged and misunderstood. While the adoption of *-ing* for the progressive form on the written page might incline us to believe that *-in'* is just the result of a sloppy tongue, a striking linguistic division of labor emerges when we take the time to measure where our *-ing*s and *-in'*s tend to occur. In Englishes as far flung as British, Australian, and American, analysis of how our modern ING patterns shows that the velar /iŋ/ form (i.e., *-ing*) is more often what we use when we say nouns like "the building" or "the dancing." However, when we use progressive participial forms such as "I was building" or "they were dancing," we have much higher rates of an alveolar /in/ (-*in'*) pronunciation, as in "they were dancin'."

This suggests that, though we have no recollection of its long-convoluted history, we still somewhere understand this fundamental -*ing*/-*inde* division that descended from our Old English morphology. In essence, -*ing* is a noun thing and -*in* is a verb thing. This is why it stands out more when someone says *puddin'* or *darlin'*—we are less used to -*in'* on noun forms as it is not as grammatically intuitive. Saying -*in'* is a trace of the -*e*/*inde* ending that once was used on verbs that functioned as participles. As well, the degree to which we find -*in'* used by modern speakers also seems to be related to where this original ending stuck around the longest during the Middle English period. In areas such as northern Britain, Scotland, and Ireland, where the -*ande* remained distinct from -*ing* on verbs until the fifteenth century, we still find higher rates of -*in'* pronunciation in modern speech compared to the south of England.

While use of these forms might attract notice, they reflect the ending's historical progression rather than any linguistic transgression. Time, it seems, has a way of reimagining even our grammatical complexity, instead making us view those who -*in'* more as less sophisticated. In truth, they simply retain more of the original pattern. But as we have seen over and over again in these pages, the linguistic patterns driving how we speak—and why we differ—often take a back seat to the social assumptions we make because of it.

Are you *-in'* or *-ing*?

Our inability to commit to one pronunciation versus the other might seem to speak to our lack of grammatical conviction, but I assure you that if one side was to emerge victorious, it would have happened by now. We find written indications of this alternation for hundreds of years, and it's still going strong into the modern era. The big question given all these sound changes and grammatical shifts since Old English is why we didn't just end up with *-ing* and be done with it? Why do we still, a thousand years later, alternate between *-in'* and *-ing*?

Because we humans are remarkably good at finding ways to communicate not just informational content but also how we feel about each other and about who we are. In the midst of great linguistic upheaval, ING adapted to say something social, rather than something grammatical. And now, choosing *-in'* or *-ing* has become a stylistic choice illuminating our social circumstances more handily than most of us even realize. Even in writing, e.g., in comics or quoted dialogue, using an *-in'* rather than an *-ing* communicates something about a speaker or what the writer is trying to get across far greater than simply the semantic meaning of the words. To try to figure out exactly what our ING reveals, recent research on the *-ing/-in'* variation has spanned the globe— Scotland, Ireland, Australia, Canada, Britain, and, of course, the United States—and remarkably, all these varieties of English exhibit the same socially relevant shift between these two different forms. It will come as no shock that most of us associate the use of *-in'* with informality, but as we will see, this is merely the tip of the iceberg in terms of ING's social message.

The earliest socially focused study on the use of this variation was by social anthropologist John Fischer in the 1950s. Fischer and his wife were studying child-rearing practices, not just language per se, but he noticed that the kids in the study alternated between the *-in'* and *-ing* endings. What attracted his attention was not just the alternation itself, but which kids seemed to use it more. He noted that the boys used *-in'* much more than the girls, and even more curious, the "model" boy, whom he describes as an exemplary child, used *-ing* far more than the "typical" boy, described as "physically strong, dominating, full of mischief, but disarmingly frank about his transgressions." This boy's *-in'* use, echoing what we find with things like vernacular *ain't* and other nonstandard features, seems to help build his image as a somewhat nonconformist kid.

Fischer also suggested that *-in'* was used more often by working-class speakers and was, of course, more common for everyone in casual speech. His was the first in a long line of research that suggested that alternating between *-in'* and *-ing* says something about a speaker's attitude and relative status as well as aspects of their personality and mood more generally. If you have ever been in conversation with someone who adopts an overly formal style, it is likely that one of the ways they do this is by overusing *-ing* endings, which lends an air of haughty pretension. And indeed, later, more rigorous linguistic studies have overwhelmingly confirmed Fischer's initial hypothesis that high *-ing* use comes across as more professional, formal, and feminine, but potentially at the cost of communicating that you're an uptight, rule-following stick-in-the-mud.

In a detailed dissertation on the history and use of ING, Ann Houston notes that pre-nineteenth-century grammar books provide no evidence that early grammarians, who normally did not hesitate to call out anything they viewed as linguistic indiscretion, even noticed the ending. In fact, contrary to its present-day rep, early-twentieth-century language historian Henry Cecil Wyld suggests that *-in'* might even have carried some cachet among high-falutin' seventeenth- and eighteenth-century folks. In looking back at commentaries on language at the time, he finds Jonathan Swift writes of "learnen" as the polite form used at court, and elocutionist John Walker writes that the best speakers do not rhyme "ing" with *king*, but instead with "*in*." So it certainly seems that, before the nineteenth century, you could *-in'* to your heart's content with hardly a raised eyebrow. But such linguistic harmony lasted only until the early 1800s, when linguistic busybodies start to comment on what they saw as incorrect and lazy participle use.* And so opened the floodgates of *-in'* backlash.

---

* Otto Jespersen, in his *A Modern English Grammar on Historical Principles, Part 1: Sounds and Spellings* (London & Copenhagen: George Allan & Unwin/ Ejnar Munksgaard, 1961), notes there were some stray curmudgeons as early as

As one English-language purist would so eloquently lament in a letter to the satirical British magazine *Punch* in 1902, those who "deprive present participles of their final 'g' lobby a disloyal crusade against the Queen's English." Though Queen Elizabeth II might have agreed, Queen Elizabeth I would debate this point, as her letters show she had no problem using an *-in'* here or there.*

In pondering the reason for the nineteenth-century elevation of *-ing*, Wyld suggests the rise of literacy along with the codification of the *-ing* form sealed *-in'*'s colloquialized fate. The written word became more impressive than the spoken one, with the *-ing* form emerging as a marker of education and class. It's only at this point when we start to see the colloquial form spelled with an apostrophe, and this new *-in'* became a popular way for writers to mark the speech of the lowly commoner versus the cultured one. Take, for example, this excerpt from a book written by Arthur Sketchley in 1870 following the travails of Mrs. Brown, a lower-class British woman:

> . . . they're all a-runnin' about in nothink but beads and a few features as ain't common decent; a-yellin' of their war 'oops, and flourishin' about their Tommy 'awks.

the late 1700s who dismissed *-in'* as imperfect pronunciation, but both he and Wyld note that it was prevalent in writings from aristocratic, or as Jespersen so aptly puts it, "horsy" types, suggesting it was not considered an uneducated form.
* Wyld notes an example found in Queen Elizabeth's letter to James VI, where she wrote *-en* instead of *-ing* (e.g., "besichen" for "beseeching").

Her robust *-in'* use, along with a splash of *ain't* and a lack of *h*'s, helps ensure none of us get the wrong impression about which side of the tracks Mrs. Brown is from.

This image of a working-class woman's speech replete with *-in'* might seem to run counter to our present predilection toward more masculine *-in'* use, but remember it is women who have often popularized new variants. While contemporary women may follow the straight and narrow when it comes to *-ing*, Wyld discovered the *-in'* form appeared often in letters from the seventeenth and eighteenth centuries—and especially those written by women. As even upper-crust women were less literate than their male peers, their spellings more accurately reflected the au courant pronunciation in their circles at the time. This aligns with early twentieth-century language scholar Otto Jespersen's suggestion that, though it was not considered "proper," *-in'* carried some prestige as being "fashionable." Fashionable women, as we have seen many times, are often the linguistic cutting edge. But as time went on *-in'*'s growing stigmatization as a working-class form fueled its popularity with men.

Socially revealING

When sociolinguist Scott Kiesling studied fraternity men in Virginia, not only did he do a deep dive into the many faces of dudes, as witnessed in the last chapter, but he also spent a lot of time with ING. Given that the most common word in frat-boy vocabulary also has four letters but is much less family friendly than *dude*, it is not a stretch to say that ING occurs pretty often, if you know what I mean.

In looking at how frat brothers varied their use of *-in'* vs. *-ing*, Kiesling found that it wasn't about being casual or formal, but rather about the type of machismo they were going for. In frat meetings, men who wanted to make power moves but didn't have the seniority or rank to necessarily back it up sometimes shifted to higher rates of *-in'* use. Why? Because *-in'* draws on a working-class sensibility that includes a physically commanding presence that middle-class *-ing* just doesn't provide. As we learned from our foray into the development of *dude*, boys get traction from speech habits that help them build an image of tough physicality. Think of the banter of longshoremen, soldiers, or athletes in locker rooms—theirs is not the talk of college professors but of swagger and solidarity. For these men in a college environment surrounded by standard speech, the attraction of using *-in'* comes from the in-group masculinity associated with vernacularity. In other words, *-in'* is a verbal power move when structural power doesn't get the job done. As Kiesling suggests, "power is central to men's identities," and language use is key in building a powerful persona.*

---

* The relationship between certain language features and the perception of power has been well studied. So-called "powerful" language can take the form of that sanctioned by certain institutions and corporations (e.g., bald directives from

This connection of -*in'* with both masculinity and vernacular culture is not something unique to Kiesling's research. In fact, since Fischer first noted this pattern in the 1950s, almost every modern study looking at ING from Australia to Britain to the United States has found -*in'* to be more of a male and blue-collar thing. When we look at other vernacular forms like double negatives or glottalizing one's *t*'s (*bu'ah* for "butter"), we find men more often take up language forms that evoke both non-standardness and a macho heteronormative camaraderie, especially in adolescence. While slang and vernacular speech might forge the banter of bros, women -*ing* more because, as we've seen in past pages, they just don't get the same social bump for tougher talk or nonconformity. Women, especially those in the middle class, are instead drawn to forms that help them inculcate social influence, by impressing others, being fashionable, or coming across as appealingly hip. That doesn't mean women don't use -*in'*; they just don't generally use it as often, since the ethos of working-class culture tends not to up their social cred the same way as it does for men.

When it comes to ING, social class is king. Pretty much all major studies of ING, of which there have been many, show that speakers in lower socioeconomic class strata use -*in'* at a higher

---

superiors to inferiors) or forms that are perceived as "weak" features, such as using tag questions (isn't it?) or hedges (I think, perhaps). Nonstandard forms, in contrast, do not get their power from institutions but from their associations with specific speakers or social groups or how they represent nonconforming linguistic behavior.

rate than those in the middle class, be they male or female. Such associations mean nothing in terms of linguistic "correctness," for as we've discovered this is really a figment of our prescriptively trained imagination, but is more about what type of speech is valued and advantageous depending on where one is in the social hierarchy. If you are aiming to be a lawyer or a banker, then buying into codified standard language benefits you and aligns you with others on a similar track. But we are all drawn to the appeal of language that communicates more than just high status. Even CEOs go hang with friends and family after work and use talk that signals friendship and intimacy rather than poshness and economic advantage. While we may all -*ing* when we feel more formal standard speech is required, we also all -*in'* when it's not. These differences measured in the use of -*in'* are only a matter of degree.

It seems that friendship, community, and solidarity are at the heart of what we signal when we shift from using -*ing* to -*in'*. For example, in a study looking at both American and Australian English, linguists Benji Wald and Timothy Shopen found that, even more than we do with family, we shift to the most -*in'* use when we are kickin' it with friends. As the saying goes, you can pick your friends, but you can't pick your family, and we might feel more pressure to speak "proper" English when around mom and dad. They suggest using -*in'* invites greater intimacy, while -*ing* establishes status and regard. In the same study, they also found that both men and women used more -*in'* forms when they were joking with each other, in contrast to when they were arguing, which makes sense assuming -*ing* works to command respect and signal distance. This now puts the friend versus family contrast in much greater perspective, especially around the holidays. So be warned—when grandma starts giving you nothing but -*ing*, you better plan to move to the kid's table.

The power of perception

The important question is whether, based on such usage patterns, -*in'* or -*ing* matters to those who listen to you. Is your ING telling them something you might not want them to know?

The short answer is yes. Your relative rate of -*in'* and -*ing* speaks volumes to anyone who happens by. Researchers are able now to use computerized speech synthesis programs to alter recorded speech to have more or less of a specific feature, like more -*in'* or more -*ing*. Much like a physical disguise, we refer to these synthesized versions of the same speaker's speech as guises. The intriguing part is that you can play these guises for listeners and ask them questions about the speaker's social characteristics to see how much changing only that one feature affected the way the speaker was evaluated.

Of course, you could have some fun by radically altering someone's speech, like changing "normal" sounding voices into Mickey Mouse–sounding voices, a linguistic version of sucking the helium from a balloon. This is amusing perhaps, but not all that useful from a scholarly perspective. It is more interesting to make identical speech samples that only differ on one dimension—for instance, whether they use more *-in'* or more *-ing*—to see how it changes the way listeners rate that speaker on dimensions like pleasantness, articulateness, and professional competence.

So, what do we find when we tinker away like Frankenlinguists? Well, when it comes to using ING, we find that higher *-in'* use may predispose people to want to hang out with us more, but only if they can get over finding us lazy and less articulate. Even as few as one uttered *-in'* among many *-ing*s can shift how listeners hear one in terms of professionalism, as found in a 2006 study where listeners' ratings dropped after the first time a speaker used *-in'*, no matter which endings were used afterward. So, once you *-in'*, even subsequent *-ing* use can't save you from harsher evaluations. Ouch. When we *-ing*, though, we might seem more employable but less friendly and laid back. This probably doesn't surprise you much. But digging deeper, we find there is more nuanced social meaning behind whether we say *-in'* or *-ing*. For one, the American South is strongly inscribed with *-in'*. In a very intriguing study,* non-Southern speakers

---

* Linguists Charlotte Vaughn and Tyler Kendall performed a series of experiments that tested how much listeners unconsciously knew about the *-ing* and *-in'* variation. When asked to use *-in'* instead of *-ing*, speakers added things into their talk like monophthongal *ay* vowels (i.e., saying "tied" as *tod*) and drawling (i.e., longer vowel duration), which are essentially recognizable Southern-sounding

were asked to say *-in'* instead of *-ing* when reading speech prompts. But despite the fact that the researchers made no mention of any associated dialect in the instructions, they found that speakers spontaneously adopted other types of Southern features, apparently subconsciously associating the *-in'* form with Southern speech. Just using *-in'*, even without hearing any overt mention of a specific regional identity, seemingly leads us to channel a particular speech style triggered by that one form, the use of *-in'* being linked in our minds with certain types of speakers.

To see how strongly *-in'* has become tied to down South ideology, consider country music, a genre that carves a living on the back of tough Southern grit. And you can't get more Southern or gritty than the legendary man in black, Johnny Cash:

We crashed through the wall and into the street
Kickin' and a-gougin' in the mud and the blood and the beer

In these lines taken from his classic song "A Boy Named Sue," a treatise on toughness being passed down from an irascible father to his son, would singing *-ing* instead of *-in'* get across the

---

features. Even more interesting, when they played nouns such as *ceiling* or *duckling* pronounced as *ceilin'* or *ducklin'* for listeners, they reported hearing a stronger accent than when the researchers had manipulated verbs in the same way. As described in C. Vaughn and T. Kendall, "Stylistically Coherent Variants: Cognitive Representation of Social Meaning," *Revista de Estudos da Linguagem* 27, no. 4 (2019): 1787–1830.

same physicality and masculine bravado? Not so much. The songwriting credit was not given to Cash, but actually goes to Shel Silverstein, the poet and storyteller known to children everywhere for his book of humorous and relatable poetry, *Where the Sidewalk Ends*. Here using *-in'* to help paint the scene of a rough and rowdy bar fight draws on the social associations with *-in'* we already have at the ready. Certainly a bit of a different sensibility than Silverstein writes of in *The Giving Tree*, an allegorical story about a selfless tree and the boy it loves. Note in that story, he didn't make it about the Givin' Tree—seriousness and stature lean on *-ing*. Choosing *-in'* or *-ing* goes far beyond just being a feature of informal or formal language to being a stylistic choice that, when combined with other recognizable features, communicates such social nuances.

Of course, every compelling story has a dark side, and for *-in'* it is the way that *g* dropping seems to bring up redneck or hillbilly stereotypes alongside its Southern overtone. Remember those *Beverly Hillbillies* who struck oil and scored big-time? The picture of Appalachian vernacularity and uneducated-ness, hillbilly daughter Ellie May, in solidarity with cousin Jethro, who aims to go to school to learn cipherin', offers, "I can hep him fight if the big kids in the fifth grade get to pickin' on 'im." The humor here coming by virtue of the fact that six-foot-tall Jethro is far from a fifth grader, at least in size if not smarts. *The Beverly Hillbillies* and *The Dukes of Hazzard* constructed

Southern outsider-ness not just by what their characters did, but crucially by how they were represented in their speech. Would James Dickey's compelling novel and John Boorman's classic film *Deliverance* have struck the same chord had fast-talking, *r*-dropping New Yawkers been strumming that banjo down-river? I doubt Jon Voight, Burt Reynolds, or Ned Beatty would have felt the need to paddle quite as fast. It seems that *-in'* use is low-hanging fruit to help deliver rural, and typically male, characters.

But, obviously, using *-in'* in songs, movies, and sitcoms picks up on the strong leanings we have in terms of how we think Southerners talk. While we might charitably figure that this is because *-in'* sounds warmer and more friendly, as Southerners are held to be, a study by linguist Kathryn Campbell-Kibler suggests it is also tied to how we associate *-in'* users with lower education and class. Since this is also a stereotype about Southerners more generally, tossing a bit more *-in'* into their speech just ups the ante. In listener ratings of speech guises, the term *redneck* was used to describe speakers who used more of the *-in'* variant, and also who were perceived to sound more Southern and rural. The exact same speakers were considered more educated, more articulate, and less rednecky when their speech, identical in all other respects, had more *-ing*. Obviously, the same speakers can't be both redneck and not redneck, articulate and not articulate; the shift in ratings reflects a bias listeners had when hearing *-in'* based on the beliefs they had about what type of person *-in'*s and what type of person *-ing*s. In reality, we all use *-in'*, but Southerners and lower-class speakers seem associated with it on a much grander scale.*

In an unexpected twist, Campbell-Kibler also found that altering a speech guise to have more *-ing* affected how listeners perceived one of the speakers as more gay than when he used more *-in'*. The idea that there exists something such as a gay accent is a bit of a unicorn—often talked about but rarely empirically proven. Though listeners do appear to be able to recognize sexuality from speech at rates better than chance when listening to self-identified "gay" versus "straight" speakers, research looking for these elusive homosexuality-cuing speech features have not found many that have consistently proven to serve as cues of gayness or straightness. But Campbell-Kibler discovered that, whether true or not, listeners seemed to think there is a gay style and that *-ing* articulation plays into it. Since *-in'* has developed a masculine appeal as so amply demonstrated by Kiesling's frat boys and our boy named Sue, the association with gayness may reflect the less macho but more refined rep associated with *-ing*.

---

* Southerners are not the only group who has received some ridicule for the way they say the -ING ending. Young Californians (or Westerners more generally) are often called to task for their pronunciation of the -ING ending as *een*, as in "I went out bik-*een* and then run-*een*" (for "biking" and "running"), which involves not only a shift to an alveolar nasal but also a change to a more stressed vowel quality, which is what seems to attract the most notice.

BeING ghosted

ING's ability to not only survive but thrive through sharp regional divisions, incursions of Old Norse and French, and the sharp eyes of grammar mavens throughout the centuries has been remarkable. Even more remarkable still has been its spread as both a social and linguistic resource throughout the English-speaking world, an unanimity that no world leader has yet to rival. And though you probably hadn't realized it, you have been privy all these years to a historical documentation of this process of merger and -*ing* territory expansion in the form of a little jingle we all know and love, otherwise known as "The Twelve Days of Christmas."

For those of us whose caroling days are far behind us, here is a bit of a refresher:

On the tenth day of Christmas
My true love gave to me
Ten lords a-leaping,
Nine ladies dancing,
Eight maids a-milking,
Seven swans a-swimming,
Six geese a-laying,
Five golden rings,
Four calling birds,

Three French hens,

Two turtle doves

And a partridge in a pear tree.

A catchy tune certainly, but haven't you ever wondered why the lords were a-leaping or the maids a-milking? It's doubtful they were all from Appalachia, where *a*-prefixing is still rumored to be a thing.* But now with your newfound insight (or ingsight?), the mystery can be solved. This well-known shibboleth, i.e., He's a-huntin', is actually a residual trace of what was once none other than the OE noun-making *-inge* suffix, derived from forms like "He wæs on huntinge," back in the day. As we have seen happened a lot back then, the preposition *on* gradually lost the final consonant sound, becoming just the vowel *a*, which was also lost over time. Eventually, this morphs into the simplified verbal progressive "He was hunting." If deletion is really a sign of linguistic decay, *a*-prefixing Southerners should be the ones accusing the rest of the country of degrading the English language. I would dare say over the centuries we have all been pretty guilty of such petty crimes. As we have seen in this chapter, what one might say based on the morphosyntactic structure

---

* Though *a*-prefixing is still found in Appalachian dialects, its association as a relic feature of Appalachian English has unfortunately become part of a common stereotype of a stuck-in-the-past hillbilly dialect. It is also this Southern variety that has attracted the most pejorative commentary as well as negative portrayal in movies and TV shows (e.g. *Deliverance*, *The Beverly Hillbillies*) because of misunderstandings about the evolution, origin, and status of several Appalachian features.

and historical development of a language is often vastly different from what one feels they *should* say based on the social preference and prestige of certain times and in certain places. It is only in the last couple of centuries that anyone even started paying attention to the ins and outs of our *-in*'s and *-ings*. By having both endings, what have we lost? Nothing, once you realize that *-in'* is not incorrectness but instead a salute to our far more complex participial past, and simply brings a social richness to our talk. So perhaps the next time we are feeling grammatically smug and a-singin' "The Twelve Days of Christmas," we will remember that the ghosts of English endings past are there to remind us not to be so judgmental.

6

A Little Less Literally

Speaking of being a tad bit judgmental, my husband has been known to accuse me of a fondness for exaggeration, especially when describing things like the wait at the DMV (horrifically long!) or my fingers when I forgot my gloves on my morning run (literally frozen!). But I am not the only one who calls on a little linguistic support to amplify my expressivity. Everyone from Winston Churchill to Buffy the Vampire Slayer shares this same proclivity when it comes to making liberal use of one of the most rapidly evolving and innovative areas of the English language: adverbial intensity.

Don't worry, you didn't miss any memos about strange new features of English. This term just refers to the way that we boost or amplify adjectives to add more punch—like *"really* happy," *"so* rad," and *"extremely* annoying." You've used them with impunity all these years without knowing they had such a sophisticated name. From presidents to pundits, from toddlers to teenagers, intensification is all the rage. Intensifiers feed our need for hyperbole and help us emphasize what we are saying, though not everyone is a fan. Never one to shy away from exaggeration, former commander in chief Donald Trump has been taken to task on intensity, with tweets like "You are *sooo* lucky to have me as your President" and a predilection for using "very" and "very, very" a lot when he talks. But Trump, along with his penchant for overemphasis, is just one of many who find such boosters very, very useful.

We all lean on intensifiers because they allow us to be more expressive about what we want to say. Why be just happy when you can be *really* happy? Why just be awesome when you can be *totally* awesome? And even more to the point, why would anyone not want to be *super* sexy? Intensification provides a way to communicate the degree to which something applies, ramping up our impact. We use intensifiers because we want to convey emotion, something anyone who has a spouse, a child, a parent, a bad boss, or a relationship with a pet does extremely often. Note the intensifier "extremely" scaling up the frequency right there. They are just tremendously useful. Intensifiers are a lot like potato chips—it's hard to stop at just one.

But once we start using a certain intensifier a lot, it loses its zing and we need to come up with a novel way of persuading our listeners that what we are describing exceeds the norm. If we're Trump, we add on the *very*s, but the linguistic innovators around us start adding *ly* to fun, unexpected words to see what will stick. This constant rejuvenation makes the intensifiers du jour very noticeable, which is the goal, but also often makes them subject to disdain, aka our scoffing at the rise of *super* or *so*, and our dismay at the expansion of *literally*. Popularity has a dark side, even for intensification. Of course, this brings up the question from a grammar perspective of what, exactly, are intensifiers. Where did they come from? And how do new ones come to exist, given that they seem to multiply like bunnies on a farm in July?

The power of intensity

From the Bible to the Bard, we have always been ones for heightening the dramatic effect of what we say. Would Paris Hilton have been as popular if she hadn't coined "That's so hot"? So not. This shouldn't be surprising—we need a way to communicate where on a relative scale we view a particular person, thing, or event. Otherwise, everything would be equally banal or blasé or we would understate the degree to which something occurred. When I invite people over for a dinner party and spend ten hours in the kitchen stirring the roux for my gumbo, I expect a bit more from my guests than a simple "It was good." Compliments are one example of where intensification was born to thrive.

We often try to capture the height of emotional experiences, and we would be much less expressive if we did not have the boosting power of intensifier words. Take this quote from a critical-care fellow describing being in a New York City hospital during the COVID-19 pandemic of 2020: "It was a very scary, very overwhelming experience. It was a nightmare." Here intensifiers are used to amplify the descriptiveness of the words *scary* and *overwhelming* to come closer to encoding verbally the loss of life and the frightening uncertainty during this time. Even though we might find that our adjectives fit the sentiment we are trying to get across, sometimes they still don't have quite the right amount of zing. Since a huge part of language is to encapsulate moments and feelings as well as to transmit information, we need ways that can adequately translate and express the depth of our experiences and emotions linguistically.

Intensifiers are a part of speech that is referred to as a degree adverb, or adverbs that modify adjectives or other adverbs, but specifically ones that boost or add emphasis to what one is trying to say. Remember those *Mad Libs* fill-in-the-blank books that were popular when you were a kid? The ones that asked for parts of speech to make a zany story that you helped write? Intensifiers are the adverbs that would go in the slots like, "She is [insert adverb] knowledgeable about [insert body part]." Of course, at age eight when Mad Libbing is cool, our understanding of adverbs is limited to "ends with -ly" and our ideas about body parts slightly devious, so we usually end up with something like "She is awfully knowledgeable about butts."

What sent us into peals of laughter was the strangeness of these combinations—they surprised us and were noticeably unexpected. Innovation in how we use language garners attention, and it is this same drive motivating the use of ever-changing intensifiers to amplify our speech.

Most intensifiers, ones like *absolutely, horribly, wholly, completely*, and *totally*, are derived originally from adverbs of manner. But how do we go from the meaning of an adverb like *horribly* describing a frightful incident, i.e., "They perished *horribly*," to uses such as "He is horribly handsome"?

We start using the adverb in contexts more and more removed from its original sense through a process referred to in linguist lingo as delexification. Linguist Michael Israel more descriptively refers to this process as "semantic bleaching." Over time, the word's literal meaning wanes until what remains is only its boosting capacity. We find such a weakening in the meaning for *horribly* as early as Shakespeare's *Much Ado about Nothing*, where Benedick, speaking of Beatrice, says "I will be *horribly* in loue with her." This use of *horribly* metaphorically describes the extent of his love as being so strong that it evokes horror. Since many a love story ends in horror, this may not be such a stretch. But as we use it more often in contexts that only very loosely reference its original sense (i.e., a sound that is *horribly* loud), the takeaway becomes mainly the intensity of emotion and not the feeling of horror itself.

The sign that the delexification process is complete? When we finally reach the point where its use no longer brings up any horribleness, making us *horribly* happy. This process has happened to countless words. If you are *fairly* poor, I doubt you think much is fair about that. And if you are *terrifically* angry, that doesn't seem so terrific. Being *dead* posh, as one can be in the UK, doesn't mean you are a corpse with a fashion sense. What separates true intensifiers from the rest of the adverb lot is that they have lost their original meaning and now denote scalar qualities like "somewhat" (*pretty*), "a lot" (*very*), or "the most" (*completely*) instead.

Why *literally* can't get its groove back

We can see delexification at work very clearly with the adverb *literally*, which gets more than its fair share of shade. For some reason, this intensifier has met with great resistance, not by those using it in its hyperbolic sense, but by those unwilling to release it from the confines of its former self. Put *literally* in a search engine and you will be rewarded with a cornucopia of headlines about the "misuse" or "abuse" of the word, rebukes of politicians like Nick Clegg and Lindsey Graham, and even presidents like Joe Biden who dare to utter it, and if that wasn't illustrative enough of our moral decay, a compilation of reality stars using *literally* wrong. One comedian even calls himself the

Literally Tsar and claims to be on a mission to take *literally* back from the figurative edge. Everyone seems to have something to say about *literally*: a bar in New York posted a sign reading SORRY, BUT IF YOU SAY THE WORD "LITERALLY" INSIDE THE CONTINENTAL, YOU HAVE FIVE MINUTES TO FINISH YOUR DRINK AND THEN YOU MUST LEAVE. And then there are the many blog posts devoted to cataloging its rampant abuse. One would think *literally* was the equivalent of linguistic Armageddon given the rancor its use seems to provoke. But as we have learned about many of the pet peeves we hold, while these naysayers might be literally right, they are linguistically wrong; the evolution of literally is as principled as any other semantic bleaching witnessed in English over the years.

The word *literal* comes from French *literal* and Latin *littera*, both meaning "of a letter" or "pertaining to the letter." According to the *Oxford English Dictionary*, the meaning of *literally* in English as "in a literal, exact or actual sense" can be dated back to 1429. Even such use was already a figurative extension of the meaning inherited from French, which referred to copying a text letter by letter. More surprising perhaps is that *literally* used figuratively as we despise it today has been with us a lot longer than we might think. The OED notes an early use in 1769 in Frances Brooke's *The History of Emily Montague*: "He is a fortunate man to be introduced to such a party of fine women at his arrival; it is literally to feed among the lilies." Given the women are metaphorically the lilies, we can assume the intent is not actually to feed on them, unless zombie lit was more popular than we thought at the time. And thus began a great literal literary tradition. Jane Austen, James Fenimore Cooper, Charlotte Brontë, Charles Dickens, and James Joyce were all guilty of taking license with *literally*. As *Oxford English Dictionary* editor Jesse Sheidlower notes in an article for *Slate*, if it was good enough for Mark Twain in *The Adventures of Tom Sawyer*, where "Tom was literally rolling in wealth," and F. Scott Fitzgerald describing Gatsby's radiance with "He literally glowed," then why all the fuss?

We certainly can't be suggesting writers shouldn't use words in ways they were not originally intended. Wordplay and figurative language is often a show of their acumen. But what the long history of its use versus today's hullabaloo tells us is that this supposedly new use of *literally* has attracted our attention in a way it hadn't before. It's not until the early 1900s when we first start seeing it mentioned in usage guides, intimating it had become widespread enough at that point to gain notoriety. Irritating though those with prescriptivist leanings may find it, semantic change is the daily bread of language, as we have seen often throughout these pages. And *literally* is hardly our first time on the semantic merry-go-round. We use *awful* to describe something bad or traumatic, though its original meaning was "filling with awe." When we say *hardly* to mean scarcely or very little as in "hardly tired," this doesn't accurately portray the word's original sense of vigorously or with difficulty. And don't get me started on how *bad* is now actually *good*.

The use of *literally* in its emphatic sense gets its force specifically from the contrast with its traditional meaning. Besides being a thorn in the side of linguistic progress, our resistance to this intensifying sense comes a couple of centuries too late. We didn't mind Jane Austen or Mark Twain using it because we never noticed it, but it bugs us now because its use has pervaded more spaces and places where *literally* had never dared go before, a sure sign of semantic bleaching at work. Our thirst for novel ways of expressing intensity has never been easily quenched, and grammarian efforts are often too little, too late. By the time a new intensifier goes mainstream, linguistic trendsetters are already off to the races with a new one.

The intensity of our past

What's linguistically unusual about intensifiers is that they are much more prone to reinvention and recycling than any other adverbs. Since they are part of our expressive repertoire, they require creativity to stay fresh and engaging. When you hear someone say that was *hella* good or *f@#king* awful, it draws your attention because it's not your average everyday adverb. And this is precisely the point. An innovative or slang form will be more noticeable and more expressive than one that has been around the block a few times, like boring old *very* or *really*, two well-worn intensifiers. Think about the last time someone said a book was "very good" compared to another friend telling you a book was "amazingly good." Which one do you reach for first? *Very* just doesn't carry the same weight it used to because we've used it so much that its lost some of its expressive value. Even back as far as Old and Middle English, we find the same need for rapid innovation in intensification that we heed today. After all, given all the conquests, jousts, royal backstabbing, plagues, and the arrival of the Renaissance, there was a lot to be expressive about.

The most popular intensifier during the early history of English was *swiþe*,* a word now gone the way of the dodo. Though the word's original meaning was "strong," it developed early on the intensifying sense of "extremely." We find, for instance, "He hine lædde upon swiþe hea dune," from an Anglo-Saxon sermon dated from before 1000 AD, translating to: "He led him up on an extremely high hill." Not the most scintillating sermon, perhaps, but it leaves no doubt that the hill was high. Shortly after, we find *full*† starting to make an appearance in an intensifying function, and by 1300, it supplants *swiþe* as the most frequently used. We find *full* used this way, for example, in the general prologue to *The Canterbury Tales*: "Frensh she spak ful faire and fetisly" where *full* intensifies how fairly and fluently the Prioress spoke French, despite her lack of the "right" (Parisian) dialect.

---

* Pronounced something like "swee-the" in case you were wondering.
† Usually written in Middle English as *ful*.

Such intensifying traces remain even still in modern English. For instance, what does it mean when you know *full well*? Though this would be a very useful term to describe how I feel after Thanksgiving dinner, it really means that you are *very* certain.

Around this same time period, the adverbial (as opposed to adjectival) *well* begins its foray into intensification. We see such examples in old manuscripts like the fourteenth-century alliterative romance *William of Palerne*—for instance, in the line, "in flat forest . . . fler woned a wel old cherl," which describes an old man in a forest. Unfortunately for him, *well* doesn't describe his health status, but instead emphasizes his very ripe old age. By 1400, even *well* itself was getting old and *right* had moved in to become the shiny new intensifier, as we find a bit later in Shakespeare, "The better angel is a man right fair." This intensive use of *right*, afield from its original meaning of "exact" or "just," may have come to us circuitously from Viking influence via Old Scandinavian *rätt*, as *rätt* was also commonly used as an intensifier in Swedish. But by the sixteenth century, the intensifier *pretty* had taken over the top spot, used similarly to how we use it today, i.e., "That's pretty cool." Yet despite being supplanted, not all was lost for intensifier *well*—we see remnants of this meaning in modern expressions like *well worn* or *well done*, which describe things that are "very" worn or cooked. In a true testament to what goes around comes around, after being dormant for several centuries, this type of *well* is having a resurgence in modern British English, where it can be found as a colloquial intensifier, as in "That's well good."*

But of course, the hardest-working intensifier has to be *very*, with the longest run of any intensifier throughout history. This longevity seems only fitting given that it descends to us through the Old French *verai*, meaning "true," now *vrai* in modern French. The Anglo-Norman version *verrai*, as found in Middle English, was first used to mean "true" or "truthful." We see it carries this meaning still in verse from the William Tyndale Bible, written in 1526: "All men counted Ihon, that he was a veri prophet," identifying Jesus as a true prophet. Traces of this earliest meaning can yet be found in *very*'s rare modern nonintensifying use in expressions like "on this very day" or "in this very spot," referring to something true, in the sense of exact, being described. But we also start to find evidence of *very* used in an adverbial sense to mean "to a high or full extent" as early as the fourteenth century. We can locate such an emphatic meaning in Chaucer's work, "That he nys but a verray propre fole,"† though Chaucer also used it elsewhere with its original sense of true or actual. This early variability is a classic example of how mean-

---

* By the fifteenth century, intensification of regular adjectives like *good* or *happy* with *well* had become obsolete and intensifying *well* was only found before adjectives derived from verbs (e.g., *educated*, *experienced*) or with a few specific adjectives (e.g., *well aware*, *well able*). Today, though, it is the original wider distribution of *well* that seems to be reemerging in colloquial British speech, as in "She's well happy."

† Meaning something akin to "That he is nothing but a complete fool."

ing shifts via a slow process of delexification, until today *very* maintains mainly its boosting or emphatic sense.

Despite these few early appearances, our modern sense of *very* doesn't occur too often until the early modern era. But when it makes an entrance, it comes in with a bang. In the sixteenth century, *very* was everywhere. And former President Trump's aforementioned penchant for using the word *very* very, very much? Such repetition too has been around for a while. We see examples starting as early as the sixteenth century, and even find it among some of our literary greats, such as Daniel Defoe, for example: "It was indeed very, very, very dreadful," and later, Charles Dickens. Of all intensifiers tracked over the centuries, *very* is the veritable grande dame, having graced English for more than four hundred years and maintaining its position as the top intensifier up to the twenty-first century. *Very*, it seems, has become the little black dress of the intensifier set.

Despite its longevity and its ubiquity, even well-worn *very* has its detractors. In a 1916 newspaper editorial, Winston Churchill was taken to task for his "unconquerable fondness for the word 'very.'" Perhaps its former life attesting truth made *very* a favorite of prime ministers and presidents, or maybe just the frequent need for hyperbole. Even more than in speaking, we find grammar guides and writing experts like Jane Friedman warning of the dangers of its overuse. *Very*, along with *literally, totally,* and several other intensifiers, qualifies as one of the "9 Words You're Literally Beating to Death," according to an article in *Forbes*.

Compounding *very*'s overuse image problems, *v.*, an abbreviated form of *very* used often on Twitter, is making inroads into spoken language as an intensifier ("He was v. upset"), much to the dismay of those for whom tweeting is still reminiscent of birdsong. Maybe *very* getting its wings clipped tells us the time for change has come.

Really is the new black

In a study looking at how Toronto teens used intensifiers, sociolinguist Sali Tagliamonte found that young speakers used comparatively more intensifiers as well as a rapidly evolving set of new ones. While stalwart *very* still hung around to some degree, it was now a reliable fallback rather than an intensifier of first choice. These newer intensifiers were associated with casualness and youth culture. After several hundred years of use, *very* has become blasé.

And what innovative new form came in to displace *very*? You might be surprised to find that it is none other than *really*, which can be found used sparingly as an intensifier as early as the eighteenth century. In comparison to *very*, *really* might be a neophyte but it is well on its way to becoming the latest in intensifier fashion. When we say language change in intensifiers is rapid that doesn't mean that the introduction of a new form instantly becomes the most popular. As with *really*, it sometimes takes a while to delexicalize to the point where, like *very*, the new intensifier loses almost all other associated meanings and is used widely and with essentially all adjectives and adverbs. Some, like *horrifically*, still carry for quite some time a modicum of their original sense, so we don't see them co-occur with words that don't have some natural affinity to this meaning; that is, you might say "horrifically traumatic" but not "horrifically good." *Really* might have taken about two hundred years to get here, but now studies looking at its frequency and distribution across modern speech corpora show that it has expanded to become, in essence, the new *very*.

Although Americans were embracing *really* as the new it-intensifier by the 1980s, the British took a bit longer to warm up. But research suggests that, for the under thirty-five set, *really* has now also emerged in Britain as a contender to knock *very* off its throne, sort of the new duchess of intensifiers. *Very* still reigns in more formal written contexts and among older speakers, but *really* has become the most popular intensifier in spoken contexts, and especially for young women.* Generally, older intensifiers stick around, but just get used less often. What might be more unexpected is that *really* has been found to increase along with education level, at least where it has been studied in this capacity. Along the same lines, in a study in Scotland by linguist

---

* The rise of *really* as intensifier du jour is quite pervasive. Research on Australian English and New Zealand English shows *really* tops the charts there as well, while *very* use is simultaneously decreasing. And guess who's leading the charge down under? You got it. Young women.

Ronald Macaulay, intensifiers were more common in the speech of upper-class speakers, surprising perhaps given our sometimes jaded view of them. Macaulay hypothesized this stems from an upper-class tendency to want to provide a more evaluative take on what is being reported, something being *very* good, *quite* funny, or *utterly* dismal. Intensifiers have also been found to occur more often with emotional language (*glad, scared*) rather than descriptive words (*red, thin*), a fact that has been proposed as an explanation for what makes them more popular with women. In a study that examined how intensifiers were scripted in the popular TV show *Friends*, adjectives that expressed emotion did encourage intensifier use, but this was true of both male and female characters, so the jury is still out on that one.

After unseating *very*, even the popular *really* is now barely holding its own against an emerging set of newcomers. The intensifier *so* is fast on the heels of *really* both in Britain and the United States, suggesting that *really* has started to wane in its ability to boost our expressiveness. Despite the sheen of novelty, *so* itself is no babe in the woods, having appeared in Old English documents in the form of *swa*, meaning "in the manner of" or "as," as early as 888. But it has only drawn attention in an intensification capacity for the last century or so, where we find it mentioned in 1901 as a favorite, no surprise, among the ladies. In Tagliamonte's study measuring the rise of *so*, being young and female still mattered in its use, but as found with *very*, this gender difference decreases among young adult speakers, where first-year college-age men actually used *so* slightly more than women. This echoes the pattern of young male catch-up we've seen before when looking at the use of discourse markers *um* and *like* over time. But *so* was not the only new intensifier on the horizon. *Pretty* and *totally* were also found as frequent up-and-comers, and in comparing *pretty*'s use by gender, Tagliamonte found adolescent men were actually prettier than adolescent women, at least in terms of their intensifiers. What this likely means is that *so* and *pretty* are on their way to being the next well-worn intensifiers more generally, though *pretty* does seem to be primarily the domain of North American users, at least in its modern, rather than sixteenth-century, incarnation.

While research suggests *really*, *so*, and *pretty* have hit the big time and made it out of the trenches of the young, very new intensifiers like *hecka*, *hella*, *all*, and *way* in the United States, *proper*, *enough*, and *well* in England, and *pure* in Glasgow wait in the wings, still relegated to pockets of youthful users. These intensifiers might sound funny to outsiders, but such adolescent social groups are the lifeblood of what makes or breaks an intensifier's rise to expressive glory.

Identity through intensity

One of the reasons that intensifiers are useful, beyond satisfying our penchant for hyperbole, is that they provide clues to who we are in terms of the identity we project and the groups to which we belong. For example, *wicked* smart marks a New Englander, while *bloody* brilliant marks a slightly bawdy Brit. Like *totally*, *so* gained traction as a SoCal feature, immortalized by Moon Unit Zappa who was *so* bitchin', but has now also gone more mainstream. Though Southern Californians are the last who should be casting intensifier stones, someone saying *hella* in Los Angeles would definitely be an outcast; every self-respecting Californian knows that *hella* is a NoCal kind of thing. And of course, intensifiers like *f@#king*, *freaking*, *crazy-ass*, and *-af* (short for *as f@#k*, as in *happy-af*) say something else entirely about the vibe you are giving off. Their shock value makes them popular as a symbol of nonconformist youth culture or to project a rougher or tougher persona.

They say imitation is the sincerest form of flattery, but once intensifiers get picked up and used more widely, they lose their in-group mojo. Such imitation then becomes the mother of linguistic invention, starting the cycle of inspiring new intensifiers over again. And what's the social force behind our linguistic ingenuity and the driver of whether others pick it up? Who we are hanging with and who we are trying to impress.

In the cult favorite *Buffy the Vampire Slayer*, a teen girl finds out that she is destined through ancient prophecy to kick demon butt. Between her slaying activities and surviving high school, the main character, Buffy, has a pretty active social life. You might be wondering what Buffy the Vampire Slayer and intensifiers have in common. A focus on youth culture, for one, and the attempt to use a variety of superpowers, be it vampire slaying or linguistic innovation, to navigate social life in high school. Perhaps, then, it should come as no surprise that writers for the show mined the use of these expressive forms to richly represent characters' social and cultural leanings.

Examining how intensifiers were used for characterization in the show, linguists found that intensification varied based on character type. For instance, the more refined (and non-evil) British character, Giles, was often scripted with *very* and *quite*, displaying his upper-crust Britishness.* Spike, the British vampire with street cred and a bad attitude, instead used the intensifier *bloody*, fitting perhaps, given his drink of choice. Handily, when a cyborg controlled by Spike tries to pass for Buffy, the Buffybot's use of "bloody" serves as a clue to its true identity. This correlation of intensifier choice with Britishness makes sense, as *very*, *quite*, and *bloody* are, of course, associated with British more than American speech. Yet this play on intensifiers also goes further to provide a refined versus punk contrast for the characters. In a similar vein, linguist James Stratton's analysis of the distribution of the intensifier *well* in the British show

---

* The British use of "quite" is often different from the American "quite," where it generally only expresses intensification. In Britain, it can sometimes be used in this same way (e.g., *quite brilliant*), but is used more often as a down-toner to express the sense of "somewhat" or "moderately," as in, "the book was quite good, but it was a bit slow at times."

The Inbetweeners found the scripting of the colloquial intensifier *well*, as in "well embarrassing," was used to mark a social difference, with *well* intensification associated with mainly boys, and especially those from a comprehensive or public school background. Such usage is in contrast to research that finds intensification with *well* to be used more by upper-middle-class boys, but Stratton suggests that, as a stigmatized colloquial form, it is used in the show to help portray a class-based stereotype. On the other hand, like the upper-crust Giles, the higher-class and private school–educated character, Will, is portrayed instead as a heavy *very* user.

So, the incoming new trendy intensifier, also helps build characters' identities on *Buffy*, particularly for the young women. Cordelia, the "queen bee" cheerleader at the beginning of the show, uses a high rate of *so*, aligning with her popular in-group status. Willow, Buffy's somewhat nerdy friend, uses far less *so* in the early seasons, and not surprisingly is not in the same sphere of influence as Cordelia. But as the show progresses and these characters move into the same social circle, Cordelia's use of *so* falls as Willow's increases. The frequency of *so* use marks a transition in their social roles and relationships, particularly as it relates to high school popularity and cliques. While this is obviously scripted rather than natural speech, these intensifier patterns show a recognition of how use of newer intensifiers is tied to highlighting in-group membership. And it is exactly this salience as a noticeable feature that brings with it the fun, popular, or hip vibes that give rise to its spread into the larger community.

The mother of invention

As with many of the features appearing in these pages, critics of intensity have long associated its use with women. Such notice of the female affinity for novel intensifying forms captured the not-so-admiring attention of Lord Chesterfield in the eighteenth century, when he suggested that women have a tendency to "take a word and change it, like a guinea into shillings for pocket money . . . vastly obliged, or vastly offended, vastly glad, or vastly sorry." Grammarian Cornelis Stoffel, writing in 1901, suggests "ladies are notoriously fond of hyperbole," and labels the intensifier *so* as "highly characteristic of ladies' usage." Likewise, famed linguist Otto Jespersen, writing in 1922, also finds that women have a "fondness for hyperbole" that drives their preference for adverbs of intensity. But while they were right about the fact that women led the charge, they were vastly wrong about why.

What these fine gentlemen did not seem to realize was that the female patterns of innovation they remarked on were far-reaching and prescient. Given the pressure to adhere to the norms of what one knows (and what butters one's bread), the staying power and communicative value of innovative forms are underestimated and instead often derided. But what women are saying today is what we will all be saying tomorrow, and the reason people scoff is precisely because what's new is notable. Women, as usual, are the vanguard. This is as true for intensifiers as for next season's must-have accessory.

The fact that women were less literate and formally educated than men in those days may have allowed them to use language more creatively, less tied to the oppressive written conventions that, by the eighteenth century and later, stifled natural linguistic variation. Indeed, a study of linguistic changes in Early Modern English by historical linguist Terttu Nevalainen found that female-led changes such as using *you* for *ye* and *does* for *doth* started as oral or regional forms and rose to become new norms because they became a regular part of conversations and daily life. Early plays and personal correspondence allowed a view into these more informal patterns. Men appear to have led some changes, but mainly those that were awarded prestige in learned domains, for instance, the shift from double negation to single negation that we find occurring in early modern texts and court documents.

Women, much like the lower classes during the reign of the Normans in Britain, were less constricted by the social conventions prescribed by formal usage and more attuned to using language in innovative and fashionable ways. But language outside prescription is clearly not always appreciated, especially when women and other undesirables are at the helm. It should come as no surprise then that this pattern of change did not pass unnoticed by the ever-watchful eyes of the grammar gate-keepers. Our friend Lord Chesterfield, for one, found it most distasteful that "most women and all the ordinary people in general speak in open defiance of all grammar."* Still, women didn't invent hyperbole as they were often accused, just new ways of delivering it.

What Jespersen, Lord Chesterfield, and many others since failed to recognize was that intensification was nothing new in English or exclusively the domain of women. What women brought to the fore was novelty in the form of this expressivity, not greater expressivity itself. In fact, intensification surrounded them in the literary examples we've discussed, and these written documents from which we have come to understand intensifiers across time were written predominantly by men. Clearly, boost-ers are not just the domain of women, but because of women's role in linguistic change and adverbial innovation, they have de-veloped quite a reputation.

But let's think of the other language features that we tend to love to hate: hedges such as *I think*, *I suppose*, or *maybe*, dis-course markers such as *you know* and *like*, and sentence initial *so*. What type of speaker comes to mind? Probably not stalwart and tough Arnold Schwarzenegger or Clint Eastwood, but more

---

* This quote comes from a letter Lord Chesterfield wrote to his son dated 1741, as cited in Jennifer Coates, *Women, Men and Language* (Abingdon-on-Thames, UK: Routledge, 2016), 16.

Reese Witherspoon or Alicia Silverstone, actresses known for portraying airheaded but popular young women, usually with a heart of gold and surprising smarts. Borrowing a line from Witherspoon's movie *Legally Blonde*, "Whoever said orange was the new black was seriously disturbed." Or from *Clueless*, a rich girl coming-of-age movie, when Silverstone describes her failure to stop at a stop sign, saying, "I totally paused." Both of these instances of appealingly airheaded female characterization are accomplished with the help of intensification, a mistaken but longstanding association that shows that we have not moved all that far from the dismissive contentions of Chesterfield and Jespersen, who discount women's innovation as frivolity instead of function.

While men can rely on physicality or economic advantage to pump up their power and presence, women, and young women in particular, find other symbolic resources to make a way in the world. Language helps women (and others) negotiate status and a sense of belonging, providing a form of social capital as valuable as fists and finance. For young speakers more generally, but especially young women, linguistic style is a tour de force in establishing a persona and fitting in with a group, similar to other sociostylistic markers like whether you wear a letterman jacket or one with black leather and studs. But because of this association with novelty and colloquialism (a phase through which much of what has now become our standard has passed), the view of such innovation has often been negative.

A future full of intensity

Do you recall those AT&T ads in which invested parties inquire about the skill set of a moving company, a skydiving instructor, or a doctor? The response is a less than reassuring, "They're OK," with the tagline "Just OK is not OK." A more perfect plug for the utility of intensity would be hard to make. We want to hear about a moving company being "extremely careful" with our stuff or a skydiving instructor who is "very experienced," and certainly not about a doctor who tells you, "Nervous? Yeah, me too," as you head into surgery. These commercials are a great highlighting of why we need ways to boost what we say to be more informative and to help others assess how things are evaluated.

The good news is that intensifiers are perceived much better than we might think given the bad press these adverbs attract. In looking to speech-communication research, using intensifiers enhanced perceptions of certainty and control, increased perceptions of authoritativeness, and raised ratings on sociability scales. While this might seem to run counter to what we would expect, intensifiers communicate one's conviction about what they say, or how strongly we feel about something. The more certain or committed you come across, the more likely others are to buy what you are saying, hook, line, and sinker. In other words, who goes for just great, when *absolutely* great is on the table?

Particularly true when it comes to assessing surgeons, job offers, attorneys, and spouses. Boosting your expressive power boosts your persuasive power. It's safe to say that it's not a very totally tremendously so awfully bad thing to use an intensifier or two.

Of course, these studies examined intensifiers that were already mainstream, not those that still lurked in the margins. And many of these new forms will end up fading away, never breaking out of a group-identity function and into the mainstream. *Crazy-ass*, for example, likely does not represent the kind of intensification that people might go for more widely. But many, like *literally*, *totally*, and *pretty*, have already begun the slide past the grammar mavens and into the grammar books. So whether you find this fantastically awesome or traumatically upsetting really depends on your willingness to embrace language change. But rest assured that much of what we find conservative and formal today, like *very* or *highly* or *quite*, were once trendy and even colloquial, and now we hardly notice them. This, of course, pretty much sums up the problem with intensity. The only difference between the intensifiers of today and those of yore is how the passage of time has influenced our perspective. While they may have begun their journey out of the mouths of young women, they ended up in the books and conversations of men. And the rest, as they say, is history.

The Perfect Pitch

What Kind of Person Fakes Their Voice?" read the headline of a 2019 piece in *New York* magazine's *The Cut*. The voice in question? That of disgraced Theranos CEO Elizabeth Holmes, suspected of having adopted a deeper voice than her "natural" one. For those who missed it, Holmes was the founder of a biotech start-up that purportedly developed a revolutionary new blood-testing technology. Turns out, there was no such technology, only a lot of smoke and mirrors, and she was convicted of fraud for bilking investors. And while the story of her meteoric rise and fall is the stuff of a reporter's dreams, the interest in how her voice dropped as her fortune rose is a great example of how our linguistic choices are viewed as specific social and stylistic moves. The irony here being that, of all her sins in defrauding investors and health-care institutions, shifting to a baritone voice would be called out as one of the biggest flags of her inauthenticity.

This intense focus on Holmes's voice sums up something linguists have known for a long time: namely, that aspects of our voice can have very real consequences on how we're perceived. Even when not guilty of any criminal activities, everyday women find themselves scrutinized for, and sensitive about, the way they sound. I hear about these concerns from all sides—from the perspective of the people who can't stand things like vocal fry or uptalk, as well as from the perspective of those who habitually use them. A lot of my female students mention they have been called out for the throaty fry that slips into their voice, especially by employers or older relatives. The result is that they have become very self-conscious about how they sound.

And it's no wonder. Take a gander at the clamor over what has been referred to as the "vocal fry epidemic," plus gloom-and-doom headlines like "Vocal Fry May Hurt Women's Job Prospects" (*The Atlantic*), and it becomes quickly apparent that you don't have to have achieved great notoriety to face the perils of talking while female. But beyond being a magnet for bad press, what is the real social and linguistic story behind this seemingly strange new vocal characteristic otherwise known as vocal fry?

While vocal fry might sound painful, in lay terms, it just describes speech with some gravelly-ness, a bit like the sound created when running a stick along a metal railing. For most English speakers, vocal fry, or creaky voice, as it is more commonly called outside pop publications, occurs at the end of a phrase or sentence, alongside a "getting to the end" drop in pitch. Though Kim Kardashian is often held up as the model vocal fry user, many a man walked that road long before a Kardashian made it worthy of comment. Famed linguist Noam Chomsky displays pretty awesome fry, as does aristocratic-sounding William F. Buckley, as measured by the "Creakometer" created by linguist Mark Liberman on the *Language Log* blog. There too we find action hero Bruce Willis and Western movie icon Lee Marvin mentioned as frequent friers.

Though it didn't attract nearly the popular notice back then as it does now, vocal fry started being studied about thirty or forty years ago in its role as a voice register, where it was found to serve "an array of linguistic (phonological), pragmatic (turn-taking), and metalinguistic (emotional) purposes in American English." At the time, it was being taken seriously as part of our communicative arsenal. And intriguingly, none of this early work suggested fry was more common among women. In fact, work in Britain in the 1970s and '80s suggests quite the opposite— finding men used more fry than women and that it carried an upper-class high-status association. This certainly leads one to wonder how vocal fry became known as the female-led "verbal tic of doom."*

---

* According to a writer for *Fast Company*, who further details how hearing vocal fry turned him off hiring an otherwise qualified, and not surprisingly female, applicant.

Bring on the sexy babies

In several interviews for her role as voice-over talent in her 2013 movie *In a World*, actress Lake Bell complains about women using what she calls "sexy baby voice" or "squeaky toy voice." For those of us who have never met a sexy baby, she describes this voice as a combination of higher pitch, vocal fry, and uptalk (ending sentences with an intonational question mark), a nice summary of the most common complaints regarding women's unpleasant verbal habits. To set herself far apart from such vocal shamefulness, Bell says she adopts a deeper voice during interviews to sound more professional. Now, no shade on Ms. Bell for expressing her opinion, but it sure feels like she's adopting a pretty patriarchal system that privileges the way men sound—something Ms. Holmes seems to have embraced as well.

The truth is that most highly recognizable voice types, including vocal fry, start out simply as a product of our body size, hormones, and the way we manipulate our vocal apparatus. But out in the world, we start to view such voice types as proxies for personality types, or perhaps more critically, vocal stereotypes. But there is nothing inherently gentle, dumb, sultry, or unprofessional about someone because of how they sound. Instead, these are the voices of the cultural models we have formed that represent our expectations for how people with particular attributes or in certain roles should talk.

But of course, Lake Bell is far from the first to dis women's voices. Women's talk has long been held aside as discordant, disruptive, and even dangerous. As classicist Mary Beard has documented, as far back as Roman antiquity, speech was the domain of men, something the *Odyssey*'s young Telemachus makes clear to his mother, Penelope, when he tells her essentially to shut up and go busy herself with her weaving. This view can be traced back to classical philosophical texts by Cicero and Aristotle and early Christian theologians like Augustine, all cautioning against women's voices in public spheres. For example, Aristotle reminds us of the value of women being seen but not heard when he writes, "Silence gives grace to woman." When women in ancient Greece or Rome did make their voices heard, they were ridiculed and ostracized. We find just such an example in Roman litigator Gaia Afrania. Her courtroom advocacy so disturbed the powers that be that her behavior is rumored to have been the impetus for an edict forbidding women to plead cases for anyone but themselves. Not only was her speech compared to that of dogs barking, but her very name, Gaia Afrania, became a generic reference for a woman of low morals.

Things didn't get much better for the so-called gentler sex in the Middle Ages, when disagreeable speech, particularly that associated with women, was criminalized. Women who spoke out publicly were often accused of and prosecuted for "sins of the tongue." As punishment, they were forced to don a scold's bridle, a contraption rivaling Hannibal Lector's face mask. Though the coming of the Age of Enlightenment brought with it fewer tongue-inhibiting accessories, etiquette booklets and manuals became increasingly popular and often cautioned women not to babble, talk too much, or use loud voices. The focus had shifted from criminalizing women's voices to properly socializing them. For instance, in the nineteenth-century etiquette guide *The Woman Beautiful*, author Ella Adelia Fletcher warns, "The commonest defect of a woman's voice is pitching it too high," which, unfortunately, "imparts an unpleasant rasping, dead or shrill timbre to the voice." Probably not a winning combination of vocal attributes at the ball.

Even as we get to more modern times, women entering the workforce received much unsolicited voice-directed counsel. Broadcasting guides from the 1950s advised women to adopt a lower pitch to avoid sounding "shrill," the preferred adjective to describe the tone of women's talk. And even with the growing movement for equal rights for women in the 1970s, it apparently didn't hold for their voices, as feminist literature also suggested that women avoid using high-pitched speech because it came across as timid and lacking in authority. It would seem that all this advice has had the desired effect; an Australian study comparing women's speech in the 1940s to more modern data from the 1990s suggests that contemporary women have significantly lowered their pitch over time. And vocal fry is just the next step on the road to vying for linguistic equality.

The mechanics of fry

To appreciate how and why we fry when we drop to a lower pitch, we have to understand a bit about the vocal magic that happens behind the scenes. To make speech sounds, our first order of business is to create our basic pitch. To start this process, we push sustained lung air through muscular flaps (the vocal folds or flaps) that attach to the glottis at the top of our larynx, aka our voice box (hiding behind your Adam's apple). Most of the time we do this with a decent amount of subglottal air pressure, while also holding the vocal folds long and tense, so that it creates a fluid and rhythmic vibrating pattern, the pattern we basically recognize as someone's pitch. But when air pressure is weak (or the folds are larger), the vocal folds vibrate more slowly. If we also bunch up the vocal folds, making them shorter and thicker, we produce a slower and more irregular pulsing pattern. The result? What we hear as fry is simply the result of this reduced glottal airflow pushing up through stiffer vocal folds, producing a more irregular vibration that comes across as something like a low popping sound. Since the vocal folds are moving slowly, and our pitch is related to how fast our folds vibrate, vocal fry only occurs at a lower pitch. From an objective standpoint, vocal fry is simply a part of our natural pitch variability and something speakers can draw from for contextual and stylistic effect.* Though we might not notice when it is not part of our usual speech style, most of us creak sometimes when we shift to a lower pitch. Just try saying "Yeah, I know that" while dropping to a low pitch and elongating the "that." Did you hear a little fry get by?

Doubtless there are many who don't enjoy fry's scratchy staccato sound, but we tend to forget that voice is a very personal attribute. Telling someone that you find their voice unpleasant is a lot like telling someone to change their name because you don't like it. And despite press to the contrary, there is not a pathology or disorder with this type of voice quality, though it is possible for creak to be a signal of damage to one's vocal folds. However, in such cases, creak is much more pervasive throughout one's speech and not in the sociolinguistic pattern we see in its more typical use—as a signal that we are getting to an end of a sentence.

Journalistic creakiness

Recall that early research on creak found it to be a tool in a speaker's stylistic toolbox. It really was not until the recent

---

* Vocal fry is by no means just a feature of English. Many other languages use creaky phonation either for sociolinguistic purposes (Finnish, Swedish, Serbo-Croation, Hanoi Vietnamese) or linguistic purposes (as a clue to the meaning of a word or identity of a sound as in Tzeltal, Zapotec, and Salish).

2000s, and mainly via the popular press, that vocal fry became demonized as an unsuitable vocal affectation. It is no coincidence that this attitudinal shift seems to have emerged alongside the increasing presence of women in professional contexts, and particularly in radio/broadcasting forums where women had long been subject to criticism for their high-pitched voices.*

Analyzing the voices of newscasters in 1996, researchers Laura Dilley, Stefanie Shattuck-Hufnagel, and Mari Ostendorf found that the female radio newscasters used greater amounts of creak compared to the male broadcasters. A more recent study of newscasts returned similar findings, but intriguingly, the researchers also analyzed the speech of nonprofessional speakers and found that they did not show the same gendered pattern. This suggests, first, that women are feeling the pressure to lower their voice in professional contexts, especially those for whom voice makes their living (à la Ms. Bell), and, second, that using fry helped give the perception of a lower voice to sound more authoritative. This increase in vocal fry as a broadcast vocal style for women has absolutely not gone unnoticed.

Case in point: Public radio's *This American Life* received so many complaints about how women sounded on the show that

---

* The disdain for women's voices in the early broadcasting years is well documented ("Are Women Undesirable—Over the Radio" explores the topic as early as 1924 in the periodical *Radio Broadcast*), and much of the rationalization for their unsuitability was based on their "shrill" voices over the airwaves. Ironic that today it is their lower-pitched tones via vocal fry that seems to attract negative notice.

they even devoted a special episode to addressing the prodigious amount of female-oriented hate mail they receive. Listeners, both male and female, condemned the female journalists not for one-sided pieces or thin content, but for something much more personal—the way they delivered it. Not surprisingly, much criticism centered on the use of vocal fry. One writer complains, "The growl in the woman's voice was so annoying I turned it off." Another says listening was "too much to bear." One particularly incensed writer posits the pressure to hire women created the conditions that led to this sad state of vocal affairs and wonders if NPR holds a contest to find the most annoying voices possible.

According to host Ira Glass, these missives about his female colleagues' voices are "some of the angriest emails we ever get." What is it exactly that makes listeners so irate? Glass suggests that the verbal habit itself is not the issue, but rather it represents a larger bias against features associated with women, echoing our common theme that women's use of innovative linguistic forms attracts attention. Over the years, Glass says complaints have looked unfavorably upon whatever linguistic aspects were most conspicuous in women's voices. First it was uptalk, then *like* use, and now vocal fry. The frequency of comments about uptalk or *like* has waned as vocal fry has increasingly taken first place as the object of the belligerent tirades. What's particularly interesting is that Glass himself fries quite a bit, but that was never called out or criticized by listeners.

This American Life has not been the only radio show surprised by the volume of mail inspired by female voices. Katie Mingle, producer of the radio podcast *99% Invisible*, set up an auto-reply to respond to the jarring number of complaints they get about the quality of women's voices on the show. Her auto-response to the voice hate? Complaint lodgers are told that they are being directed to a special folder that will be responded to "Never," and she includes the savvy advice to listeners unhappy with the show's response that "there are plenty of shows that don't feature women's voices at all." Remarkably, Mingle notes they don't need a special folder for the complaints they get about men's voices. Why? Because they've never gotten any.

These observations would seem to suggest that vocal fry is predominately the purview of women. After all, we have seen many times before it is common for women to lead in the novel use of forms. But it is also the case that the perception of a feature as specifically female emerges because we tend to linguistically scrutinize women in particular. As a result, media reports of women's verbal habits misrepresent the more equitable distribution of that feature in the youthful population in general. We have seen this with *like* use in an earlier chapter, where a trend in young women using *like* more, despite a pattern of use in young men as well, gets exaggerated because we perceive it more. The increasing use of words like *so* and *totally*, part of a larger pattern of innovation in intensifiers, has also been used to characterize the ditzy or airheaded language of women, even though young men also use the forms. Part of the difficulty with being linguistic leaders and with being female is that both things seem to get you noticed, and often not in a good way.

Frequent fryers?

On a segment called "New Speech Pattern of Young Women," *Today* show medical editor Dr. Nancy Snyderman declared that men don't fry. Any speech pathologist or linguist knows this is simply incorrect. In fact, one of the earliest studies on vocal fry pointed to its potential as a "hypermasculine" feature in some British English varieties. But Dr. Snyderman is clearly not alone in her misconception. And it begs the question of whether there is actually any evidence that women really do fry more than men, at least outside of newscasters.

When we look to more general scholarly research, do we indeed see a pattern of female-fueled fry? In short, yes, at least if we look only at speakers in the United States. Yet, despite the "epidemic" reported by the media, we certainly don't see a pattern of exclusive fry use by women even there. In her study looking at young English speakers in California, linguist Ikuko Yuasa found that young American women used creak or vocal fry about twice as often as a comparative group of males. As well, she found that this was culturally specific, as young Japanese women used about the same amount of fry as the American men. A similar finding was reported by Stanford linguist Rob Podesva, when comparing men and women in the Washington, D.C., area,* and another study noted the same trend, though small, in midwestern American speakers.

Not all studies turned up women as the most frequent friers. For example, in a study from 2016, psychology student Sarah Irons and her professor Jessica Alexander discovered men using more fry than women in their Southern U.S. sample, a study that focused on spontaneous speech rather than the reading style used for most of the other studies. A separate study done the same year by communication-science researchers found no significant gender difference in overall vocal fry using an automatic detection algorithm. Regardless of which gender fried more, in all these studies, both men and women tended to use it in the same way—namely, as a signal that they were coming to the end of a phrase or sentence, a usage pattern that has been widely reported across various studies both inside and outside of the United States.

This trend of female-led frying seems uniquely American. As mentioned before, much of the early research on creaky voice

---

* Though vocal fry has been characterized as part of a white female linguistic style, as discussed by Tyanna Slobe in her work on "mock white girl" persona (*Language in Society* 47 [2018]), linguist Rob Podesva found vocal fry also used by African Americans in the community he studied, and he found women used fry more often than men. This suggests the sociocultural attractiveness of fry appeals across ethnic lines.

was done in Britain, where the predominant pattern was male. Though some recent coverage in the British press portends a trend of fry influenced by the Kardashians and other young female American celebrities, this appears to be driven more by the contagion view of vocal fry than any solid evidence. In fact, harnessing the power of the modern cell phone and our desire to tirelessly talk into them, a recent study analyzed crowdsourced recordings made via a dialect app from 2,500 (willing) smartphone users across Britain and confirmed that this male fry preference is still the rule in the UK.* Not only that, but the researchers also discovered more fry in older male speakers and, echoing its earlier upper-crust vibe, by those with more education. This "Americanness" of (female) vocal fry seems to be something picked up on both sides of the Atlantic. A study examining actresses' accents when they portrayed British versus American characters, such as Gwyneth Paltrow in *Shallow Hal* versus in *Sliding Doors*, found that American actresses used vocal fry in their American but not British roles, showing that fry has social nuances for which one needs to be culturally savvy.

While it may be the case that vocal fry is more common in American women's voices, what we don't have is a lot of data on whether vocal fry is actually increasing in prevalence, despite

---

* The idea to combine the reach and easy access of the smartphone with linguistic analysis is recent but has been used not only for data collection but even to assess the likelihood that one might have COVID-19 (via measurable vocal changes) or to monitor illnesses as wide ranging as depression and Parkinson's.

our firm conviction that it is. Instead, it very well might be part of what has been labeled as a "recency illusion" by linguist Arnold Zwicky. What this means is that it simply appears to be a new thing because you only just noticed it. You might have been blissfully unaware of its existence until someone pointed it out and—damn that someone!—now you can't unhear it. Couple our tendency toward recentism with the fact that we see discussion of creak as far back as the 1930s, as well as serious study of its use beginning in the 1970s, and vocal fry doesn't seem all that new. Unfortunately, there have not been any rigorous studies comparing speech from an earlier period to speech today to determine whether vocal fry use is actually increasing or just feels that way. The few studies we have just looking across different age groups are fairly inconclusive in terms of showing any trends that would suggest change. For instance, a 2016 study comparing young and middle-aged women suggests that there is not much difference between these two age groups in terms of creakiness, with both groups exhibiting a similar degree of vocal fry. Finally, reviews of creaky voice literature also fail to turn up much empirical support for an increase in prevalence of vocal fry. In fact, the tendency to focus only on young women's voices when it comes to studying creak might inadvertently create the appearance that women are frying more. In surveying previous research, speech pathologist Katherine Dallaston and linguist Gerard Docherty found that many studies examined young female college speakers to the exclusion of others at a rate of almost 3 to 1. This really makes it hard to say whether any vocal fry measured was more or less than in any other group of speakers, and strongly suggests male and older speakers' patterns of use might be undermeasured. So, our fear of fry's epidemic potential—and the alarm bells rung about its increase—seem somewhat unwarranted.

This doesn't necessarily mean that vocal fry isn't on the upswing in American speech (or elsewhere), just that we can't say that it indeed is. For we might also be suffering from the "frequency illusion," also coined by Zwicky, which suggests that once you notice something, you notice it seemingly everywhere. In other words, it might also be that fry has become more discernable to us rather than more frequent. What does seem to be the case, though, is that it is a voice type that establishes a particular social identity, and one that appeals to women, at least in the United States, more than men. And though vocal fry has been around in our speech for some time, it was less salient because men occupied professionally visible positions more often than women until quite recently. And since vocal fry requires one to drop down into a low-frequency range to get it going regardless of where in pitch one started, the greater frequency shift from a typically higher pitch for women would tend to increase its perceptual salience.* As a result of this greater shift drop,

---

* In fact, examining the differences in pitch drop of male and female participants between their normal voice register and their creaky voice register showed a

women using creaky voices would draw more notice as exceptional or atypical.

It might just be a figment of our imagination that vocal fry is actually on the increase, but we do have good empirical research that suggests it is definitely present in the speech of modern women and men. What might explain its attractiveness as a vocal style in American speech? One likely driver is that it is viewed as a feature that carries confidence and weight. Early research on perceptions, mainly in the UK and Australia, clearly showed a relationship between creaky voice and perceptions of authority and higher status. And turning to the perceptions that drive its current popularity in the American college-age population, Yuasa's research with young Californians suggested students hear fry as upwardly mobile, urban, and educated, a clear contrast to what *This American Life* listeners seem to take away from listening to it. This difference in perception says a lot about our own speech and social perspective. On the NPR show *Fresh Air*, Penny Eckert, a sociolinguist from Stanford, tells host Terry Gross that she was also not originally a fan of the way vocal fry sounded, but that her students report that they think it sounds authoritative. Her takeaway? Eckert realized she was probably just getting old and so didn't "get" what this speech style conveyed to younger speakers.

So what does it help convey to those who use it, beyond

---

significantly larger distance for women than for men in preliminary work by Shannon Melville and Cynthia Clopper (2015).

signaling that you are getting to the end of a sentence? Vocal fry, at least within the social cadre that does get it, can also be used affectively—signaling to others a certain attitude or how you feel about a situation or context. For instance, it can convey a disaffected or bored air, something also mentioned regarding its use by Received Pronunciation speakers in Britain in much earlier discussions of creaky voice, when phonetician John Laver suggested it gives the impression of bored resignation (something perhaps tied to its association with a higher-class affected vocal style). More recently it has been found to parlay a sense that you are relaxed or "chill," to quote an adjective frequently selected when exploring the social meaning of fry.* These meanings seem to be communicated particularly when fry is used throughout speech, or in a creaky-sounding "yeah" to signal acknowledgment of what was said, but disinclination to continue a topic further. In fact, it might be a shift in usage pattern— away from the far edge and into the center of our sentences—that draws our notice, especially since teens and their ilk are more inclined to use features in less typical ways. In other words, all creak is not created the same, but the pattern in terms of how it is distributed in a sentence seems to give listeners a clue to its users and its function.

---

* In a study by speech pathologist Clare Ligon and colleagues, which asked graduate students to assign adjectives to different voice qualities, vocal fry was heard as chill and relaxed, but also bored, vain, and disengaged, and some students also mentioned it as trendy and professional.

A wolf among the sheep?

The most common complaint about young women's perceived vocal habits is that they will undermine career advancement, lobbed not only by the usual language prescription suspects but perhaps more surprisingly, by those with feminist leanings as well. For instance, well-known liberal feminist writer Naomi Wolf penned a widely read article for *The Guardian* that made her side of the fence clear from the title: YOUNG WOMEN, GIVE UP THE VOCAL FRY AND RECLAIM YOUR STRONG FEMALE VOICE. Targeting not only vocal fry, but also women's breathier and higher-pitched voices, she spends much of the article blaming young women for qualities she, like much of society, associates with their voices—pronouncing young career women doomed by their soft-spoken, weak, run-on, and insecure uptalking. Her thesis is that women's voices are the problem that needs to be fixed to be successful in male-dominated areas like data analysis, leadership, and engineering. But she doesn't examine the larger issue of how our beliefs that these features lessen women's power and authority are tied to the historical view that women's voices don't belong in public spheres, nor does she consider whether these speech habits might be used by both men and women but policed more in women's voices. It is the fact that the ones talking are women, not the voice quality, that damns young women in the workplace from the get-go.

A lot of the press about how vocal fry ruins women's job prospects emerged after a study published in the scientific journal *PLoS One* reported that the use of vocal fry came across as less competent, educated, and hirable. Such listener judgments were taken to suggest that women would be disadvantaged in the labor market.* Though the article showed male fry also decreased listener ratings, the effect was larger for women, and the whole men-fry-too part seems not to have made the cut for popular press coverage. While it might indeed be the case that some people find fry unprofessional (especially, it seems, on the radio), this study asked speakers to imitate fry when creating the stimuli voices, which is a questionable way to ascertain people's perception of a feature that has a specific pattern and form in natural speech. This is a lot like asking non-Southerners to put on a Southern drawl and then being surprised that raters liked their natural voices better.

But despite its shortcomings, what such research shows is that we are very socially aware of voice differences. In particular, we are quick to evaluate women on voice qualities, while men rarely get called out for features like creaky voice. And when we look at preferences for voice pitch more generally, research overwhelmingly finds that we are a heck of a lot more

---

* Suggesting listener response to speakers is more complex than just such a single dimension, a different study showed that vocal fry alone did not create unfavorable impressions of female speakers—voice pitch and whether they had a fast or slow speech rate were also key factors. For instance, when using a low pitch and slow speech rate, vocal fry actually increased ratings of intelligence and solidarity.

inclined to think highly of lower-pitched voices, especially for qualities that really count in the workplace.

Hey, Siri, why do you talk like a lady?

While one consequence of this is certainly that it affects women in terms of employment and promotion opportunities, these sorts of biases also affect how we create and interact with technology. For example, consider the development of synthetic voices. Why is Siri generally female (as the generic standard issue voice)? Why does our digital assistant go by the name of Alexa rather than Fred? And does it matter to us anyway, since we know these are not real voices?

It certainly seems that it does matter. For example, when BMW first introduced voiced navigation systems in cars in Germany, drivers were so unhappy with a synthetic female voice giving them directions, they demanded a product recall. Evil, commanding, or authoritative machines, such as HAL in *2001: A Space Odyssey* or AUTO in *Wall-E* are almost always male, whereas digital assistants that are designed to oblige and be helpful, like Siri and Alexa, are almost always female, as this is overwhelmingly the preferred synthetic voice—reflecting larger expectations and stereotypes. In a somewhat ironic twist given BMW's experience using a female voice for navigation, James Bond's highly specialized and custom-designed BMW in the movie

Tomorrow Never Dies included a soothing and obliging female voice—a feature the notoriously womanizing Bond very obviously enjoyed.*

Looking at this empirically, social and evolutionary psychology research indicates that acoustic properties of voice, and most especially pitch, are deeply intertwined with our assessment of a speaker's personality, gleaned even from something as simple as hearing a single "hello." A general finding in much of this work is that low-pitched voices are heard as more dominant, while high-pitched voices come across as more submissive and deferential. And in turn, this plays out in the finding that men receive higher ratings on attractiveness and status scales when they have lower-pitched voices. In contrast, while women tend to get better reviews on their looks and their youthfulness when they have a higher-pitched voice, a lower pitch improves their ratings on power-based qualities like leadership and assertiveness.† Sure makes "You had me at hello," to quote a famous line from the 1996 film *Jerry Maguire*, take on a whole new dimension.

The evolutionary psychologist would say this low-pitch power and status correlation reflects our association of low-frequency voices with larger body size, so that a deeper voice is taken as a

---

* To learn more about Bond, BMWs, artificial voices, and gender bias, a good read is "Why Your Voice Assistant Might Be Sexist," at bbc.com (bbc.com/future /article/20220614-why-your-voice-assistant-might-be-sexist).

† However, this is less consistent a finding than for men. For example, McAleer et al. (2014) found that Scottish raters felt higher-pitched women were more dominant.

proxy for physical dominance. As a result, at least according to evolutionary theories, lower-voiced men are more attractive to mates and more intimidating to their competition. But even in a world where we don't need to beat on our chests and emit low-pitched growls to prove our worth, lower-pitched voices, regardless of body size, still often translate into better rankings on dominance and authority scales. In essence, what might have been a sign of physical dominance at one point in our evolutionary history has now instead come to symbolize social dominance in the modern day.

Don't think social associations with pitch are that one-sided? Think again. A multitude of studies show people rate lower-pitched voices as more confident, competent, and authoritative, while high-pitched voices are heard as less competent, lower in status, and even less trustworthy. There is also research that suggests that lower voice pitch communicates leadership potential in work or organizational settings. One study in *The Journal of Experimental Psychology* showed that when subjects were given group tasks to accomplish, those adopting a higher pitch (from their baseline) while working on the task assumed a lower rank in the group, while those adopting a lower pitch took on higher-rank roles. Likewise, in a study published in *The Journal of Nonverbal Behavior* that compared how professionals changed their voices when taking on the role of "expert" rather than in regular conversation, speakers were found to lower their pitch when taking on an authoritative role. This was true of both sexes, but women actually lowered their pitch more than men. The end result? Lowered-pitch voices were heard as relatively more competent and authoritative, but the perception bump was greater for men, even though they actually changed their pitch less. It seems that women feel more pressure to lower their voice to be taken seriously, but still don't benefit as much as men when they do.

Our preference for lower-pitched voices also guides other aspects of our behavior—for example, predicting our mating preferences. A number of studies have shown that we have strong voice-pitch preferences when picking a date, with lower-pitched men and higher-pitched women coming out on top in terms of mate selection. From an evolutionary perspective, this presumably began based on the cues that voice pitch and voice quality could provide about physical attributes such as body size, health status, and age, all things that might factor into picking a young, healthy, and fertile mate. While such criteria are probably not at the top of the list when screening prospective dates on Tinder, these preferences for voices still seem to guide whether we find someone attractive.

And that's not all—all these various associations with voice pitch also play into our preferences for things as unexpected as whom we vote for. In an experiment where the voices of former U.S. presidents were acoustically manipulated into higher- and lower-pitched versions, subjects were much more likely to vote for the lower-pitched versions compared to the higher-pitched versions. In other studies, a similar pattern of low-pitched preference in presidential candidates was found to be particularly true for conservative voters and in conservative countries, compared to those with more liberal leanings. The evolutionary psychology take on this pattern is that this is due to a conservative outlook on the world as more dangerous, thereby requiring a more powerful leader, with deeper voices again standing as proxy for dominance. In several studies that looked at the outcome of actual elections, this type of vocal preference held out—candidates with lower-pitched voices were more likely winners of elections ranging from senatorial races to presidential contests. Outside of politics, in studies of preferred traits in business leaders, lower-pitched CEOs were found to lead larger companies and make more money.* A lot more money, in fact. Of course, it is exactly this type of social conditioning and economic incentive that makes women feel that they need to change their speaking style and harkens back to admonitions on women to avoid sounding "shrill."

As more women move into professional contexts where lower voices and men long held the floor, it is not surprising they are making more use of the bottom part of their pitch range to capture some of the benefit of the qualities associated with low

---

* William J. Mayew, Christopher A. Parsons, and Mohan Venkatachalam studied almost eight hundred CEOs, finding that a pitch drop of 22 hertz was associated with a "$440 million increase in the size of the firm managed, and in turn, $187 thousand more in annual compensation." Now that is the kind of pay raise worth lowering one's voice for. See "Voice Pitch and the Labor Market Success of Male Chief Executive Officers," *Evolution and Human Behavior* 34 (2013).

pitch. Because what does using a high-pitch voice gain for women? Not much professionally, unless someone thinking you're hot is the key to your success. Of course, this creates a problem for women that doesn't exist for men—men with lower-pitched voices get to enjoy both dominance and attractiveness. The problem for women is that we have set up a system where they are always on the losing side, as we view pitch characteristics that are more prevalent in women, such as higher or more variable pitch, as deferential and emotional even if attractive.* Then, when women try to adopt features such as low pitch, they are also viewed negatively because of its sociocultural baggage as a masculinized norm. Pretty much a no-win situation if you happen to be on the wrong side of the gender divide.

So those of the female persuasion find themselves in a double bind. While actor Josh Brolin might be able to pull off playing macho demigod Thanos *and* the president of the United States with his singular low pitch, for women there is a continual conflict between the competence and dominance associated with low pitch and the vocal attractiveness associated with high pitch. You might be able to talk like Marilyn Monroe and gain a lot of

---

* Women, without the pressure to come across as physically powerful, might be freer to use their natural range, and this might be why we associate women with greater pitch variability, giving rise, most likely, to the stereotype of women and emotionality. But the reason women have more pitch volatility is not hysteria but history—the pressure to speak with mainly a monotone low voice has been more salient for men, at least until recently. As well, using a higher range of the acoustic spectrum (as women's voices typically do) creates some compression of the sound waves perceptively, requiring women to make larger frequency shifts to achieve the same perceived shift in loudness to a listener.

admirers, but they probably won't vote you into office or hire you as CEO. As a result, professional women have to navigate this type of voice bias in areas like broadcasting, politics, and business, fields traditionally dominated by men, where there is a delicate balance between being professional and being feminine, with pitch playing a pivotal role.

All of this suggests why vocal fry seems to be on our radar so much all of the sudden: Vocal fry is a low-pitch style, meaning that it is only possible when a speaker shifts to a lower-pitched register. By using fry, you can have an excursion into using low pitch while still maintaining a higher average pitch overall—two birds, one stone. Just call it a creative way to solve the high pitch/ more attractive, low pitch/more dominant conundrum that young women in the workforce face. In other words, using a bit of fry is a compromise between still sounding like a woman while talking like a man for career success.

We certainly see evidence of young female role models using fry and pitch to inculcate a more professional persona. For example, a number of news outlets reported on a shift in Ivanka Trump's use of low-pitched register and vocal fry as she took on more extensive roles in her father's presidency. Likewise, media reports also comment on how Paris Hilton had much higher pitch in her early TV appearances than in her later, more mature appearances, where she uses some vocal fry. And then, of course, there are the frequent frying Kim, Kourtney, and Khloe of the Kardashian empire. Though perhaps not the poster children for serious professionalism, these women are under similar pressure as other young women who are rewarded for femininity on some levels, but punished for it on others, particularly when trying to be taken seriously.

Fry really is fly

Of the many speech tics that are covered in this book, vocal fry might just be the one that is the vocal equivalent of nails on a chalkboard to those who have taken a dislike to the feature. And those who use it—for instance, the journalists who talked about how all the haters made them feel self-conscious on the special episode of *This American Life*—have been shamed into vocal insecurity. But as should be clear by now, vocal fry is neither pathological nor detrimental, and it is far from exclusively female despite the lack of noise about men's use. What it is, instead, is a way to have one's voice heard in domains where women and high pitch have, to quote *Star Trek*, never gone before.

Of a young woman she quotes who claims to use uptalk to please older authority figures, Naomi Wolf laments that "surely we older feminists have not completed our tasks if no one has taught this young woman that it was not her job to placate her elders." Ironically, Wolf herself, and all those who decry fry, are expecting just that—that young women speak like older professional men and women want them to, rather than assert their own style and identity by using features that have naturally evolved to serve functional and social needs in their own speech. When young men use vocal fry (and, trust me, they do), take up the conversation floor (ditto), or even use voices that violate expected norms, where are the articles decrying the downfall of man? Instead, they get articles in *GQ* titled "Male Celebrities with Surprisingly High Voices: A Celebration." In other words, no one is telling Mike Tyson he needs to sound more like a man to be successful.

Though we may not notice it, fry is also a tool in a young man's toolbox. As we become more used to it—and given how we now seem to notice it everywhere, we will—it will become the new normal, and our current disfavor will fade away. So, again, don't like it? Wait a generation or so and you won't remember what you found so unpleasant about it. If you use it yourself? Consider yourself ahead of the game and stop apologizing for it. And looking to the future, perhaps when we elect our first female president, it will be that low-pitched creak in her voice that finally got her our vote. Or maybe, just maybe, it will be the qualities of the woman, and not the sound of her voice, that guides our choice.

8

Who Are *They*?

Merriam-Webster declared it *the* word of the year in 2019, and the American Dialect Society named it the word of the decade. Newspapers and magazines have recently changed their protocols and usage manuals to make room for it. Controversies have been ignited by it. What is this powerful and mysterious new word, you ask? No, it's not the name of some earth-shattering new invention or technology. It's not *cryptocurrency, Zoom,* or *Siri.* Instead, the most contested word of our time is a simple little pronoun that's been around for centuries. But in a testament to how language evolves to meet the needs of all its speakers, *they* used in the singular form has become somewhat of a linguistic celebrity, making headlines and changing editors' minds when deciding to whom *they* can refer.

In contrast to words that entered our language to help us tackle emerging frontiers of technology and science, singular *they* arose to offer a solution to an old and intractable problem—that of the limits of the English pronominal system. And while the use of *they* in this way is certainly a different kind of linguistic feature than the ones we've been talking about, how could we not come full circle in our discussion of language and innovation by considering what, despite centuries of prescriptive proscriptions, led to one of the most useful linguistic developments of the twenty-first century?

Just as with *dude* and *like*, there is a surprising linguistic backstory behind the evolution of *they* and all our other English pronouns. Although most of us tend to think of words like *you*, *they*, *he*, and *she* as being pretty stalwart and stable, the reality is that the pronouns we use when talking about ourselves and about others have changed vastly over the past thousand years. What is most revealing about tracing the patterns of our pronominal past is that our yearning for a way to talk about people without gender getting in the way is not as new as we think it is. Nor is the "immoral" and "ungrammatical" party line often invoked to argue against using pronouns in a novel way. Looking back, we will see that our pronouns have been no stranger to drama, and the often bumpy road to modern *they* has involved a cast of characters ranging from Vikings to British lords to literary giants, and of course, not just a few grammarians. Translation: *they* ain't scared of a little controversy.

A *they* for every occasion

Pronouns, it seems, are everywhere these days. On name tags, on signature lines, on emails, in the newspaper. Everyone wants to know which ones you use, and for some on the far side of the millennial generation, this can be awkward and uncertain territory. Part of what makes people uneasy is the lack of clarity around what choosing one's pronouns means exactly—and the necessity to wrest back control from our inner grammar nerd. So, to help us unpack this new pronominal world, we need to understand why changing pronouns are simply par for the course in the history of English.

Before we go digging into our past, let's dive into what all the modern fuss is even about. Why do we regularly find headlines mulling its uptake, like the recent *Time* magazine article "This Is Why Singular 'They' Is Such a Controversial Subject." Or even more to the point, the opinion piece featured in *The Atlantic*, "The Singular 'They' Must Be Stopped!"* Though more and more respected language authorities like dictionaries and the APA, MLA, and Associated Press style guides have welcomed singular *they* into the fold, its appropriateness for use

---

* Since this article was written in 2013, author Jen Doll has tweeted that, after others helped expand her perspective on singular *they*, she changed her mind about its grammatical acceptability.

in a singular capacity continues to be hotly debated by grammarians.*

Part of the complication is that there are different ways in which singular *they* has been used over time. The first more familiar and somewhat less controversial one is the use of *they* as what is called an epicene or unisex pronoun, meaning basically a replacement for generic *he* or the clunky *he/she*. This type of *they* is often used when the gender of the person being talked about (the antecedent) is nonspecific, as in, *A student should study hard if they want to succeed.* Such usage seems fine to most people, especially if used in spoken language or casual writing. In contrast, the allegedly generic *he* seems cumbersome and exclusionary in the same context: *A student should study hard if he wants to succeed.* It is the inherent tendency to read "he" here as, well, a he, that really promotes the use of a more gender-neutral *they*. Most of us use *they* as a singular form in our everyday conversations without even being aware of it.

Such usage is even expanding to more formal writing, especially from the pens (or keyboards) of the young. This, of course, is where we start getting into the gray area of whether people

---

* Of course, there is an entirely separate debate about the validity of the social identity represented by *they* used in a nonbinary way. Here, we approach the topic from a linguistic and grammatical perspective, as this book takes the view that language develops to meet the needs of its speakers—and that this innovative capacity of language to represent the gender diversity of speakers is a strength, not a detriment.

find its use acceptable or not. I fall firmly on the side of singular *they,* as do a growing number of my English professor colleagues. Papers turned in for my classes almost always evidence some *they* in places where *he* or *she* used to be, and if I marked them in red, which I typically don't, I would likely have that student in my office asking what was wrong with it ten minutes after class let out. And who would I be to cast stones? I readily own up to using *they* regularly, and unfailingly when talking about anyones, everyones, and someones.

This type of nonspecific usage is now becoming so common that only hard-core prescriptivists get worked up over it anymore. But, never ones to sit grammatically idle for long, the novel use that seems to agitate naysayers these days is the expansion of the pronoun *they* to refer to a person whose gender identity is neither strictly male nor female, contrasting *they* with the constraining confines of *he* or *she*. While evidence of *they* in generic contexts has been with us for about seven hundred years, using *they* as this type of nonbinary alternative appears to be a very recent innovation,* which might explain why some still find it hard to use. We have had several hundred years to get used to *they* in its generic form, but many are still working on getting comfortable with the cultural and grammatical shift that

---

* The *Oxford English Dictionary* first notes it in 2009 in a tweet ("What about they/them/theirs") by @thebutchcaucus, though it certainly was used before that, particularly in trans and nonbinary speech communities. Still, at most, we're looking at a few decades of familiarity.

rides shotgun to *they* in this new role. Not to mention the number and gender agreement quandary it seems to present.

As with many of the innovative linguistic features that catch our attention, part of the term's attraction is precisely its socially symbolic function. In discussing their use of *they* instead of gendered pronouns, Daniel, a friend living in the Bay Area, tells me that using traditional pronouns reinforced the dichotomizing separation of masculinity and femininity that they felt did not represent who they were. Discovering the pronoun *they* a few years ago felt like finding part of themselves that had linguistically been rendered invisible. So, when others make the effort to use *they* when referring to them, Daniel feels really seen and affirmed. Who they are is being represented and, importantly, acknowledged by others.

Despite the social dexterity it offers, research suggests *they*'s use in reference to a specific person stands out more than a generic use because, for some, it leads to a grammatical clash. In their work looking at changes to singular *they* over time, linguist Kirby Conrod found using *they* to refer back to proper names like John, Kelly, or Sue seemed to evoke the most negative ratings in terms of grammatical acceptability compared to generic uses like "the ideal student" or "each professor." Their work suggested that there is a cline of acceptability determined by how strongly marked for gender an antecedent is. For instance, "Sue was waiting for their coffee" was more difficult for some respondents than a context like "That teacher always spills their coffee," with a definite antecedent (e.g., "that teacher") whose gender might be known or unknown. But this was still less acceptable than using *they* as a truly generic pronoun, i.e., "Everyone spills their coffee sometimes." Not so surprisingly, Conrod's research found that age played a role in how acceptable people found these different pronoun patterns. Millennials and those born after were the least bothered by *they* that referred back to proper names, while older speakers found this use less grammatically acceptable. This suggests that, like many of the features we've already encountered, for younger speakers, nonbinary *they* is becoming a natural part of their grammar, while older speakers experience it as grammatically incongruent and need to reset a few things to make it work. Their research also pointed to greater acceptance and use of *they* among transgender and nonbinary respondents, reminding us that language change often takes root in our most boundary-pushing groups.

Living on the edge

Just as we saw with the rise of the modern *dude* from its association with zoot-suit counterculture, subcultures are very powerful progenitors for language change because speakers on the social edges have little to lose linguistically and much to gain, both from a perspective of earning recognition and establishing community. The push for adopting language to increase linguistic visibility of nonconforming gender started really taking hold in genderqueer writer and activist communities in the 1990s,* with writer Kate Bornstein's 1994 *Gender Outlaw: On Men, Women, and the Rest of Us* explicitly articulating the need for nonbinary language and pronouns. This push for both social and linguistic recognition of nonbinary identity has overlapped the wider feminist movement toward more gender neutrality in English that started in the 1970s, with shifts toward terms like the nongendered *chairperson* and *flight attendant*. Language change is part and parcel of social change, dynamically reflecting it and fueling it at the same time, so it should be no surprise that as we have become more gender aware, changes to our pronouns—from including *she* with *he* or introducing *they*—have arrived alongside.

Certainly, the idea of a utopian world in which gender is irrelevant or more fluid is not a new one. The concept of androgyny became prominent in the 1970s and '80s, both in the fantasy worlds of writers, starting with Ursula Le Guin's 1969 classic *The Left Hand of Darkness*, which portrayed gender-bending aliens (though still called *he*), and in pop culture more widely (think Boy George or glam rock). We also have plenty of

---

* An early and influential discussion of genderqueer identity—referring to "gender outlaws" that do not identify within the socially constructed he-she dichotomy—can be found in writer-activist Leslie Feinberg's short work *Transgender Liberation*, which called for acceptance of a range of types of gender variation.

evidence that gender fluidity has been around far longer than this modern conception, as nongender-conforming Hijras in India, eunuchs in Europe, and Machi in South America attest. The concept of gender variation beyond the framework of just *he* and *she* has existed a lot longer than English has had terms that adequately incorporate it, an open door to linguistic innovation if ever I've seen one.

As nonbinary *they* use has increased, so has the backlash to using *they* this way, with arguments against it ranging from its lack of necessity to its ungrammaticality in singular form to its association with an identity that some are simply unwilling to accept. Yet, whether or not one feels ready to embrace its use, the linguistic story behind the development of our modern pronominal system offers us the long view that this isn't our pronouns' first time at the rodeo of competing public opinion.

The battle cry of prescriptivism

Early grammatical sticklerism over pronouns started back in the sixteenth century, when influential grammarian William Lily wrote in support of the supremacy of *he*, borrowing from Latin what to him seemed most obvious—that masculine forms should be elevated above all others. Luckily, *she* took precedence over *it*, so at least women ranked higher than animals and things. This sentiment (known as the worthiness doctrine) was later taken up by eighteenth-century male prescriptivists such as Robert Lowth,* Lindley Murray, and John Kirby, who found particularly distasteful the practice of using the clumsy and cumbersome co-allocated *he or she* or the agreement-violating *they*.

The pronoun debates of this century were of course not driven by the interests of gender equity (which was, unfortunately for women of the era, not yet really a thing), but more an attempt to correct what was seen as a grammatical shortcoming of English— namely, the lack of a way to have pronouns properly agree in *both* number and gender when referring to mixed or undetermined sex. To take an oft-quoted linguistics example, "Everyone loves his mother," "his" in this sentence grammatically only agrees with a segment of "everyones," assuming women and nonbinary folks love their mums as well.† As the mother of a teen girl, I am not sure of the veracity of that statement, but let's just assume it so for the sake of argument. In contrast, the widely used (even in the eighteenth century) singular *they* in this context ("Everyone loves their mother") would instead violate the

---

* To be fair, Bishop Robert Lowth has gotten a bad rap over the years as the great-grandfather of prescription. Sociohistorical linguist Ingrid Tieken-Boon van Ostade's research suggests that Lowth was not trying to be prescriptivist in writing his famous grammar, but just wanted to help illuminate the rules of English to serve his son in his studies of Latin. And don't we all just want to give our kids a leg up where we can? Still, describing and documenting the grammar of a language does set the bar a bit high for the rest of us parents, who feel that reading *Llama Red Pajama* twice in a row gets the job done.

† It is also the case that "his" here leads to what is referred to in semantics as scope ambiguity, meaning that the sentence could mean either that everyone loves his own mother or that everyone loves one particular individual's mother.

grammatical rule requiring pronouns to agree in number. Going with generic *he* was deemed the lesser of two evils, at least to a bunch of men arguing over grammar rules.

This disdain for the disarray of eighteenth-century pronouns was part of a larger movement of the time toward linguistic "purity" and standardization. The intense focus on grammatical rights and wrongs accompanied a changing class structure with increased access to literacy, education, and economic opportunities, which made those at the top of the food chain a little uneasy. Language was one of the few remaining clear markers discerning the haves and have-nots. Establishing standards and writing grammar books based on upper-crust norms was a great way of cementing one's status linguistically and socially. Add to this a strong interest by the growing middle class in glomming on to anything that might help them with upward mobility, and a booming business in dictionaries, usage guides, and linguistic etiquette was born. Not a bad way to solidify your dominant position while making a solid buck at the same time.

This push toward prescriptivism with generic *he* culminated in an Act of Parliament in 1850, known as the Act of Interpretation or Lord Brougham's Act,* declaring *he* the proscribed correct generic pronoun (a similar act was passed a few years later in the United States). The motivation? To decrease the wordiness

---

* Or by its amusingly long-winded full title, "An Act for Shortening the Language Used in Acts of Parliament."

in Acts of Parliament, a problem obviously driven by that pesky need to add in the "or she" when it was relevant once every decade or so. Of course, getting rid of long-winded politicians would have done more toward that purpose. But this raises the question of how we should refer to a room full of men in powdered wigs making laws about the gender of a generic pronoun. Might I suggest *they*?

And the pronoun war wages on

This legislation was by no means the end of the fight over generic *he*. As many an English teacher has learned, instructing people on what they "should" say and what they actually say are often at odds. Our speech has long had a habit of sidestepping any efforts to contain it, as language standardization efforts are often post hoc attempts at control. And once the proverbial *they* got out of the bag, it was hard to get it back in. By the twentieth century, the argument over generic *he* and its alternatives moved from being about grammar to being about gender representation. As sociologist Ann Bodine wrote in an influential article discussing the androcentrism surrounding efforts to relegate the use of alternatives to generic *he*, two hundred years of focused grammarian effort still could not halt the use of singular *they* or *he or she* among those not satisfied to leave at least half of the population out to linguistic pasture.

But that doesn't mean many a so-called language expert wouldn't try. In the 1970s, two female divinity students at Harvard challenged classmates in one of their courses to avoid the use of masculine generic terms, complete with paper noisemakers to blow whenever the ban was violated. In a well-publicized rebuff of their effort to bring attention to male-centered language, the Harvard linguistics faculty wrote an open letter to the newspaper *The Crimson* mansplaining the basics of linguistic markedness (meaning s*he* stands out) and informing these linguistically wayward women that the masculine generic is "simply a feature of grammar." They followed with the patronizing sentiment that it is "no cause for anxiety or pronoun-envy on the part of those seeking such changes."

Despite the Harvard linguists' argument to the contrary, part of the problem with generic *he* as an inclusive pronoun is that historically it has only been treated as inclusive when it served the interests of men. For example, according to linguist Dennis Baron in his book *What's Your Pronoun?*, the suffragette Susan B. Anthony argued that if *he* only referred to men in terms of voting rights, why did it not then also exclude women when it came to taxation and criminal penalties? While this argument did not prevent her arrest, it did highlight a double standard behind claiming the pronoun *he* could stand for all people, but mainly when it suited those of the male persuasion—for instance, when used to challenge the right of women to sit for the bar exam (as happened in Maryland) or to win a congressional seat (as in Montana) on the basis of a *he*. While lip service, like that of the Harvard professors, might be paid to *he* representing all people, that has certainly not been the experience of many whose rights have been trampled on by a pronoun.

The function of pronouns in the crafting of important documents and laws is not superficial or just a thing of the past. The Constitution, for instance, problematically refers to elected members of our government, from the president to Congress, only as "he." This male-centric language reveals a culturally ingrained bias many female politicians have worked hard to overcome. Politicians like Elizabeth Warren, Hillary Clinton, and Kamala Harris, in using feminine pronouns in place of the generic *he* when talking about the duties of a future president, have called attention to language's part in normalizing men in that role. Using pronouns that only reference a portion of our population, excluding both women and those whose identities fall outside the male/female binary, has increasingly come under scrutiny. In fact, upon taking office as California's attorney general, Harris had all legislated *he* references to the position changed to more inclusive pronouns as part of her attempt to bring language in line with the face (and gender) of modern politics.

All these attempts at prescriptivism and subsequent language reform have certainly brought attention to the lack of equity inherent in the use of a masculine generic. But this leads us to the question of why *they* has emerged as such a long-standing and strong contender. For that, it seems, we must begin by thanking the Vikings.

A brief history of *they*

Though the pronoun *they* is now a well-established part of English, it wasn't always that way. Old English had multiple ways to refer to *me, us, you, it,* and *him,* but not to *them,* a pronoun we instead inherited from Old Norse via our Scandinavian friends when they came on holiday to the balmy British Isles. Although we arguably could have lived without the accompanying looting and pillaging, it was very handy to have a new way to talk generically about a group of people, as Old English just wasn't hitting the mark. While Anglo-Saxons certainly had lots of conversations about third parties not present (notably, "Beware the Vikings!"), they relied on a derivative of the Old English third-person singular masculine pronoun *he* (*heo* for feminine), which appeared typically as *hi* or *hie.* Problematically, *he, heo,* and *hi,* especially after the loss of grammatical gender and other weakening processes started in the twelfth century, sounded pretty much the same.*

As a result, the early issue with pronominal reference was not

---

* Case on pronouns would have been marked as well, giving rise to a number of varying forms, but *he, heo,* and *hi/hie* are the nominative (or subject) case forms.

gender identity but preserving grammatical distinctions that were being lost due to sound changes. In a letter dated 1844, London Philological Society founder Edwin Guest noted that older texts from several dialects confused the highly similar-sounding masculine and feminine singular pronouns, particularly in cases where unspecified (male/female) subjects were discussed. As an example, he points to the poetry of Edmund Spenser, which uses *her* for *he* in his pastoral poem *September*, a common trait of West Country dialects. According to Guest, this habit was not a particularly favorable one, at least in the eyes of grammarians like Samuel Johnson, who likened Spenser's words to "studied barbarism." It appears that not much has changed in the jaded view of prescriptivism.

It was also very common for feminine and masculine pronoun confusion to be in the direction of *he*, which perhaps men found more acceptable, but ended up being a bit confusing when talking about one's true love. Linguists Thomas Pyles and John Algeo cite just such an example, "Bote he me wolle to hir take," meaning "Unless she will take me to her," as written by an anonymous lovelorn poet in the late thirteenth- or early fourteenth-century lyric poem "Alysoun." Of course, when we find variations like this appearing in written documents, it is very probable that the confusion was even more pronounced when speaking. This overlap between the Old English pronunciation of *he* and *heo* is hypothesized to have been the motivation of the development of a more discernable female pronoun, namely *she*.* And of course, also what inspired the need for a new and more distinguishable third-person plural pronoun. And through this open pronoun door entered *þei*, the early form of our contemporary *they*, first appearing around the thirteenth century in texts written in northern British dialects with extensive Old Scandinavian (Norse) influence. The *þ* that graces *þei* is the letter known as "thorn," and it was used in Old English to represent a *th* sound.

At first, *þei* was only used to denote that our third parties were indeed plural, as in, more than one *he* or *she*. But by the fourteenth century, singular *they* referring to an unidentified person had begun to make an appearance. We find the first example of this type of *they* in the poem "William and the Werewolf," namely "*þei* neyȝþed so neiȝh," translatable, for those of us whose Middle English is a bit rusty, as "'til they grew near," a reference back to an earlier singular subject, "each man."

From this point on, singular *they* can be found increasingly in every century that follows. We see it, for instance, in a very early manuscript of *The Canterbury Tales*, where, in the Pardoner's Prologue, singular "whoso," meaning "whoever," is referenced in the next line as "they." As well, in the Knight's Tale, Chaucer

---

* The path to modern *she* is pretty murky. Some suggest it developed from the masculine *he*, while others suggest it came from *seo*, the feminine form of the demonstrative pronoun. There is also an etymological underdog that has been proposed—namely, *si* (pronounced "she") from Irish English. What does not seem in doubt is that the emergence of *she* was tied to the confusing similarity among the original OE third-person pronouns in the twelfth and thirteenth centuries.

falls back on *they* instead of *he* when referring back to "euery wight," translating roughly to "every person":

> *Made euery wight to been in swich plesaunce*
> *That al that Monday iusten they and daunce**

And who can blame Chaucer for trying to come up with a creative solution for how to refer back to indefinite pronouns such as *whoever, anybody, everyone, anyone,* or *each*? Though we might not talk about knights or whosos quite as often, we still use this very same strategy when talking about *somebody* and *everyone*. And as it turns out, Chaucer was just the beginning of a great literary tradition.

Sir Walter Scott was known to do it too, as was Lord Byron. Jane Austen even got in on the action, so enthusiastically in fact that there is a website devoted to tracking how often she did it. While this certainly suggests someone has way too much time on their hands, it also provides a useful measure of how often celebrated writers used singular *they* in works held in high esteem. In addition to use by these notable figures, singular *they* also can be found in venerated works produced by Dickinson, Swift, Dafoe, and Shakespeare. Singular *they* has, very early on, been quite successful at fulfilling our need to talk about people

---

* Found in the fourth part of the Knight's Tale, reading as "Made every person to be in such delight, That all that Monday they joust and dance."

without having to talk about their gender. If it was good enough for the Bard, not to mention the King James Bible, who are we to stand in *they*'s way?

What's *ze* problem?

But as has been suggested by many an exasperated grammarian, why not just come up with an entirely new pronoun—one that violates no rules of agreement? Surely, if we can create new words like *she* or *Ms.* that seem to have stuck around, if Lewis Carroll can *chortle* from *chuckling* and *snorting*, and Jonathan Swift can come up with *Yahoo* (just look at it now!), creating one tiny little new pronoun shouldn't be a problem, right? Well, been there, done that, and pretty much to no avail. According to Dennis Baron (aka Dr. Pronoun), who keeps a running list of the invented terms proposed since the eighteenth century, more than two hundred alternatives for a gender-neutral third-person singular term have been suggested.* None have had the impact, or the promise for longevity, of singular *they*.

But it certainly hasn't been for lack of trying. In 1912, one Dr. Funk of *Standard Dictionary* fame, wrote *The Chicago Daily Tribune* enthusiastically supporting the coinage of a new "common gender" pronoun reported in the previous week's

---

* Such new pronoun coinages are also referred to as neopronouns.

paper. As it would turn out, the new words, *he'er*, *him'er*, and *his'er*, came from Ella Flagg Young, superintendent of Chicago schools, who decided to take the lack of a generic pronoun to task. In the article reporting the inspiring coinage, Young allegedly "made principals gasp" (in pleased astonishment) with his'er creative combination of *he/his/him* with the female *her*. While these blended forms didn't end up catching on, it was definitely a memorable two-for-one. And *he'er* was certainly an improvement over the common gender suggestion *hor* (and, yes, pronounced just the way you think it is), made by a correspondent to the *Tribune* in 1890. I can't imagine why that one didn't quite catch on.

Dr. Baron also cites *ne*, *nis*, and *nim* as some of the earliest documented examples of unisex pronouns and dates them back to roughly 1850. Since most of us don't use *ne* except to form negatives in French, the life span of these terms was clearly not too impressive. Slightly longer-lasting success at coining a new singular pronoun was achieved by lawyer and concerned citizen of grammar Charles Converse, who counted hymn-writing as well as legalese among his talents. In 1858, Converse came up with another combination of existing words, namely *thon*, from *that + one,* in deference "to the beautiful symmetry of the English tongue and a due reverence for etymologic consistency." Now, *thon*, though never as pervasive as singular *they*, was brought out on occasion here and there when discussion came up about the need for a third-person pronoun. In fact, it appears to have been momentarily influential in the late nineteenth/early twentieth century, when it not only made it into several dictionaries (including an edition of *Webster's*) and was applauded by a number of notable professors, but was also used in writings by the founders of chiropractic medicine, Bartlett and Daniel Palmer. Thus, it was not only talked about, but in the spirit of language, was actually used, especially when a patient needed to get thon's back adjusted.

Not to be daunted by this recurrent lack of success, neologists (a fancy label for new-word creators) from all walks of life still enter the pronoun fray. Some even using the paradigm of pronoun coinages past. Who can forget, for instance, the (joking) suggestion in *Forbes* in 1976 that *he/she/it* simply be condensed to *h'orsh'it* for a common pronoun? More recently and using a different approach, D. N. DeLuna, a writing instructor at Johns Hopkins University, came up with the gender-neutral pronoun *hu* (pronounced "huh"), founding what *hu* called the Archangul Foundation to support *hu*'s diffusion into the world. DeLuna also simultaneously published an edited collection of academic essays that makes use of the *hu* pronoun (and includes papers with subheadings like "Why cyborgs have boobs," so it may not make everyone's reading list). The word, quite literally, does not seem to have gotten out. In a review of the book that appeared in an academic journal, *hu* is noted as "a misprint that curiously occurs several times in the text."

Working within alien or alternative worlds, science fiction

writers have always been a great source of inventive non-gendered terms as evidenced by the multiple writers who have taken up the use of the relatively popular *ze/hir* or *per*, short for "person," inspired by Marge Piercy's 1976 novel *Woman on the Edge of Time*, which imagines a nonbinary world of the future. And of course, the internet has proven fruitful as well, for example, spurring some popularity for the pronoun *ey* and its derivatives (*em, eir*), which caught on in the 1990s after mathematician Michael Spivak used them in a textbook (*The Joy of TeX*). But alas, few of these invented pronouns have picked up much steam outside of their originating subcultures of use. The problem is that constructed language is rarely as successful as that which evolves naturally. After all, you don't see Esperanto around much, do you? Along the same lines, it is hard to get the word out about a neologism, particularly when there are already functioning alternatives out there.

A more organic strategy in the face of the generic pronoun problem is the rise of *yo*, noted regularly in the speech of middle school and high school students. After hearing sentences like, "Yo handin' out the paper" in reference to the teacher and "Peep yo!" (translated into old-people-talk as "Look at him!"), teachers put together a study examining the growing use of this novel pronoun.* Since *yo* was not an invented but an emergent pronoun

---

* As mentioned in this study, *yo* has long had a number of other uses in vernacular speech, e.g., as a greeting ("Yo! What's hangin'?") or as an attention-focusing discourse marker ("Yo, he better watch himself"), but the *yo* discussed here shows a

that seems to have sprung without conscious effort from the mouths of babes, reminding us of the pattern of youth-led language change more generally, it already had more traction than *hu, ey,* or *he'er.* Like *they, yo* is a repurposed word already used in conversational speech, which tends to have a much better shot of being adopted by speakers.* Its continued slanginess and strong association with youth culture, however, will likely keep it from contention to unseat singular *they.*

As we can see, in the years since *ne, his'er,* and *thon,* many a new pronoun might have come and gone, but what really shifted was the sociocultural impetus that prompted the need for such pronouns. Though the early attempts behind invented words were driven by grammar concerns (and mainly men), later efforts at coinages often recognized that the use of generic *he* could be—gasp!—interpreted to exclude anyone not male. So, in the late 1960s and the '70s, the women's movement put some teeth behind the argument for a unisex pronoun as part of a larger reform movement that popularized the use of terms like *person* for "man" and *Ms.* for "Mrs." This effort spawned numerous ideas, running the gamut from *Ta* (from Chinese), *heris,*

---

novel repurposing specifically as a generic pronoun as in "Yo hit the floor." This probably developed from its discourse-marking use.

* As discussed in chapter 4, another example of an organically repurposed word used as a personal pronoun is *man* in place of "I" in Multicultural London English (MLE), where we also find the use of "mandem" to refer to a group of men (particularly when speaking of one's own male posse). Clearly given that these words derive from the use of the male-oriented term "man" in colloquial speech, they don't do much for those in search of nonbinary expression.

ve, co, na, tey, em, shem, to *zie.* A few of the suggested alternates, like *ze/zir* and *hir,* are still found with some frequency, particularly in trans, gender-fluid, genderqueer, or nonbinary social media forums.

Despite no lack of innovative efforts, singular *they* still looks to be the only nonbinary pronoun that has managed to slide past those in the trenches and the grammar gatekeepers and really stick. What might be the reason for *they*'s success where many invented pronouns have failed before? While we might not all see ourselves in *ze* or *thon* or *yo*, we have all, at one point or another, been part of *they.* Whether it's the *they* that refers to that generic "someone" or "anyone," or the *they* that names us along with our friends as troublemakers at school, or the *they* that transcends the gender binary, *they* is still that well-worn old pair of shoes resoled and shined up. They may feel a little different at first, but they are a hell of a lot more comfortable to put on than that new pair that gives you blisters because you've never worn them before.

In short, *they,* like so many of the changes that have taken root over the centuries to bring us to how we speak today, had natural linguistic evolution on its side. Since we already used *they* in other contexts, its expansion into a true unisex alternative synergistically developed from several hundred years of flexibility. The variations among pronouns throughout history remind us that language is remarkably adaptable. Add in a seismic cultural shift toward greater acceptance and legislated rights for different gendered communities, and voila, singular *they* becomes mainstream.

Why *they* is the new *you*

While it might feel as if English pronouns have been chiseled in stone since time eternal, this is far from the first time our pronouns have shifted to adjust to a changing sociocultural landscape. When Moses (aka Charlton Heston) unveils the Ten Commandments in the movie of the same name, you might notice that the proclamations against killing, stealing, and coveting don't read exactly as they would in modern English. Instead, the stone tablets are inscribed with the pronouns *thou* and *thy* rather than the much more au courant *you* and *your*, a good reminder that *they* is not the only pronoun that has undergone a bit of an evolution over time. Echoing the hubbub surrounding the shift toward singular *they* today, getting from *thou* to *you* was no small feat and definitely had its fair share of semantic and social bumps in the road. So, to understand our problems with pronouns a bit more, it is well worth a diversion into the history of *you*, which, as double entendre would have it, is also the history of you.

During Middle English up through the beginning of the Early Modern period, the second-person pronoun paradigm was a veritable cornucopia of options. No simple "hey you" back then. First, you had to figure out the necessary number and case and then decide how polite you wanted to be to your addressee. In 1300, this meant you needed to know the difference between subjects (thou/ye) and objects (thee/you), something we still seem to have problems with in modern English when it comes to deciding things like whether it is "Zoe and I" or "Zoe and me" going to the party.* By the time that all was figured out, you had already forgotten what you were going to say. So it is no surprise that by around the seventeenth century, we had gotten wise and figured out we really just needed to call people *you* and leave it at that. Away with all this fancy *thou/thee/ye/you* stuff. This transformation toward a less complicated second-person pattern started as far back as the thirteenth century, when *you* began slipping into use in singular *thou* territory, and was fairly complete by the eighteenth. Since language change never occurs in a social vacuum, a lot of what drove the shift away from the *thou* of our past was a realignment in cultural thinking about how society should work and changes toward a more egalitarian worldview. So what exactly happened to prod our pronouns toward democracy?

In Old English, the difference between the *thou/thee* set and *you/ye* set was pretty straightforward—basically whether the *you* in question was singular or plural. But then came the Norman French, and with them a new political and cultural climate. In French, the singular/plural (*tu/vous*) distinction also existed,

---

* And don't forget there was also the possessive, e.g., *thy* or *thine*.

but it was complicated by what has been referred to as power semantics, which is not only something we find in marital disagreements and Senate confirmation hearings, but also the way French linguistically paid heed to hierarchical relationships among speakers. When talking with a social superior, the plural (now polite) *you* form was used. Talking down in status, to lower classes or children, for instance, would elicit the singular *thou* form. *You* was reserved mainly for the influential and the powerful, while the rest of us were just *thou*. Over time, though, a solidarity semantic instead became popular, where using the *you* form with each other was viewed as a good way to be respectful and polite more generally (unless on more intimate terms), whereas shifting to *thou* was, to put it in modern English lingo, a good way to dis someone.

As a result of all this power negotiating and making nice, *you* expanded into a great many more contexts and was particularly directed to singular referents, where it had not been used as much before. When unsure of how to address someone, it was much safer to use the high-status *you* rather than risk insulting someone by the presumed informality of *thou*, unless that was the intention. For instance, Shakespeare's writings reflect this *you/thou* distinction, and he often used *you* and *thou* shifts to illustrate nuanced changes in character attitudes or relationships. In *Twelfth Night*, Shakespeare explicitly references the superior/inferior power dynamics of *thou* use when Sir Andrew Aguecheek is encouraged to use *thou* as a demeaning insult, "If thou thou'st him some thrice, it shall not be amiss." However, *thou* had begun to be lost in the everyday speech around him, evidenced by Shakespeare's own inconsistency in use in his works, and it became more of a rarity by the middle of the seventeenth century.

The demise of *thou/thee* was also nudged along by its uptake by the Society of Friends (aka the Quakers). Quaker founder George Fox suggested that the expanding use of *you* and the social realignment it represented were founded in sinful pride and spoken only by "idiots and fools." Instead, adherents were directed to use only what he referred to as "Plain Speech." *Thou*, as the humble form, was adopted as a symbol of the Quaker belief in the equality of all and the need for humility over vanity. A noble cause, but one that put the nail in the coffin for *thou*, as its association with Quaker speech did not do much for its popularity. Being a Quaker advocating language reform in the seventeenth century seems to have been about as popular as being a feminist divinity student at Harvard advocating much the same in the twentieth century.

So, much like the grumbling we still hear about using *they* in singular contexts today, the switch to *you* from *thou* did not happen without comment and concern from the language guardians of the day. George Fox and fellow friends feared the moral downfall of society it portended and warned that such use went against the will of God and Christ. And if that is not sounding a familiar note in tune with today's anti-*they* rhetoric, coming at it instead from the grammatical correctness angle, eighteenth-century grammarians like Robert Lowth and Lindley Murray decried the vulgar violation of using *you* when a good *thou* should do. Spiritual ruin and linguistic decay all in one fell swoop. Yet here *you* remains, and *thou* is all but a distant memory. And our language is seemingly none the worse for wear.

Verbal confusion

To anyone who came to this chapter with a bit of uncertainty about how to appropriately use nonbinary *they* in your daily life, you are not alone. Even those of us who are linguistically wizened had a thing or two to learn about how to respectfully approach *they* in this new way. For instance, the first time I encountered singular *they* used in a nonbinary way was a number of years ago in my role directing my department's graduate studies program. Part of my job was to recruit and woo prospective students. One particularly promising candidate already had a contract on a novel, making the student quite a catch for any graduate program. It was important, in other words, to make a good impression. Right before I went into a reception to meet and introduce around the applicants, another faculty member mentioned that this particular student had asked to be referred to as *they*. Having never been acquainted with the pronoun used in this way, I had a lot of trepidation around both how to use it and exactly how I should interpret it. For example, was the student expressing nonbinary gender identity themselves? Or just wanting not to be defined by the constraints of a traditional gendered ideology?* Was I supposed to use a singular or a plural verb? And lastly, what if I slipped up and used the wrong pronoun when introducing them to other students and faculty? I might be a formally trained linguist, but that didn't mean I knew how to navigate this uncharted territory any better than anyone else.

Truth be told, in this first experience using singular *they*, I admittedly had the kneejerk reaction of many a linguistic curmudgeon that using it was somehow grammatically incongruent. After all, I had gotten down pat using *they* as an indefinite pronoun instead of generic *he*, à la the "everyone one loves *their* mother" pattern, but this was different. This felt like a *they* as no *they* that had gone before sort of deal. But then I remembered—I have this system down too! I just didn't realize it. And so, it turns out, do you.

Many of us are completely on board with the desire to talk about third parties without making gender part of the equation. And if the grammatical aspect is making your head hurt, luckily, you've already been using a singular pronoun with a plural verb for most of your life. Namely, *you*, not you personally, but *you* the second-person pronoun.

---

* Of course, the reason they expressed their gender identity with the pronoun *they* is beside the point and was actually none of my business. However, in the interest of full disclosure of my first experience with using *they* in this way, it was part of my processing of this new form's use in context.

In another interesting parallel to our modern *they* conundrum, the early shift from *thou* to *you* goes from using *you* only for plural contexts (directed to more than one *you*) to using it as a singular, much like *they* today. Fine and dandy you say, we've already been over that. But now let's consider the problem of how we have been getting our verbal agreement to, well, agree. This is where past pronominal experience can help us understand how some people are simply overthinking it when it comes to *they*.

When using *you* today do you stop and stress about how you use a plural verb when referring to one person? In other words, do you say "you is" when talking to Maria, and switch to "you are" when their friend Tamika walks in the room? Probably not, and no one has ever called you out on your lack of proper subject-verb agreement. Singular *they* use is no different, other than the fact that this change is happening during your lifetime, while the change to *you* (and the acceptance of the plural verb alongside it) was over and done well before you were babbling your first syllables. So, if *you* can do this, so, it would seem, can *they*. All you need is a bit of practice.

They—a primer

One of the things I get asked a lot as a linguist is how or when to use nonbinary *they*, a question I too had when first introduced to the pronoun in its nonbinary function. So, here are a few pointers I have picked up over the years that might be helpful.* First, if you are not sure, just ask. Most people who use *they* are completely aware that this is new territory for those who are used to operating within the old *he/she* system. For example, when I start teaching at the beginning of a semester, I share my pronouns and simply tell my students to give me a heads-up about theirs—but I give them the option of saying nothing at all, saying something to the whole class, or just letting me know privately. And if you get it wrong, just apologize quickly and move along. Daniel, whom I mentioned earlier, admits to having used the wrong pronouns to self-refer in the middle of a business meeting after just having explained their preference for *they*. Compassion, they said, is key, and also why it's worth the effort to use the pronouns people have requested, even if it is not yet a choice you find grammatically easy to accommodate.

Remember those using the pronoun *they* are not one and the same; it can mean a variety of things ranging from seeing yourself as not fitting within the boundaries imposed by *he* or *she* to not wanting to play into traditional gender expectations. There is no one type of person who uses *they*. Finally, as just mentioned, go ahead and feel free to use plural verb agreement even for singular *they* use, i.e., "They are a good friend to me," rather

---

* For more tips, linguist and *they* expert Kirby Conrod has written several posts for Medium on pronouns and how to use them entitled "Pronouns 101" and "Pronouns 102."

than "They is." This both solves the internal grammatical struggle of how to use a formerly plural pronoun with a singular verb and makes it feel more natural to say. After all, in your years of using *they* as an epicene pronoun (e.g., "If anyone has a preference, they are welcome to share") you probably didn't waste much angst on subject-verb agreement. Like *you*, the shift to generic and nonbinary *they* will benefit from time and distance. As folks get used to using it in nonconventional contexts, such usages will become normalized and, as happened with the shift from *thou* to *you*, will no longer feel awkward.

They's future looks bright

Despite a lingering undercurrent of prescriptivist and social conservative dismay, it looks like *they*'s time has come. Beyond becoming sanctioned by grammar authorities like dictionaries and style guides, the true test of any novel form is whether it is shared and embraced not only in limited ways, but across age, gender, and class divides. And *they* seems to be breaking the glass ceiling. In 2019, Goldman Sachs, a Wall Street stalwart, announced an initiative to help bring pronouns to the forefront, not just for those with nonbinary gender identity, but for everyone. Tagged "Bring your authentic self to work: Pronouns," the company launched an effort to destigmatize pronoun diversity and foster a positive and supportive working environment for all gendered

273

identities. Their initiative included coaching on how to broach the subject with colleagues, lists of possible pronouns (ranging from the traditional *he/she*, singular *they*, and the coined gender-flexible *ze/hir*), and provided ways for gender fluid or nonconforming workers to self-identify in directories and documents. Even the friendly skies have gotten friendlier. When booking a trip on American or United Airlines, nonbinary choices allow passengers to be true to their identity. We also find the new openness to gender diversity extended to options for marking gender identity on identification cards in a number of places such as San Francisco, Washington, D.C., and New York.

English is not alone in this development—in Swedish, a coined form of a third-person generic *hen* now exists comfortably alongside feminine *hon* and masculine *han*. The experience in Sweden shows that initial opposition to such forms fades and a more favorable view and general use comes with time. And even in France, long known for its linguistic conservatism and efforts to preserve traditional language forms, the nonbinary pronoun *iel* (a combination of *il* and *elle*) was recently included in a prominent dictionary. The magic ingredient for success is, of course, our desire to make inclusivity and acceptance a priority. Arguments on the basis of grammatical incorrectness are, as we have seen throughout this book, often only cover for a discomfort with social changes or the groups that such linguistic changes represent. And get used to it we should, as although it may have taken about seven hundred years of evolution, our expanded use for the third-person pronoun appears to be here to stay. What might seem to some a sudden shift to a nonbinary meaning is in fact just the culmination of a long history of linguistic reinvention.

9

Linguistic Badasses

One time, at a linguistics conference, several colleagues and I were in the elevator wearing our shiny Linguistic Society of America name tags, heading down to the lobby. But before we made it there, the doors opened and a couple came in. After the wife assessed us with our gleaming conference badge bling, she remarked, "Oh, you all must speak a bunch of languages." After a brief pause, the entire elevator of linguists burst out laughing, not because what she said was not true (I am sure the elevator was packed with much multilingual ability), but because of how often linguistics is misunderstood to be about speaking languages, rather than about understanding language speakers. Speakers, and their social lives, are the force that drives the linguistic train, and as this book has shown, truly knowing about language means much more than knowing how to construct sentences or speak a foreign tongue. It means recognizing that identities and communities are built through very small aspects of our language use—along with the realization that, though we don't always like the way others talk, our disdain is rarely justifiable based on linguistic grounds.

So, as we come to the end of our tour of the speech habits we love to hate, let me pose to you one final question: What if, Cinderella-like, we were visited by a linguistic fairy godmother and were granted the chance to make one wish? Being an ambassador for the greater good, no doubt one would want to make it a wish that would solve many of the world's problems. It might be tempting to wish to eradicate all linguistic variation, casting off linguistic bias and cross-cultural misunderstanding. Overnight, we could all speak the same language, say *-ing* instead of *-in'*, have the perfect pitch, and most enticingly, never utter another *like* or *um*. And pronouns would magically be both uniquely specific and universal. A great idea, right?

The basic problem with such a wish is that in these differences lie our greatest strengths. Eradicating what helps us stand out decreases our diversity, limits our creativity, and stamps out the very thing that helps us find each other and commiserate over our shared experiences. What do we have to talk about if everyone is the same? While from an educational, political, and cross-language perspective, a common language with no variation might appear to make things a lot easier, few of us would find this a satisfying linguistic state of affairs, particularly those whose varieties would disappear. By eradicating the very thing that allows us a range of social expression—that renders visible our similarities as well as our differences—we lose much more than we would gain.

The irony is that, over the past few centuries, we have often behaved as if this would be the right approach, despite the fact that drastic change has been the very foundation upon which our modern tongue has been built. Viewing the new and distinctive as a threat to our linguistic future, we treat it as something negative, something divisive, but instead it is a powerful testament to our adaptive, innovative, and creative abilities.

A little appreciation

Language is universal, true, but also it is intensely personal and social. We use language to incite revolution, to explain ourselves, to share beliefs, to talk to and about each other, and of course, to declare love or to declare war. Yet it is amazing how little time we have spent getting to know the ins and outs of this amazing capacity we have for revealing our deepest thoughts and expressing our most powerful feelings beyond what we learned in grammar school.

Throughout these chapters, we have used seemingly small questions about how we use language (why we fry, how we *like*, and why *they* is the new *you*) to explore the big questions (why languages changes and how English came to be the way it is today). We have looked at how we judge, and are judged, on the basis of often misinformed biases we hold about the origin of new and "annoying" linguistic features and about the social status of their speakers. This awareness gives us the power to decide how our linguistic choices will define us and the way we see others. Though such knowledge may lead some to try to alter the way they speak, perhaps we can also learn to appreciate how language variation and change is the nature of the linguistic beast and part and parcel of what it means to be a diverse and social species.

Even if we might feel smug in our own linguistic prowess, chances are that, at one point in history, features in our own speech were held suspect by those whose language or dialect held the sway of the times. Power has always been intimately tied into which features we applaud and which we deride under the cover, unwitting perhaps, of linguistic superiority or purity. For instance, in the eighteenth and nineteenth centuries, to the ears of those speaking proper British English, the language of the rebellious American upstarts was feared as the end of English, with Americans "corrupting the beauty and well-ordered norms of the metropolitan standard through slovenly pronunciation and careless use of words and syntactic patterns." Um, why does that, like, sound so totally familiar?

While certainly no one would claim that our fondness for words formed from using -ass as a suffix has necessarily raised our global profile, surely Americans have not quite brought the

English language to its knees. But the strange thing about linguistic prejudice is that it has a way of infecting those who themselves at one time have stood on tenuous linguistic footing. The judged have now become the jury.

Hot or not?

Many years ago, my department was wining and dining a prospective hire for a position as an English professor. At a cocktail party for one of the candidates, a colleague casually mentioned that she had recently been at a conference in Budapest, Hungary. The candidate, clearly lacking the wisdom that comes from gainful employment, corrected her pronunciation with "I believe it is pronounced 'Budapessht.'" Needless to say, she didn't make the top of the hire list. But she lived on as a key example of what not to do in job interviews, alongside "Don't wear a crop top," also a nugget gathered through lived experience. The point here being that, while she might have been right about a more native-like pronunciation, telling others that their speech is wrong has rarely ended up a successful endeavor in changing what people actually say (or in making a good impression).

If there is anything that the history of the features laid out in these pages can tell us, it's that we really can't predict or control what will catch on and what won't. But it's a good bet that whatever does become popular and eventually makes it into the grammar books probably started with the very folks whose speech is most criticized and reviled. The disenfranchised? Check. The young? Check. The female? Check. And while many of the curiosities heard in the speech around us may die out as quickly as a trending TikTok, some will go the distance and become the speech that our grandkids rebel against. And yes, that is a sentence-ending preposition, the likes of which Shakespeare, a preposition strander himself, would be proud. In fact, the Elizabethan era was rife with such gratuitous linguistic behavior, at least until seventeenth- and eighteenth-century authorities and writers like John Dryden put the kibosh on such wayward syntactic behavior. Again, a perfect example of how what we now think of as a grammatical no-no is more a matter of subjective convention than linguistic improvement. And a reminder that we are a fickle crowd when it comes to deciding what's hot and what's not.

This is in part because, just like reminiscing about our favorite childhood candy (Pop Rocks, of course) and watching *Breakfast at Tiffany's* for the tenth time, we all pine for a bit of nostalgia, and language is no different. Take, for instance, the very recognizable pronunciation of words like *rather* and *aunt* with the *ah* vowel as in *rah-ther* or *ahhnt*. When you run into a New Englander who talks about their summers growing up in Nantucket, you can bet your bottom dollar that it was with *Ahhntie* Elizabeth, not Aunt (*Ant*) Bess like the rest of us whose summers were spent counting how many mosquitos got killed by the bug zappers in our backyards. Though a few more *ahhnt* speakers were around in North America in the early twentieth century, nowadays when one hears *ah* in words like *half, after,* or *glass,* it stands out as formal and refined, limited to the descendants of scattered groups along the Eastern Seaboard who hobnobbed with Brits far longer than the rest of the country.

But how does this have any relation to what we've talked about here? Well, at one point in the developmental history of our low vowels, the ash vowel, the one most Americans still have in *ask, bath,* and *glass,* was the prestige pronunciation in Britain, and *ah* just the unrefined linguistic upstart. Indeed, advising on proper pronunciation in 1791, early elocutionist John Walker suggests this new *ah* pronunciation gaining traction in words such as *after* or *answer* "borders very closely on vulgarity." But wait a hundred years, and *ah* is all the rage. As is often the nature of language change, one person's trash has become another person's treasure.

Since a side effect of winning the Revolutionary War was the dampening of our fondness for Briticisms, only those areas of the former colonies that had had regular exposure to more modern British forms, such as the seaports in Boston and Virginia, and of course, the still-hitched-through-the-Commonwealth Canadians, fully embraced the new London norms. And, despite Noah Webster's attempts to redefine how our speech was viewed, the American language was still shiny and new and yet to have made a deep grammatical impression. As a result, British norms continued to be viewed by many as more cultivated and refined, leading to the haughty highbrow association that using *ah* in words like *tomahto*, *ahnt*, and *rahther* gets you today.

So if such a linguistic turnabout could raise British *ah* to the heights of gentrified proper speech and American English to the level of global prominence it now enjoys, then maybe we can cut ourselves and others some linguistic slack on those other speech features we love to hate today.

Coming around again

We have a hard time separating our feelings about the way people sound from our ingrained beliefs about the groups to which they belong, be it a nationality, an ethnicity, a class, or a gender. But we tend to forget there have always been differences in how people speak—be it the nobles versus the servants, or Norman French versus English—and it is these very differences that created the rich language we speak today.

While prescriptivists cling to grammar books and usage guides, the reality is that most of what has been set down in them was the result not of divine inheritance, but rather the codification of the norms of those in power. Whether it was Samuel Johnson noting the upper-crust norms of the day in his well-regarded dictionary, or Noah Webster legitimizing New World coinages in his first American dictionary, or the contemporary usage panels who curate for modern dictionaries, we all come to look at language from a perspective born from our standing in the world. The fact that the downtrodden and overlooked rarely get a say, much less a vote, in determining how language forms will be viewed makes it hard for the features they use to ever meet the standards those who are the gatekeepers proscribe. But as we have seen here, from the novel intensifiers that ramp up our sentential sentiments to the *dude* that helps us commiserate or the pronouns that include us all, whether we approve of a new form or not is rarely what paves the path to the language forms of our future. Nor should it be, because the very language we hold so dear is the fait accompli of hundreds of years of tumultuous change and reinvention that those at the top of the linguistic food chain now unquestionably accept.

The goal of this book has been to share the fascinating stories that brought to life so many of the linguistic features we notice around us and to present contemporary research that explains why they have become so useful and popular today. Perhaps seeing the commonalities between the development of such features with those from yesteryear once considered uncouth and improper will allow for more empathy toward those who take up the linguistic vanguard. As the research reported in these pages confirms with great regularity, linguistic principles and patterns underlie even the most reviled features, such as *like* and vocal fry, with the negative views we hold about them by and large a matter of long-standing biases toward those who lead in language change, such as the young, the female, and the lower classes.

Even after reading these pages, some may very well still cringe at the sound of creak or struggle to comfortably say nonbinary *they*, but we should all have come to appreciate the linguistic merit of such forms. The sounds we make, the way we structure our sentences, the words we choose—these are the building blocks of language, the little black dresses of the linguistic world. But the linguistic flourishes each of us adds—these are the accessories that, in the end, make us who we are. Function *and* fashion, hand in hand.

Acknowledgments

So many ideas, so much research, and so many hours of revision helped create this book that it's hard to know where to start in recognizing the long line of people who helped along the way. One thing for sure is that none of these chapters would have been possible were it not for the work of so many great linguists, whose research is not mentioned much outside academia. Indeed, tell anyone you're a linguist and most people just think you speak a bunch of languages. In reality, the work that linguists do is far-reaching and fundamental to our modern-day chats with Siri, our understanding of children's and adult's language impairments, our efforts at language policy and planning, and, most important to my task here, for understanding how language changes over time. This book is for all these language researchers working in the trenches in quiet anonymity. And while there are numerous amazing scholars cited in these pages to whom I owe a great debt, a few stand out in need of special recognition for the inspiration their work has provided as well as their willingness to read over drafts and give me feedback: Tyler Kendall, Kirk Hazen, Sali Tagliamonte, Alexandra D'Arcy, Marisa Brook, Charlotte Vaughn, Dennis Cronan, Natalie Schilling, Ian Clayton, and Mignon Fogarty—I can't thank you enough for taking the time to help this book be an accurate reflection of the types of work we do. I would also like to acknowledge the help I received from the National Endowment for the Humanites. Without their fellowship award, it would have been much harder to carve out the time to write this book. I would also be remiss to not recognize one of my graduate students, Ruth Sylvester, who helped with proofreading. And speaking of students: to all the students in my classes who have been so inquisitive about why we say the things we say, this book was very much inspired by you. These pages represent the language features that emerged from your mouths, the questions that hung from your lips, and the tireless curiosity you brought when you entered my classroom.

To my dear friends and fellow writers, Michael Branch and Mark Herschberg, I hope you know how much I appreciated your guidance in making this whole book thing a reality. Likewise, to my editor at Viking, Terezia Cicel, who painstakingly read each version and was always spot-on about how to improve it; thank you for believing in this book and its subject from the get-go and for sharing with me a deep love of language and all its intricacies. A shout-out also goes to my agent, Becky Sweren, who taught me to write less as a professor and more as a story-teller. You and your "come to Jesus" read made it possible for my book proposal to find the perfect home, even if I learned to dread your prolific (but so helpful) red lining.

And speaking of home, without parents who illustrated all the richness that language has to offer, I would never have started down the path that brought me here. Thanks, Mom and Dad. I know that at the beginning you were not too sure what the heck someone does with a linguistics degree, but you supported me anyway, and I think it all turned out okay. My biggest debt, though, might be to my son, Cole, and my daughter, Taylor, who inspired many of the anecdotes in these pages, and whose lin-guistic innovation often attracted my attention, much to their dismay. You may not always have appreciated having a socio-linguist for a mom, but thank you for only rolling your eyes some (okay, most) of the time when I analyzed your speech and peppered you with usage questions. And, dude, one day when you have kids of your own, you'll be glad I helped you recognize the value of adolescent lingo. Last but not least, to my wonder-ful husband, Craig, who was the first and only person to see these pages for many months; thanks for sharing this journey—and this life—with me.

Notes

Introduction: I hate when you say that!

8 **self-described "nerd" girls:** The linguistic practices of nerds (and other high school social groups) and how they were tied to stylized and racialized identity formation were explored by linguist Mary Bucholtz in her 2011 book, *White Kids: Language, Race, and Styles of Youth Identity* (Cambridge: Cambridge University Press).

8 **Orthodox Jewish boys:** This finding on the use of *t* comes from linguist Sarah Bunin Benor's work in a community of Chabad Jews in California, which was published in 2001; see "The Learned /T/: Phonological Variation in Orthodox Jewish English," University of Pennsylvania, *Penn Working Papers in Linguistics* 7, no 3: 1–16.

17 **the go-to authority:** The *Oxford English Dictionary* (or *OED*), which holds itself to be the "definitive record of the English language," was an invaluable source for me throughout this book to help explore the early usage patterns and literary history of terms and expressions. For those unacquainted with its marvels, a search of this online resource provides access to the meaning, pronunciation, original forms, and the history of hundreds of thousands of English words.

1: Linguistic Fashionistas

32 **"better brought up sort":** The growing esteem with which London-area English was associated in this period is implied by the use of this phrase to describe many of its inhabitants by poet and writer George Puttenham in

his 1589 handbook for poets, *Arte of English Poesie*. Cited by Terttu Nevalainen in "Processes of Supralocalisation and the Rise of Standard English in the Early Modern Period," in *Generative Theory and Corpus
Studies*, ed. R. Bermúdez-Otero, D. Denison, R. M. Hogg, and C. B. Mc-
Cully (Berlin: De Gruyter Mouton, 2000), 329–72.

40 **This question of why languages change:** The actuation problem was first
introduced in the seminal paper "Empirical Foundations for a Theory of
Language Change" by Uriel Weinreich, William Labov, and Marvin I. Her-
zog in 1968. This work, along with the groundbreaking research published
in Labov's book *Sociolinguistic Patterns*, established the study of language
in its social context, known as sociolinguistics. As well, Labov's subsequent research, along with that of other early sociolinguists such as Peter
Trudgill, Walt Wolfram, Leslie Milroy, and, a bit later, Penny Eckert, really
helped refine our understanding of the role of social factors in driving how
language changes over time. My work in this chapter (and this book more
generally) is greatly influenced by their foundational work.

45 **Caste could be identified by:** These examples of caste-based dialect differences were drawn from British sociolinguist Peter Trudgill's very accessible
text *Sociolinguistics: An Introduction to Language and Society* (New
York: Penguin Books, 1974). It might be an oldie, but it is still a goodie.

50 *Must* **is no longer the preferred form:** For more on changes to our system
of deontic modality, see Sali Tagliamonte and Jennifer Smith's "Layering,
Competition and a Twist of Fate: Deontic Modality in Dialects of English,"
Diachronica 23, no. 2 (2006): 341–80.

53 **how language acquisition typically proceeds:** This idea that we have an
advantage in language acquisition early in life is known as the Critical Period Hypothesis or CPH and was first introduced by Eric H. Lenneberg in
1967 in the classic *Biological Foundations of Language*.

55 **with adult expectations:** Stanford linguist Penny Eckert spent a year embedded in a high school in Detroit observing and collecting data on how changes
work their way through different social groups, like the "jocks" and "burnouts," to come out the other side as new norms. Though it is a bit technical,
her two books, namely, *Jocks and Burnouts: Social Categories and Identity
in the High School* and *Linguistic Variation as Social Practice: The Linguistic Construction of Identity in Belten High*, stand out as the most comprehensive research into how new forms emerge via adolescent social structure.

2: Umloved

69 **for example,** *eh* **and** *ehm* **in Dutch:** Japanese, in fact, has more filled pauses
than just the two mentioned here (e.g., also *eto* and *sono*), and these forms
serve more functions than the simple *uh*s and *um*s found in English. Many

languages, like Japanese and Chinese, have filled pauses that function as both demonstrative pronouns and filled pauses (such as *nà* and *nàge* in Chinese) or use conventional words also as FPs (e.g., Spanish *este*). However, distilling down to the basics, we find that *um*- and *uh*-like vocalizations are the most commonly shared across languages.

70 **not the pariah they are now:** In the chapter "A Brief History of Um" in *Um*, a book on verbal blunders and filled pauses, writer Michael Erard explores the works of the great rhetoricians of ancient Greece and Rome, finding much about how to speak boldly and confidently in public but nothing commenting on or criticizing features akin to modern-day filled pauses. This suggests either that they didn't have such hesitations in days of yore or, more likely, that they simply didn't note them as disruptive.

72 **expressed our repressed anxieties or worries:** It was in *The Psychopathology of Everyday Life* that Freud proposed that slips of the tongue and other disfluencies were reflections of our anxieties and emotional states.

72 **episodes of increased anxiety:** As found, for instance, in Mahl's 1959 article, "Measuring the Patient's Anxiety During Interviews from 'Expressive' Aspects of His Speech," *Transactions of the New York Academy of Sciences* 21, no. 3: 249–57.

73 **some of the earliest studies:** A summary of some of this early work can be found in Frieda Goldman-Eisler's book *Psycholinguistics: Experiments in Spontaneous Speech* (London: Academic Press, 1968).

74 **We see this pattern borne out:** These results were reported in S. Schachter, N. Christenfeld, B. Ravina, and F. Bilous, "Speech Disfluency and the Structure of Knowledge," *Journal of Personality and Social Psychology* 60, no. 3 (1991): 362–67.

77 **hang on a minute:** Though it has become more popular as a theory behind our *um*s in recent work, Howard Maclay and Charles Osgood first brought up the *um* as conversational floor holder idea in their 1959 article, "Hesitation Phenomena in Spontaneous English Speech," published in the journal *Word*. This view became known as the filler-as-signal view, as opposed to the view that fillers were just symptoms of processing difficulties (referred to, not surprisingly, as the "symptom" view).

78 **These findings on the communicative function:** This view, known as the filler-as-word view, was developed most extensively by Clark and Fox Tree in their 2002 article, "Using Um and Uh in Spontaneous Speaking," *Journal of Cognition* 84, 73–111, though filled pauses had been treated as words, although very superficially, by a scholar in the 1970s.

78 **that *um*s and *uh*s should be treated:** A very informative but somewhat technical summary of research on *um* and how it relates to this filler-as-word debate can be found in M. Corley and O. W. Stewart, "Hesitation Disfluencies in Spontaneous Speech: The Meaning of *Um*," *Language and Linguistics Compass* 2, no. 4 (2008): 589–602.

82 **A somewhat more complicated study:** For a fuller description of this research, see J. E. Arnold, M. K. Tanenhaus, R. Altmann, and M. Fagnano, "The Old and Thee, uh, New," *Psychological Science* 15, no. 9 (2004): 578–81.

84 **when the experimenters put:** These findings were reported in M. Corley, L. J. MacGregor, and D. I. Donaldson, "It's the Way That You, er, Say It: Hesitations in Speech Affect Language Comprehension," *Cognition* 105, no. 3 (2007): 658–68.

84 **less likely to make any anticipatory shifts:** For more on these findings, see J. E. Arnold, C. L. Hudson Kam, and M. K. Tanenhaus, "If You Say Thee Uh You Are Describing Something Hard: The On-Line Attribution of Disfluency During Reference Comprehension," *Journal of Experimental Psychology, Learning, Memory, and Cognition* 33, no. 5 (2007): 914–30.

84 **filled pauses in a native speaker's speech:** In comparing how disfluencies influenced listener prediction of low-frequency words, psycholinguists from the Max Planck Institute for Psycholinguistics found nonnative disfluencies did not have the same effect on prediction as native speaker disfluency. H. R. Bosker, H. Quené, T. Sanders, and N. H. De Jong, "Native 'Um's Elicit Prediction of Low-Frequency Referents, but Non-Native 'Um's Do Not," *Journal of Memory and Language* 75 (2014): 104–16.

85 **an hour after having listened:** Corley, MacGregor, and Donaldson, "It's the Way That You, er, Say It," 658–68.

86 **filled pauses occurring before some plot points:** S. H. Fraundorf and D. G. Watson, "The Disfluent Discourse: Effects of Filled Pauses on Recall," *Journal of Memory and Language* 65, no. 2 (2011): 161–75.

89 **women and younger speakers have:** The majority of the studies that looked at age and gender patterns in filled pause preferences compared the use of different groups in terms of their *um/uh* ratio—with a higher ratio indicating greater *um* use compared to their use of *uh*.

89 **about twenty-two years behind women:** This male lag was the estimate made by Josef Fruehwald in his 2016 article, "Filled Pause Choice as a Sociolinguistic Variable," University of Pennsylvania, *Penn Working Papers in Linguistics* 22, no. 2.

89 **might be more pervasive:** Though it hasn't been that deeply explored, gender and age are not the only things that seem to affect how much we *um*— several studies have also pointed to higher-class or more-educated speakers using it more. This might be tied to the trend of *um* becoming more prevalent in written text.

90 **Germanic languages that share similar *uh*s and *um*s:** For a full picture of how the change is progressing across languages and social categories, see M. Wieling et al., "Variation and Change in the Use of Hesitation Markers in Germanic Languages," *Language Dynamics and Change* 6, no. 2 (2016): 199–234.

91 **for euphemistic intent or disagreement:** These examples were both mentioned in the 2017 article "From Pause to Word: *Uh, Um* and *Er* in written

American English," by linguist Gunnel Tottie, who has explored the function of *um* and *uh* in recent oral and written corpora in a number of articles. Referring to them as "slippery customers," she suggests *uh* and *um* have been put to work stylistically in a variety of ways that seem to be outgrowths of some of their "hesitancy" functions in our spoken exchanges. And to what end? "Almost without exception it is the writer's attitude to the message . . . which is signaled to the readers" (p. 120).

92 **Corpus of Historical American English turns up:** Created by Mark Davies in 2010, the Corpus of Historical American English (COHA) provides a searchable database of American English texts, newspapers, and magazines dating back to 1810 and is a great resource for those interested in early and literary usage in American English.

92 **filled pauses don't seem:** In their separate investigations of *um* and *uh* in written works, both Andreas Jucker and Gunnel Tottie don't find much evidence of filled pauses used in writing (outside of quoted forms) until the 1950s and '60s.

3: What's Not to Like?

102 **Discourse markers are by no means new or unusual:** Linguist Laurel Brinton has analyzed a multitude of such early English "mystery features" that appear to function as discourse markers in Old and Middle English texts; see *Pragmatic Markers in English: Grammaticalization and Discourse Functions* (Berlin: De Gruyter, 1996).

104 **transcripts of British criminal court trials:** This deep dive into the historical development of discourse marking *like*, including examples from the Old Bailey transcripts such as that mentioned in the footnote, can be found in Alexandra D'Arcy's *Discourse-Pragmatic Variation in Context: Eight Hundred Years of LIKE* (Amsterdam: John Benjamins Publishing, 2017).

104 **She also finds octogenarian speakers:** Far removed from Southern California's San Fernando Valley, the example used here, from linguist and *like* expert Alexandra D'Arcy, was spoken by a woman in rural Britain who was eighty-nine at the time. D'Arcy suggests these octogenarians in Britain and the *like* found in recordings of speakers born in the mid-nineteenth century in New Zealand point to a quite early origin for this discourse marking function. This discussion and the related quote appeared in Alexandra D'Arcy, "Like and Language Ideology: Disentangling Fact from Fiction," *American Speech* 82, no. 4 (2007): 386–419.

106 **the grammar police certainly were:** As discussed and cited in Suzanne Romaine and Deborah Lange's 1991 article detailing the grammaticalization of *like*, "The Use of Like as a Marker of Reported Speech and Thought: A Case of Grammaticalization in Progress," *American Speech* 66, no. 3: 227–79.

107 **the rise of this type of** *like*: Linguist Marisa Brook has done much recent work on complementizer *like*, finding it has increasingly replaced the use of "as if" or "as though" when introducing embedded sentences. In looking at its literary use to get a sense of its trajectory in English, she found it was predominately in the dialogue of stigmatized or vernacular characters in early use; see "Comparative Complementizers in Canadian English: Insights from Early Fiction," University of Pennsylvania, *Penn Working Papers in Linguistics* 20, no. 2 (2014).

112 **"He's, like, legendary"**: This study and the related example were described in Jean Fox Tree, "Placing Like in Telling Stories," *Discourse Studies* 8, no. 6 (2006): 723–43.

113 **"Like, wow" phenomenon associated with the beatniks**: This association with beat culture was made by linguist Alexandra D'Arcy in her 2017 book on everything *like, Discourse-Pragmatic Variation in Context*. Likewise, linguist John McWhorter made a similar suggestion in his article, "The Evolution of 'Like,'" which appeared in *The Atlantic* in 2016.

114 **increasing from 13 percent to 58 percent**: This information was drawn from the somewhat technical but fascinating 2007 article exploring the rise of *like* by Sali Tagliamonte and Alexandra D'Arcy, "Frequency and Variation in the Community Grammar: Tracking a New Change Through the Generations," *Language Variation and Change* 19, no. 2: 199–217. As is probably obvious from their frequent mention here, Tagliamonte and D'Arcy have been behind much of the most recent work on *like*'s distribution and function.

114 **"most vigorous and widespread"**: Cited from S. A. Tagliamonte, A. D'Arcy, and C. R. Louro, "Outliers, Impact, and Rationalization in Linguistic Change," *Language* 92, no. 4 (2016): 824–49, where they find that *like* is a fundamental and rapid shift in our quotative system similarly affecting English varieties from North America to Australia.

115 **alternating between** *say* **and** *like*: This use of quotative *like* to help mark a shift in narration was discussed by Suzanne Romaine and Deborah Lange in their 1991 article "The Use of Like as a Marker of Reported Speech and Thought: A Case of Grammaticalization in Progress," *American Speech* 66, no. 3: 227–79.

115 **fundamental shift in our narrative style**: This shift in oral narrative style that prompted the use of *be like* to report (first-person) speaker thought and then the subsequent extension of *be like* to third-person subjects was developed in Tagliamonte et al., "Outliers, Impact, and Rationalization in Linguistic Change," continuing a somewhat similar reasoning discussed in earlier work by Romaine and Lange.

117 *like* **use is increasing**: To see an overview of such age-related research, see Alexandra D'Arcy, *Discourse-Pragmatic Variation in Context*.

119 **to describe and devalue the talk of women**: For those interested in a deeper dive, a good overview of the history of androcentric bias in language can be found in Jennifer Coates's *Women, Men and Language: A Sociolinguistic*

Account of Gender Differences in Language (Abingdon-on-Thames, UK: Routledge, 2016).

120 **studies that have found that men:** Alexandra D'Arcy's 2007 *American Speech* paper on *like* and linguistic ideology, for instance, found women using more quotative *like*, but very little difference in terms of adverbial *like*. As well, Jennifer Dailey-O'Cain's earlier study found that men used slightly more focuser *like*, though the difference was not significant; see "The Sociolinguistic Distribution of and Attitudes toward Focuser *Like* and Quotative *Like*," *Journal of Sociolinguistics* 4, no. 1 (2000): 60–80.

4: Dude, WTF!

127 **Think "Dude, what the f@#k?":** On the larger themes here of slang, adolescent subculture, and American masculinity, a number of sources helped shape this chapter by providing theory and background. Jonathon Green's *Green's Dictionary of Slang* (Oxford: Oxford University Press, 2006) makes a very compelling argument for slang as counterculture or oppositional language and is also a great way to entertain oneself on rainy afternoons. For those interested in the history of specific slang words, check out Jonathan Lighter's *Historical Dictionary of American Slang* (New York: Random House, 1994). On masculinity, culture, and language, Scott Kiesling wrote a great article, "Men, Masculinities, and Language," *Language and Linguistics Compass* 1, no. 6 (2007): 653–73, which shaped a number of the ideas put forth here. Finally, for an overview and description of adolescent subcultures and the relation to slang, a very readable article for those with a continued interest is Teresa Labov's "Social and Language Boundaries among Adolescents," *American Speech* 67, no. 4 (1992): 339–66.

128 **appeared in the influential newspaper *New York World*:** As cited in A. Metcalf, *From Skedaddle to Selfie: Words of the Generations* (Oxford: Oxford University Press, 2016).

130 **"under suspicion of dudity":** "Is 'Dude' Defamatory?," *New York Times*, July 18, 1883, timesmachine.nytimes.com/timesmachine/1883/07/28/103440384 .html?pageNumber=4.

130 **"have invited a personal conflict":** "Is 'Dude' Defamatory?"

130 **new breed of young American male:** For details about how "dudes" played a role in political lampooning, see Harlen Makemson, "A 'Dude and Pharisee,'" *Journalism History* 29, no. 4 (2004): 179–89.

130 **threats to the sanctity of the family:** For a deeper exploration of the changing social landscape of the late nineteenth century, see Elaine Showalter, *Sexual Anarchy: Gender and Culture at the Fin de Siècle* (New York: Viking, 1990).

131 **English professor Robert Knoll:** Robert Knoll, "The Meanings and Suggested Etymologies of 'Dude,'" *American Speech* 27, no. 1 (1952): 20–22.

131 **army recruit with a spanking new uniform:** Richard Hill, "You've Come a Long Way, Dude: A History," *American Speech* 69, no. 3 (1994): 321–27.

132 **"That dude slickered me":** Hill, "You've Come a Long Way, Dude," 323.

133 **resistant to dominant mainstream expectations:** L. Alvarez, *The Power of the Zoot: Youth Culture and Resistance During World War* (Berkeley: University of California Press, 2008).

134 **modern colloquial word for clothes:** Hill, "You've Come a Long Way, Dude," 321–27.

134 **The word pronounced in two syllables:** From *Clothier and Furnisher*, 1883 (specifically vol. 13, no. 10), as cited in Barry Popik and Gerald Cohen, "More Materials for the Study of Dude," *Comments on Etymology* 26, no. 7 (1997).

136 **alongside the popular term *cowabunga*:** Suggested by Hill in "You've Come a Long Way, Dude."

137 **According to Kiesling's research:** Scott Kiesling, "Dude," *American Speech* 79, no. 3 (2004): 281–305.

139 **Multicultural London English:** Linguist Ben Rampton has looked extensively at what he refers to as "crossing" or the appropriation of ethnic markers. For a deeper foray into this topic in the context of British English, see his 2010 article "Crossing into Class: Language, Ethnicities and Class Sensibility in England," in *Language and Identities*, ed. Carmen Llamas and Dominic Watt (Edinburgh: Edinburgh University Press, 2009), 134–43.

141 **"connects the term to counter-culture":** Also from Kiesling's article "Dude," 288.

5: Wha' You Talkin' Bout?

156 **whether any kinds of gerunds:** The verbal properties (or lack thereof) for Old English ING forms have been discussed by many of the scholars cited here, but an early treatment can be found in twentieth-century grammarian George Curme's "History of the English Gerund," *Englischen Studien* XLV (1912): 349–80.

159 **Looking back at Old English homilies and texts:** The nouns formed with -*ing* in this early period are often described as nouns of action (as *plundering* most certainly appears to have been). *Hergiung* has been sometimes translated with the meaning of "raid" in Old English.

160 **lack of a grammaticized progressive marker:** The grammaticization of the progressive aspect using the suffix -*ing* is relatively new to English. Some of the ways we use these participles today, for example, in a passive progressive construction like "The house was being built," were considered uncouth and vulgar forms up to the nineteenth century. Instead, we would have said "The house was building."

162 **We are able to observe this change happening:** Betty Irwin's 1967 dissertation, which looked at the development of the ending in written records from the Old and Middle English periods, examined variation in the spelling of the endings by century. See "The Development of the -ing Ending of the Verbal Noun and the Present Participle from c. 700 to c. 1400."

163 **One potential but very subtle difference:** One of the best sources on the development and distribution of the ING suffix, and one that greatly helped inform this chapter, is an unpublished dissertation, "Continuity and Change in English Morphology: The Variable (ING)," by Anne Celeste Houston, written in 1985.

164 **Between the twelfth and fifteenth centuries:** As tracked in Irwin, "The Development of the -ing Ending."

166 **a trace of the -e/inde ending:** This idea of -in' and -ing echoing our noun and verb endings past was developed by Houston's "Continuity and Change in English Morphology," as well as in Bill Labov's 1989 article, "The Child as Linguistic Historian," *Language Variation and Change* 1, no. 1: 85–97. Finally, Sali Tagliamonte located the same grammatical constraints on -in' versus -ing in her 2004 article, "Somethi[ŋ]'s Goi[n] On! Variable (ING) at Ground Zero," supporting the idea of historical grammatical patterning.

168 **by social anthropologist John Fischer:** This finding from his early examination of ING use was published in Fischer's 1958 article, "Social Influences on the Choices of a Linguistic Variant," which appeared in the journal *Word* 14. The quoted line toward the end of this paragraph appears on p. 484 of this article.

169 **In looking back at commentaries on language:** These examples were cited by Wyld in his 1920 book, *A History of Modern Colloquial English* (London: T. F. Unwin Ltd.), 290.

170 **"a disloyal crusade against the Queen's English":** Letter written by Walker Delolme that appeared in the popular British magazine *Punch* in 1920, as quoted by Houston, "Continuity and Change in English Morphology," 338.

170 **nineteenth-century elevation of -ing:** As Wyld mentions in the section on substitution of /n/ for /ŋ/ on p. 289 of *A History of Modern Colloquial English*.

170 **"they're all a-runnin' about":** As cited in chapter 8, "The Evaluative Function of (ING)," in Houston, "Continuity and Change in English Morphology," 346.

171 **Wyld discovered the -in' form appeared:** This is discussed in Wyld's *A History of Modern Colloquial English*, particularly in the section detailing the Verney Memoirs and other correspondence he studied from the seventeenth and eighteenth centuries, 162–65.

171 **carried some prestige as being "fashionable":** Otto Jespersen's thoughts on -in's social traits are mentioned in his *A Modern English Grammar on Historical Principles: Part I: Sounds and Spellings* (Abingdon, UK: Routledge,

1961), 356, as discussed in Tagliamonte's study of ING, "Somethi[ŋ]'S Goi[n] On!" from 2004. Jespersen's exploration of *-ing*'s territory expansion (and its use by many a storied author) appears in his 1926 treatise, *On Some Disputed Points in English Grammar.*

171 **When sociolinguist Scott Kiesling:** Kiesling's findings are discussed in greater detail in his 1998 article "Men's Identities and Sociolinguistic Variation: The Case of Fraternity Men," *Journal of Sociolinguistics* 2, no. 1, 69–99.

172 **"power is central to men's identities":** This quote appears in Kiesling, "Men's Identities and Sociolinguistic Variation," 70.

173 **When it comes to ING:** One of the seminal works that first detailed this link between class, style, and linguistic variables (including ING) is William Labov's *The Social Stratification of English in New York City* (Washington, DC: Center for Applied Linguistics, 1966). Since then, both class and formality have been some of the most consistent social patterns associated with variable ING use. However, as we see in this chapter, they are far from the only thing your ING can say.

174 **when we are kickin' it with friends:** For a quite readable exploration into both the world of *-ing* and sociolinguistic research methods, see more in Benji Wald and Timothy Shopen, "A Researcher's Guide to the Sociolinguistic Variable (ING)," in *Style and Variables in English*, ed. Timothy Shopen and Joseph M. Williams (Cambridge, MA: Winthrop, 1981), 219–49.

176 **Even as few as one uttered *-in'*:** In W. Labov et al., 2006 study "Listeners' Sensitivity to the Frequency of Sociolinguistic Variables," the researchers found that the first *-in'* uttered seemed to cause listeners to downgrade speakers' ratings more than any subsequent *-in'* they heard.

179 **by linguist Kathryn Campbell-Kibler:** Discussed in Kathryn Campbell-Kibler's 2007 article, "Accent, (ING), and the Social Logic of Listener Perceptions," *American Speech* 82, no. 1: 32–64. Campbell-Kibler's dissertation on the social perception of ING is well known in the field and spawned a number of articles looking at ING's salience as a social marker, including the one discussed in this section.

182 **It's doubtful they were all from Appalachia:** As linguist Kirk Hazen details very eloquently in his 2017 article, "Combatting Stereotypes about Appalachian Dialects" for *The Conversation*, Appalachian English is much richer and has been part of modern linguistic changes (such as *like* use) much more often than our generally negative portraits of the region allow.

6: A Little Less Literally

186 **"You are *sooo* lucky to have me":** @realDonaldTrump, tweeted November 5, 2019, 8:47 a.m.

188 **"It was a nightmare":** "'Covid Will Not Win': Meet the Force Powering Brooklyn Hospital Center," *New York Times*, September, 11, 2020.

189 **Linguist Michael Israel:** Michael Israel, "Literally Speaking," *Journal of Pragmatics* 34, no. 4 (2002): 423–32.

189 **"I will be *horribly* in loue with her":** William Shakespeare, *Much Ado about Nothing*, act 2, scene 3, cited in the *Oxford English Dictionary*, 223.

191 **a bar in New York:** "Why This East Village Bar Has a Ban on the Word 'Literally,'" *All Things Considered*, NPR, January 26, 2018.

192 **Jesse Sheidlower notes in an article for *Slate*:** Jessie Sheidlower, "The Word We Love to Hate. Literally," *Slate*, November 1, 2005.

193 **like boring old *very* or *really*:** Much of the recent research on intensifiers in varieties such as British, Canadian, and American English has been done by Sali Tagliamonte at University of Toronto and her colleagues. I owe them a great debt for the ideas in this chapter (as well as for her work on *like* in an earlier chapter). In addition, Anna Stenström's work in Britain was also "right" helpful in looking at intensification across the pond.

194 **back as far as Old and Middle English:** A great source of information on intensifiers popular throughout the Middle English period (as well as those dating from the Old English period) is Tauno Mustanoja's *A Middle English Syntax* (Helsinki: Société néophilologique, 1960), though it is admittedly somewhat dry for those not used to exploring the ins and outs of syntax.

194 **We find, for instance, "He hine":** *The Bickling Homilies* 27, circa 971, cited in the *Oxford English Dictionary*.

195 **describes an old man in a forest:** James Stratton, "A Diachronic Analysis of the Adjective Intensifier Well from Early Modern English to Present Day English," *Canadian Journal of Linguistics/Revue canadienne de linguistique* 65, no. 2 (2020): 216–45.

195 **"The better angel":** From Shakespeare's sonnet 144, as cited in Jenny Cheshire, "Really, Very/Dead/So Interesting? How to Intensify in Tyneside," for Linguistics Research Digest, linguistics-research-digest.blogspot.com/2011/11/reallyverydeadso-interesting-how-to.html.

195 **an intensifier in Swedish:** Cornelis Stoffel, *Intensives and Down-toners* (Heidelberg: Carl Winter's Universitätsbunchhandlung, 1901).

196 **"All men counted Ihon":** Tyndale Bible, Mark xi. f. lxij, as cited in Tauno Mustanoja, *A Middle English Syntax* (Helsinki: Société Néophilologique, 1960).

196 **"That he nys but a verray propre fole":** From Chaucer's "Legend of Good Women," prologue 259, as cited for "very, adj., adv., and n.1," in OED Online.

197 **"It was indeed very, very, very dreadful":** From Daniel Defoe's *A Journal of the Plague Year* (1896), 46, as cited in the *Oxford English Dictionary*.

197 **and later, Charles Dickens:** For example, "very foolish—very" appeared in Dickens's first novel, *Pickwick Papers*, cited for "very, adj., adv., and n.1," OED Online.

197 **"unconquerable fondness for the word":** From *New York Sun*, February 12, 1916, cited in merriam-webster.com/words-at-play/the-problems-with -very, accessed 9/23/20.

197 **qualifies as one:** Rob Asghar, "9 Words You're Literally Beating to Death," *Forbes*, November 6, 2013, forbes.com/sites/robasghar/2013/11/06/9-words -youre-literally-beating-to-death/#3b903edb18ef.

198 **an abbreviated form of *very*:** As discussed in "'V' Is for Very," *Atlantic*, January 14, 2015, theatlantic.com/technology/archive/2015/01/v-very /384366/ accessed 9/20/20.

198 **how Toronto teens used intensifiers:** Sali A. Tagliamonte, "*So* Who? *Like* How? *Just* What? Discourse Markers in the Conversations of Young Canadians," *Journal of Pragmatics* 37, no. 11 (2005): 1896–1915.

199 **the British took a bit longer to warm up:** To read more about emerging intensifiers in British English, James Stratton's short article on the recent rise of the intensifier *proper* makes for a fun read. "'That's Proper Cool': The Emerging Intensifier Proper in British English," *English Today* 37, no. 4 (2005): 1–8.

199 **sort of the new duchess of intensifiers:** A. B. Stenström, G. Andersen, and I. K. Hasund, *Trends in Teenage Talk: Corpus Compilation, Analysis and Findings*, vol. 8 (Amsterdam: John Benjamins Publishing, 2002).

199 **study in Scotland:** Ronald Macaulay, "Adverbs and Social Class Revisited," University of Pennsylvania, *Penn Working Papers in Linguistics* 8, no. 11 (2002).

200 **the popular TV show *Friends*:** S. Tagliamonte and C. Roberts, "So Weird; So Cool; So Innovative: The Use of Intensifiers in the Television Series *Friends*," *American Speech* 80, no. 3 (2005): 280–300.

200 **a favorite, no surprise, among the ladies:** Stoffel, *Intensives and Downtoners*.

201 **first-year college-age men:** Tagliamonte, "*So* Who? *Like* How? *Just* What?"

201 **adolescent men were actually prettier:** The findings on *pretty*'s expansion into intensification territory is detailed in Sali Tagliamonte's "So Different and Pretty Cool! Recycling Intensifiers in Toronto, Canada," *English Language and Linguistics* 12, no. 2 (2008): 361–94.

203 **linguists found that intensification varied:** S. Reichelt and M. Durham, "Adjective Intensification as a Means of Characterization: Portraying In-Group Membership and Britishness in *Buffy the Vampire Slayer*," *Journal of English Linguistics* 45, no. 1 (2016): 60–87.

204 **comprehensive or public school background:** James Stratton, "The Use of the Adjective Intensifier 'Well' in British English: A Case Study of the Inbetweeners," *English Studies* 99, no. 8 (2018): 793–816.

204 **Such usage is in contrast to research:** Anna-Brita Stenström, Gisle Andersen, and Ingrid Kristine Hasund discuss the class-based distribution of intensifiers in their 2002 book, *Trends in Teenage Talk: Corpus Compilation, Analysis, and Findings* (Amsterdam: John Benjamins Publishing).

205 **"vastly glad, or vastly sorry"**: As cited in Otto Jespersen, *Language, Its Nature, Development and Origin* (New York: Henry Holt, 1922).

205 **"highly characteristic of ladies' usage"**: Stoffel, *Intensives and Downtoners.*

205 **"fondness for hyperbole"**: Jespersen, *Language, Its Nature, Development and Origin.*

207 **women didn't invent hyperbole**: Intensifiers as a means of hyperbolic expression, especially for women, was highlighted by early writers such as Cornelis Stoffel, Lord Chesterfield, and Otto Jespersen. But a more neutral and scientific approach to how and why they function so well in terms of hyperbole is recently discussed by M. McCarthy and R. Carter, "'There's Millions of Them': Hyperbole in Everyday Conversation," *Journal of Pragmatics* 36, no. 2 (2004): 149–84.

209 **enhanced perceptions of certainty and control**: L. A. Hosman and S. A. Siltanen, "The Attributional and Evaluative Consequences of Powerful and Powerless Speech Styles: An Examination of the 'Control over Others' and 'Control of Self' Explanations,'" *Language and Communication* 14, no. 3 (1994): 287–98.

209 **raised ratings on sociability scales**: L. A. Hosman, "The Evaluative Consequences of Hedges, Hesitations, and Intensifiers: Powerful and Powerless Speech Styles," *Human Communication Research* 15, no. 3 (1989): 383–406.

7: The Perfect Pitch

213 **"an array of linguistic"**: Quote from N. B. Abdelli-Beruh, L. Wolk, and D. Slavin, "Prevalence of Vocal Fry in Young Adult Male American English Speakers," *Journal of Voice* 28, no. 2 (2014): 185.

213 **upper-class high-status association**: A number of early phonological descriptions of British speech, such as that by John Wells (1982), John Laver (1980), and Caroline Henton and Anthony Bladon (1988), comment both on the apparent male predominance of creak and on its association with certain dialects more than others. And despite the professional doom predicted by modern fry detractors, work by both Esling (1978) in Scotland and Pittam (1987) in Australia showed an association between vocal fry and higher class. See J. H. Esling, "Voice Quality in Edinburgh: A Sociolinguistic and Phonetic Study" (PhD dissertation, University of Edinburgh), and J. Pittam, "Listeners' Evaluation of Voice Quality in Australian English Speakers," *Language and Speech* 30: 99–113.

215 **go busy herself with her weaving**: Mary Beard, "The Public Voice of Women," *Women's History Review* 24, no. 5 (2015): 809–18.

215 **"Silence gives grace to woman"**: From Aristotle's *Politics*, 1.5.9, as cited in Michèle Lardy's "From Silence to 'Civil Converse': Of the Attempts to Control Seventeenth-Century Women's 'Ripe Wit and Ready Tongues,'"

Revue de la Société d'Études Anglo-Américaines des XVIl et XVIIle Siècles 73 (2016).

215 **a woman of low morals:** For a general discussion on the history of free expression, including that involving women, Douglas M. Fraleigh and Joseph S. Tuman's *Freedom of Expression in the Marketplace of Ideas* (Newbury Park, CA: Sage Publications, 2011) offers an interesting read. For a look more specifically at women's voices in the classical world, Professor Mary Beard's blog post for the British Museum offers a short but fascinating synopsis of women's talk in antiquity, blog.britishmuseum.org/did-women -in-greece-and-rome-speak.

215 **prosecuted for "sins of the tongue":** For a deeper look at sins of the tongue and how prosecution of such crimes served to silence women whose voices threatened to disrupt the social order, check out Sandra Bardsley's book, *Venomous Tongues: Speech and Gender in Late Medieval England* (Philadelphia: University of Pennsylvania Press, 2006).

216 **talk too much, or use loud voices:** Michèle Lardy, "From Silence to 'Civil Converse,'" 105–22.

216 **"rasping, dead or shrill timbre to the voice":** As cited in Rachel Cote, *Too Much*, which examines how Victorianism echoes in our expectations and judgment of modern women's behavior.

216 **significantly lowered their pitch:** C. Pemberton, P. McCormack, and A. Russell, "Have Women's Voices Lowered Across Time? A Cross Sectional Study of Australian Women's Voices," *Journal of Voice* 12, no. 2 (1998): 208–13.

219 **greater amounts of creak:** L. Dilley, S. Shattuck-Hufnagel, and M. Ostendorf, "Glottalization of Word-Initial Vowels as a Function of Prosodic Structure," *Journal of Phonetics* 24, no. 4 (1996): 423–44.

219 **more recent study of newscasts:** L. Redi and S. Shattuck-Hufnagel, "Variations in the Realization of Glottalization in Normal Speakers," *Journal of Phonetics* 29 (2001): 407–29.

219 **Public radio's *This American Life*:** The *Freedom Fries* episode aired on January 23, 2015.

222 **a "hypermasculine" feature:** This association of creak with the expression of masculinity was made in Caroline Henton and Anthony Bladon's 1988 article, "Creak as a Sociophonetic Marker." Their research suggested that for the British English varieties examined, men used between three and ten times more fry than the women. See *Language, Speech and Mind: Studies in Honour of Victoria A. Fromkin*, ed. L. M. Hyman and C. N. Li (London: Routledge, 1988), 3–29.

223 **same amount of fry as the American men:** I. P. Yuasa, "Creaky Voice: A New Feminine Voice Quality for Young Urban-Oriented Upwardly Mobile American Women?," *American Speech* 85, no. 3 (2010): 315–37.

223 **in midwestern American speakers:** As reported by Shannon Melvin and Cynthia Clopper at the Scottish Consortium for the 18th International Congress of Phonetic Sciences in Glasgow, Scotland, in 2015.

223 **focused on spontaneous speech:** Sarah T. Irons and Jessica Alexander, "Vocal Fry in Realistic Speech: Acoustic Characteristics and Perceptions of Vocal Fry in Spontaneously Produced and Read Speech," *Journal of the Acoustical Society of America* 140, no. 4 (2016): 3397.

223 **an automatic detection algorithm:** While communication science researchers Nassima B. Abdelli-Beruh, Lesley Wolk, and Dianne Slavin found a female preference for vocal fry use when reading sentences in a comparison of male and female college students, in slightly later research published in *The Journal of Voice* using an automatic detection algorithm, Abdelli-Beruh et al. (2016) did not find any such gender difference.

223 **women used fry more often than men:** R. Podesva, "Gender and the Social Meaning of Non-Modal Phonation Types" (2013), in eds. C. Cathcart, I. H. Chen, G. Finley, S. Kang, C. Sandy, and E. Stickles, *Proceedings of the 37th Annual Meeting of the Berkeley Linguistics Society*, Berkeley, CA: Berkeley Linguistics Society.

224 **by those with more education:** B. Gittelson, A. Leemann, and F. Tomaschek, "Using Crowd-Sourced Speech Data to Study Socially Constrained Variation in Nonmodal Phonation," *Frontiers in Artificial Intelligence* (2021): 565–682.

224 **A study examining actresses' accents:** Barry Pennock-Speck compared voice samples for actresses Gwyneth Paltrow, Reese Witherspoon, and Renée Zellweger across their British versus American roles, finding creak more prevalent in American portrayals. His summary of this research appeared in the 2005 Proceedings chapter, "The Changing Voice of Women," in *Actas XXVIII Congreso Internacional AEDEAN*, 407–15.

225 **exhibiting a similar degree of vocal fry:** Gisele Oliveira, Ashira Davidson, Rachelle Holczer, Sara Kaplan, and Adina Paretzky, "A Comparison of the Use of Glottal Fry in the Spontaneous Speech of Young and Middle-Aged American Women," *Journal of Voice* 30, no. 6 (2016): 684–87.

226 **our fear of fry's epidemic potential:** The full review of the literature on creak, for those interested in a little bedtime reading, is K. Dallaston and G. Docherty, "The Quantitative Prevalence of Creaky Voice (Vocal Fry) in Varieties of English: A Systematic Review of the Literature," *PloS One* 15, no. 3 (2020): e0229960.

226 **examining the differences in pitch drop:** "Gender Variation in Creaky Voice and Fundamental Frequency," in eds. Maria Wolters, Judy Livingstone, Bernie Beattie, Rachel Smith, Mike MacMahon, Jane Stuart-Smith, and James M. Scobbie, *Proceedings of the 18th International Congress of Phonetic Sciences, ICPhS 2015*, Glasgow, UK, August 10–14, 2015, University of Glasgow.

228 **it gives the impression of:** Mentioned in John Laver's *The Phonetic Description of Voice Quality* (Cambridge: Cambridge University Press, 1980).

228 **found to parlay a sense that you are relaxed:** Research by phoneticians C. Gobl and A. Ni Chasaide found listeners rated their synthesized

"lax-creaky" voice as relaxed, intimate, and content, suggesting that it is heard relatively positively within social contexts. They also suggest that there are different types of creaky voice that can be produced and not all give off a "bored" vibe. See "The Role of Voice Quality in Communicating Emotion, Mood, and Attitude," *Speech Communication* 40 no. 1–2 (2003): 189–212.

228 **to quote an adjective frequently selected:** As discussed in C. Ligon, C. Rountrey, N. V. Rank, M. Hull, and A. Khidr, "Perceived Desirability of Vocal Fry among Female Speech Communication Disorders Graduate Students," *Journal of Voice* 33, no. 5 (2019): 805.e21–e35.

228 **disinclination to continue a topic further:** This pattern of creaky "yeah" has not been well documented, but was the topic of a 2004 article by Tamara Grivičić and Chad Nilep called "When Phonation Matters: The Use and Function of Yeah and Creaky Voice," which appeared in *Colorado Research in Linguistics* 17.

230 **came across as less competent, educated, and hirable:** R. C. Anderson, C. A. Klofstad, W. J. Mayew, and M. Venkatachalam, "Vocal Fry May Undermine the Success of Young Women in the Labor Market," *PloS One* 9, no. 5 (2014): 1–8.

230 **women would be disadvantaged:** As discussed in M. A. Parker and S. A. Borrie, "Judgments of Intelligence and Likability of Young Adult Female Speakers of American English: The Influence of Vocal Fry and the Surrounding Acoustic-Prosodic Context," *Journal of Voice* 32, no. 5 (2018): 538–45.

232 **hearing a single "hello":** These findings are reported in P. McAleer, A. Todorov, and P. Belin, "How Do You Say 'Hello'? Personality Impressions from Brief Novel Voices," *PloS One* 9 (2014): e90779.

232 **when they have lower-pitched voices:** There is a great deal of literature that looks at the effects of manipulating pitch on the perception of speaker traits and personality attributes. The focus of such work ranges from those that look at pitch differences and their effect on dominance and physical attractiveness ratings, for example D. R. Feinberg, B. C. Jones, A. C. Little, D. M. Burt, and D. L. Perrett, "Manipulations of Fundamental and Formant Frequencies Influence the Attractiveness of Human Male Voices," *Animal Behavior* 69, no. 3 (2005): 561–68 (or see note below for additional sources), to those that look at pitch differences and their effect on attributes such as trustworthiness, warmth, and leadership, for example, Casey Klofstad, Rindy Anderson, and Susan Peters, "Sounds Like a Winner: Voice Pitch Influences Perception of Leadership Capacity in Both Men and Women," *Proceedings of the Royal Society B.* 279, no. 1738: 2698–704, or M. S. Tsantani, P. Belin, H. M. Paterson, and P. McAleer, "Low Vocal Pitch Preference Drives First Impressions Irrespective of Context in Male Voices but Not in Female Voices," *Perception* 45, no. 8 (2016): 946–63.

232 **Scottish raters felt:** P. McAleer, A. Todorov, and P. Belin, "How Do You Say 'Hello'? Personality Impressions from Brief Novel Voices, *PLoS One* 9, no. 3 (2014): e90779.

233 **proxy for physical dominance:** David Puts and colleagues' 2007 article (with the decidedly long title "Men's Voices as Dominance Signals: Vocal Fundamental and Formant Frequencies Influence Dominance Attributions among Men") is an often-cited example of work relating pitch to both physical and social dominance, appearing in the journal *Evolution and Human Behavior* 28, no. 5: 340–44. As well, in linguistics, this view strongly aligns with phonologist John Ohala's idea of a "frequency code" as detailed in his 1984 article, "An Ethological Perspective on Common Cross-Language Utilization of F0 of Voice," *Phonetica* 41, no. 1: 1–16.

233 **more intimidating to their competition:** For those interested in reading more about such evolutionary theories of voice, see David Puts et al., "Sexual Selection on Male Vocal Fundamental Frequency in Humans and Other Anthropoids," which finds the pitch dimorphism between human males and females is greater than that of all other primates, *Proceedings of the Royal Society B.* 283, no. 1829 (2016): 2830.

233 **dominance and authority scales:** These preferences do seem to be somewhat culturally mediated, however. In other words, though listeners do form impressions about speakers based on voice qualities that impact dominance and attractiveness ratings, the qualities differ and the direction is not always the same across different cultures. This offers great evidence that our voice characteristics are greatly influenced by our specific sociocultural norms.

233 **communicates leadership potential:** As discussed in J. T. Cheng, J. L. Tracy, S. Ho, and J. Henrich, "Listen, Follow Me: Dynamic Vocal Signals of Dominance Predict Emergent Social Rank in Humans," *Journal of Experimental Psychology* 145, no. 5 (2016): 536–47.

233 **when taking on an authoritative role:** P. Sorokowski, D. Puts, J. Johnson, et al., "Voice of Authority: Professionals Lower Their Vocal Frequencies When Giving Expert Advice," *Journal of Nonverbal Behavior* 43, no. 2 (2019): 257–69.

234 **we have strong voice-pitch preferences:** A couple of examples of studies looking at vocal attractiveness are D. E. Re, J. J. M. O'Connor, P. J. Bennett, and D. R. Feinberg, "Preferences for Very Low and Very High Voice Pitch in Humans," *PloS One* 7, no. 3 (2012): e32719; and M. Babel, G. McGuire, and J. King, "Towards a More Nuanced View of Vocal Attractiveness," *PloS One* 9, no. 2 (2014): e88616.

234 **the voices of former U.S. presidents:** C. C. Tigue, D. J. Borak, J. J. O'Connor, C. Schandl, and D. R. Feinberg, "Voice Pitch Influences Voting Behavior," *Evolution and Human Behavior* 33, no. 3 (2012): 210–16.

235 **compared to those with more liberal leanings:** B. Banai, L. Laustsen, I. P. Banai, and K. Bovan, "Presidential, but Not Prime Minister, Candidates with Lower-Pitched Voices Stand a Better Chance of Winning the Election in Conservative Countries," *Evolutionary Psychology* 16, no. 2 (2018).

235 **preferred traits in business leaders:** See W. J. Mayew, C. A. Parsons, and M. Venkatachalam, "Voice Pitch and the Labor Market Success of Male Chief Executive Officers," *Evolution and Human Behavior* 34, no. 4 (2013): 243–48.

8: Who Are *They?*

246 **Kirby Conrod found using *they*:** This analysis of the distribution and perception of singular *they* appeared in Kirby Conrod's "Pronouns Raising and Emerging" (dissertation, University of Washington, 2019).

249 **as nongender-conforming Hijras in India:** For more on the history of nonbinary gender identity along with a discussion of the role of terminology and culture, a good source is archivist Charlie McNabb's *Nonbinary Gender Identities: History, Culture, Resources* (Lanham, MD: Rowman and Littlefield, 2018).

250 **cumbersome coallocated *he* or *she*:** A number of texts discuss prescriptivism and pronouns, but for a seminal discussion, see Ann Bodine, "Androcentrism in Prescriptive Grammar: Singular 'They,' Sex-Indefinite 'He,' and 'He or She,'" in *The Feminist Critique of Language*, ed. D. Cameron (London: Routledge, 1990), 166–86. A more recent treatment can be found in D. E. Baron, *What's Your Pronoun?: Beyond He and She* (New York: W. W. Norton, 2020).

250 **The pronoun debates of this century:** A helpful discussion of the internal, rather than social, issues that helped drive the development of singular *they* historically as well as its prevalence and pattern in Middle English texts can be found in Mark Balhorn's "The Rise of Epicene They," *Journal of English Linguistics* 32, no. 2 (2004): 79–104.

251 **linguistic "purity" and standardization:** The idea and impact of such linguistic purity is discussed in N. Langer and A. Nesse's 2012 chapter "Linguistic Purism," in *The Handbook of Historical Sociolinguistics*, eds. J. M. Hernández-Campoy and J. C. Conde-Sylvestre (Malden, MA: Blackwell, 2012), 607.

251 **status linguistically and socially:** S. Zuber and A. Reed, "The Politics of Grammar Handbooks: Generic He and Singular They," *College English* 55, no. 5 (1993): 515–30.

251 **This push toward prescriptivism:** A seminal (and very accessible) book on the politics, legislation, and history behind our third-person pronouns is Baron's *What's Your Pronoun?* I owe a great debt to this work in this chapter, as well as to Baron's earlier articles on the history of our pronouns.

251 **a similar act was passed:** D. Baron, "The Epicene Pronoun: The Word That Failed," *American Speech* 56, no. 2 (1981): 83–97.

253 **"no cause for anxiety or pronoun-envy":** "Pronoun Envy," *The Crimson*, November 16, 1971, thecrimson.com/article/1971/11/16/pronoun-envy-pto -the-editors-of.

253 **the suffragette Susan B. Anthony argued:** For those interested in a bit more about women, politics, and pronouns, Baron's *What's Your Pronoun?* includes a great chapter on "The Politics of He."

254 **This male-centric language:** Linguist Ben Zimmer provides a great overview of the issue of political invisibility in his *Wall Street Journal* article, "Dealing with Gender in the Pronouns of Law and Public Life," July 31, 2020.

255 **Old English had multiple ways:** Anne Curzan, *Gender Shifts in the History of English* (Cambridge: Cambridge University Press, 2003).

256 **Johnson, who likened Spenser's words:** Edwin Guest, "On English Pronouns Personal," *Proceedings of the Philological Society* 1 (1844): 277–92.

256 **feminine and masculine pronoun confusion:** Example taken from John Algeo and Thomas Pyle's well-known *The Origins and Development of the English Language* (San Diego: Harcourt Brace Jovanovich, 1993).

257 *þei* **was only used:** "they, pron., adj., adv., and n.," OED Online, www -oed-com.unr.idm.oclc.org/view/Entry/200700?redirectedFrom=they.

258 **translating roughly to "every person":** As cited in Balhorn, "The Rise of Epicene They," 79–104.

258 **tracking how often she did it:** You can check out singular *they* in action in a variety of Austen's works at pemberley.com/janeinfo/austhlis.html#X2.

259 **According to Dennis Baron (aka Dr. Pronoun):** A number of Baron's works have tracked the neologisms associated with the third-person plural.

259 **reported in the previous week's:** "Mrs. Ella Young Invents Pronoun: 'He'er,' 'His'er' and 'Him'er' as Combination of Genders Used in Address," *Chicago Daily Tribune*, January 7, 1912.

260 **made by a correspondent:** A. M. Case, "To Indicate the Common Gender: Thinks Chicago Could Establish the Word Hor as a Handy Pronoun," *Chicago Daily Tribune*, September 27, 1890.

260 **the earliest documented examples of unisex pronouns:** Baron, "The Epicene Pronoun."

260 **"beautiful symmetry of the English tongue":** C. C. Converse, "A New Pronoun," *The Critic: A Literary Weekly, Critical and Eclectic* 55 (August 2, 1884), 55.

261 **the founders of chiropractic medicine:** Fred Barge, "Viewpoints from Involvement," *Dynamic Chiropractic* 10, no. 17 (August 14, 1992).

261 **to support *hu*'s diffusion into the world:** Jeff Barg, "The Hu Sells Out. The Angry Grammarian," *Philadelphia Weekly*, November 21–27, 2007.

262 **a study examining the growing use of this novel pronoun:** Elaine M. Stotko and Margaret Troyer, "A New Gender-Neutral Pronoun in Baltimore, Maryland: A Preliminary Study," *American Speech* 82, no. 3 (2007): 262–79.

267 **a good way to be respectful and polite:** R. Brown and A. Gilman, "The Pronouns of Power and Solidarity," in *Style in Language*, ed. T. A. Sebeok (Cambridge, MA: MIT Press, 1960), 253–76.

267 *thou* **as a demeaning insult:** From Shakespeare's *Twelfth Night*, act 3, scene 2, line 43.

268 **the need for humility over vanity:** Teresa Bejan, "What Quakers Can Teach Us About the Politics of Pronouns," *New York Times*, November 16, 2019.

268 **went against the will of God and Christ:** For more discussion about how the Quakers felt about "you," see Mark Liberman's October 24, 2010, post to the linguistics blog *Language Log*, languagelog.ldc.upenn.edu/nll/?p =2732.

273 **"Bring your authentic self to work":** To see more about this initiative, go to goldmansachs.com/careers/blog/posts/bring-your-authentic-self-to-work -pronouns.html.

9: Linguistic Badasses

278 **we were visited by a linguistic fairy godmother:** This linguistic fairy-tale experiment was inspired by a thought experiment about what would happen in a world of identical bodies, proposed by linguist Rosina Lippi-Green in her book *English with an Accent* (Philadelphia: Taylor and Francis Group, 2011).

280 **the language of the rebellious American upstarts:** From Manfred Görlach, "Colonial Lag? The Alleged Conservative Character of American English and Other 'Colonial' Varieties," *African Studies* 46, no. 2 (1987): 179–97.

280 **words formed from using -*ass* as a suffix:** The use of -*ass* as an intensifier (or its use as the back end, so to speak, of a compound like *bitchass*) is another example of an African American English innovation that has spread far beyond its originating group but that follows, as we have seen, a long line of other intensifying words that are mined to help us add that extra "umph" when we are trying to get a point across.

282 **the Elizabethan era was rife:** For more on our stranded prepositions throughout the centuries, see N. Yáñez-Bouza, *Grammar, Rhetoric and Usage in English: Preposition Placement 1500–1900* (Cambridge: Cambridge University Press, 2014).

283 **proper pronunciation in 1791:** This criticism of the expansion of newfangled "ah" pronunciation appeared in John Walker's *A Critical Pronouncing Dictionary*, published in 1791 (London: G. G. J. and J. Robinson), 10.

Index